Following Percy

Following Percy

Essays on Walker Percy's Work

by

Lewis A. Lawson

The Whitston Publishing Company
Troy, New York
1988

Copyright 1988
Lewis A. Lawson

Library of Congress Catalog Card Number 87-61269

ISBN 0-87875-345-1

Printed in the United States of America

For my fellow far-gone Percy reader

Acknowledgements

I want to thank the General Research Board, Graduate School, University of Maryland, for five summer grants. The earlier ones, especially, enabled me to do the reading that was necessary.

I want to thank the several Chairs of the Department of English—Charles D. Murphy, Morris Freedman, John Howard, Annabel Patterson, and Richard Cross—for their encouragement.

I want to thank the following journals for publishing my essays and for allowing me to reprint them here:

"Walker Percy's Indirect Communications," *Texas Studies* in *Literature and Language*, 11 (Spring 1969), 867-900.

"Walker Percy's Southern Stoic," *Southern Literary Journal*, 3 (Fall 1970), 5-31.

"Walker Percy as Martian Visitor," *Southern Literary Journal*, 8 (Spring 1976), 102-13.

"*The Moviegoer* and the Stoic Heritage," in *The Stoic Strain in American Literature: Essays in Honour of Marston La-France*, ed. Duane J. MacMillan (Toronto: University of Toronto Press, 1979), pp. 179-91.

"The Gnostic Vision in *Lancelot*," *Renascence*, 32 (Autumn 1979), 52-64.

"Walker Percy's Silent Character," *Mississippi Quarterly*, 33 (Spring 1980), 123-40.

"Walker Percy's *The Moviegoer*: the Cinema as Cave," *Southern Studies*, 19 (Winter 1980), 331-54.

"Tom More: Cartesian Physician," *Delta*, 13 (November 1981), 67-81.

"Time and Eternity in *The Moviegoer*," *Southern Humanities Review*, 16 (Spring 1982), 129-41.

"Gnosis and Time in *Lancelot*," *Papers on Language and Literature*, 19 (Winter 1983), 64-78.

" 'English romanticism . . . and 1930 science' in *The Moviegoer*," *Rocky Mountain Review*, 38 (Numbers 1-2, 1984), 70-84.

"*Love in the Ruins:* Sequel to *Arrowsmith*," *Mobius*, 4 (April 1984), 71-79.

"Walker Percy's Physicians and Patients," *Literature and Medicine*, 3 (1984), 130-41.

CONTENTS

A Personal Note From the Author

Before Walker Percy, I was not much. Now this is not just a roundabout way of saying that after Percy I do amount to much, in the usual sense. I don't. What I mean is that reading Percy has forced me to think about a lot of things, which become one thing, myself. I am not claiming that I have gotten hold of some great idea that explains everything else. I don't know for a certainty much more than I did, maybe less. But I do know now what to think about, the uncertainties. In that way, I am much more now than I was before Percy. I am not always happy about this change, for thinking about uncertainties can be unsettling. But not thinking about them is a wasted life. Such thinking has not made me smug, for I have learned that I'm not unique. Many another reader of Percy has told me of the same change.

I first picked up Percy, a paperback of *The Moviegoer*, on an impulse in 1962. I can't remember the cover—the book tore up or was lent to a student a long time ago. (Lending books to students soon makes a person realize just how epidemic amnesia is in our colleges.) Seeing that it was a SOUTHERN NOVEL, I hoped to use it as an example in my dissertation on the grotesque in modern Southern literature. When I didn't find any grotesque in it, in order to get some good out of the reading of it, I had to turn around and argue that the absence of the grotesque was what was really significant. (Today, if I were faced with the same problem, I'd write a whole chapter on the novel as a text of the problematic grotesque.) I wonder that, once having used the novel for my own purposes, I didn't put it behind me forever, halfway angry—embarrassed at having been wrong, writing off the $1.45 as a bad investment. But I kept on rereading it—I can sit down today and read it just like it was the first time.

I noticed that Percy had written some essays about the same ideas found in *The Moviegoer*, so when I came to Maryland in 1963 I used the non-fiction to gloss the novel, when I made my debut before the faculty. This response was probably that of the majority: that the subject was interesting, but what did it have to do with whether or not the novel was aesthetically pleasing? I don't know what I said, for I was stricken with the discovery that not everybody felt about Percy like I did. The event—as a heart attack is an event—was salutary, for I have never since assumed that he would be, like Hadacol, a Louisiana panacea.

With the necessity to write heavy upon my assistant professor shoulders, I decided to do the almost unthinkable, write about what was really important to me. As everybody knows, such writing takes much more time than the other kind. Since Percy's essays appeared in such a variety of journals, I was afraid that I had not located all of them. So I sent him my list, to which he added two, even trusting me with the only copy of one that he had. I felt so encouraged that I wrote him again. Having read that he had written two unpublished novels before *The Moviegoer*, I asked if I could come to Covington to read them, even if he had to lock me in a motel room for security. After all, it would make a nice story someday about what I had done for literary research. He replied that it would be over his dead body that I would see them, come to think of it that might be exactly how I would see them, so he was going to take them out and throw them in the bayou right then. Fearful that I had cost literary culture part of its riches by my ambitiousness, I resolved never again to let professoring run away with me.

Before I could get my piece on *The Moviegoer* done, he had written *The Last Gentleman*. I realized then that I would always be a follower, in the plain sense of being behind. I have never been able to get one novel written about, before another one appears, in fact seem to get farther behind all the time. I keep picking up *The Moviegoer* and seeing something else in it.

I may as well confess to being a little bit of a follower in the other sense, too. My condition is actually quite mild, given the cases of literary obsessiveness I've seen; I have almost no relics. My attachment is to the writing. I began to notice that anything I had to say in class about any other writer was informed by ideas that keep appearing in Percy's novels and essays, like "coming-to-oneself," "certification," "rotation," and "repetition," and "island news" and "news from across the water." I finally understood that he was trying to bring back the nearly lost art of gaining knowledge through hearing, after several hundred years' domination by Descartes' learning through sight, and I probably preach too much on that text.

The only other manifestation of my condition is a propensity for finding a fellow far-gone Percy person wherever I go. These meetings and the opportunity to teach a course on him now and then have enabled me to avoid practicing Percy as a solitary pleasure. It would be especially ironic if there were no one to talk to about a writer whose life theme is that we must talk to one another. Student response has, I admit, never been what I always hope it will be. For one thing, he has no natural constituency, not being a Southerner (in any exclusive sense), a Jew, a Black, or a female. Even the Preacher would have to admit that a Unified Force of Alienated Persons would be something new under the sun. And sooner or later he has trod on everybody's pet belief. The occasional alienated student—more likely to be an erratic undergraduate than the rare incautious graduate—is enough, though, to keep my spirits up. And their papers—some destined for publication—have stimulated me to try yet another essay.

The following essays cover over twenty years of reading and talking Percy. There is some repetition of introduction in several of the essays, but not enough, I hope, to cause more than a slight annoyance. There is no central theme that I can see. But my aim has remained the same, always. I try to offer a reading of a novel or novels. This reading always reveals the reading I have been stimulated to do by Percy's writing. To him I owe my introduction to Kierkegaard, Sartre, Heidegger, Marcel, and others. Because of him I went back to other writers whom I had not read with enough seriousness. I first read *The Moviegoer* the year I finished graduate school; it was a lucky thing, for I knew then that I had to start all over.

Lewis A. Lawson

University of Maryland

Walker Percy's Indirect Communications

Just at the beginning of his career as a pathologist, Walker Percy contracted tuberculosis in the laboratory. As a consequence, he was forced to spend several years free of physical activity. During this period, he relates, his reading interests began to broaden: "I began to read, no longer McLeod's *Physiology* or Gay's *Bacteriology* but the great Russian novelists, especially Dostoevsky; the modern French novelists, especially Camus; the existentialist philosophers, Jaspers (also a physician), Marcel, and Heidegger."[1] The result of his reading was a realization that modern science, which as a physician he had followed unquestioningly, had almost nothing to say " . . . about what it is like to be a man living in the world."[2] He decided, therefore, to abandon medicine and to become an explorer of what he felt was a " . . . huge gap in the scientific view of the world. . . . "[3]

After a time Dr. Percy began to report upon his explorations. In the next few years he wrote two novels and a book about the philosophy of language—none of which could he get published. He was successful only in getting a few articles in print, in journals ranging from a Catholic to a scientific persuasion.[4] But then, after so much failure, in a little more than a year he wrote *The Moviegoer* (1961), which received a very warm response from the reviewers, won the National Book Award for 1962, and sold over a half a million copies in paperback. And his second novel, *The Last Gentleman* (1966), seems destined to be every bit as successful, for it received an even warmer response from the reviewers and was a contender for the National Book Award for 1967.

How does it happen that a middle-aged doctor with such an unlikely background for literature has achieved so much success as a novelist? Percy himself has no answer:

> This is an interesting question, one which, however, I do not pretend
> to be able to answer. I can only report that something did happen

> and it happened all of a sudden. . . . It is not like learning a skill or
> a game at which, with practice, one gradually improves. One
> works hard all right, but what comes, comes all of a sudden and as a
> breakthrough. One hits on something. What happens is a period
> of unsuccessful effort during which one works very hard—and fails.
> There follows a period of discouragement. Then there comes a para-
> doxical moment of collapse-and-renewal in which one somehow
> breaks with the past and starts afresh. All past efforts are thrown
> into the wastebasket, all advice forgotten. The slate is wiped
> clean. It is almost as if the discouragement were necessary, that one
> has first to encounter despair before one is entitled to hope. Then a
> time comes when one takes a pencil and a fresh sheet of paper and
> begins. Begins, really for the first time.[5]

What is significant about this statement is the cast of mind
which is revealed. The conception of despair not as an ultimate
catastrophe but as a stage on the road to hope implies a
Kierkegaardian view of human progress. One has only to substitute "dialectical" for "paradoxical." But this implication is not
surprising, for the influence of Kierkegaard on Dr. Percy's
thought can hardly be overemphasized. Allusions and
references to the Danish writer abound in his nonfiction articles,
and both *The Moviegoer* and *The Last Gentleman* begin with
mottoes from the same source. Indeed, and this statement is in
no way intended to detract from Dr. Percy's originality, much of
the success of his fiction derives from two key strategies which
resulted from his familiarity with Kierkegaard. For, by using
these two strategies, Dr. Percy is able to translate the abstract ideas
of his articles into the human action of his novels.

The more obvious of the strategies Dr. Percy admits he
derived from Kierkegaard. In a recent interview he placed Binx
Bolling in the "aesthetic mode" and Will Barrett in the
"religious mode."[6] Thus he indicated that he conceives of his
protagonists as men who live in a state of becoming, of men
who attempt to leap from one plateau of existential awareness to
another. Here Dr. Percy is following Kierkegaard's conception of
life as a series of "stages," or "spheres," or "spheres of existence,"
through which a person may or may not pass. There are three
such stages: the aesthetic, the ethical, and the religious. The aesthetic man is the immediate man, the sensuous man, the
hedonist; he is unreflective and undifferentiated from his
environment; his life is governed by the pleasure-pain principle.
The ethical man becomes aware of issues beyond the immediate;

he begins to reflect and to feel obligations; his life is governed by
the good-bad principle. The religious man becomes aware of his
individuality; he begins to know his sinfulness and to feel his
need of God; his life is governed by the principle of the absolute
task.

The less obvious of these strategies concerns the surface of
Percy's fiction.   At the conclusion of *The Moviegoer*, in the
Epilogue, the protagonist Binx Bolling says: "As for my search, I
have not the inclination to say much on the subject.   For one
thing, I have not the authority, as the great Danish philosopher
declared, to speak of such matters in any way other than the
edifying.   For another thing, it is not open to me even to be edifying, since the time is later than his, much too late to edify or do
much of anything except plant a foot in the right place as the
opportunity presents itself—if indeed asskicking is properly
distinguished   from   edification."[7]   Here   Binx   alludes   to
Kierkegaard's *The Point of View for My Work as An Author*[8] in
such a way that a great deal about Percy's fictional intentions is
suggested.

What Binx suggests about himself is that he, like
Kierkegaard, recognizes that he has no absolute authority to
speak about "universal" religious truths; he can only speak for
himself and he cannot even be certain about his own
achievement, since he, like Kierkegaard, also recognizes that a
soul's residence in a "sphere of existence" is always in a state of
becoming, not being.   Therefore, all that he can do is to relate
that something ethically rewarding has happened to him; if he
attempted to relate its value for others, the very attempt would
defeat his purpose, since ethico-religious truth is subjective.   All
he can do for others is to plant a foot in the right place, that is,
use the indirect method to attack the illusions of those who
think themselves Christians.   What Binx suggests about Percy's
methods is that Percy, very much aware of the futility of writing
about religion for an audience which already conceives of itself
as religious, must utilize the "indirect approach," must write
maieutically, by "indirect communication," in order to catch his
readers aesthetically and then—without ever directly discussing
religion or lapsing into a "serious" tone—attack their religious
illusions from behind.   In a sense, then, Percy's novels are the
"indirect   communications"   that   complement   his   "direct
communications," his nonfiction articles, even at the same time
that they are aesthetically very satisfying.

I

Binx Bolling: From the Aesthetic to the Ethical

One of Percy's nonfiction articles in particular serves as a very helpful introduction to his first novel, *The Moviegoer*. In "The Coming Crisis in Psychiatry," Percy discusses a new theme which he detects in American psychiatry. Since it is being introduced by psychiatrists themselves, such as Erich Fromm in *The Sane Society* (1955), Dr. Percy suspects that most people will misunderstand its radical nature. The new theme is not just another variation on standard Freudian thought; it threatens, on the contrary, the very basis of that doctrine. "The issue," as Dr. Percy puts it, "is simply this: is psychiatry a biological science in which man is treated as an organism with instinctive drives and needs not utterly or qualitatively different from those of other organisms? Or is psychiatry a humanistic discipline which must take account of man as possessing a unique destiny by which he is oriented in a wholly different direction?"[9]

The issue has arisen, Dr. Percy believes, because people have begun to realize that a psychiatry bound within the premises of a biological science is powerless to treat all of the sicknesses of modern man's psyche. As a result, "It is increasingly noticeable that American psychiatry has almost nothing to say about the great themes that have engaged the existential critics of modern society from Sören Kierkegaard to Gabriel Marcel. The very men whose business is mental health have been silent about the sickness of modern man, his emotional impoverishment, his sense of homelessness in the midst of the very world which he, more than men of any other time, has made over for his own happiness."[10] What is more, Dr. Percy argues, psychiatry is silent because, " . . . given its basic concept of man, it is *unable* to take account of the predicament of modern man."[11] Psychiatry, as it is currently constituted, simply cannot understand the apparently well-adjusted man who is in fact desperately suffering from alienation.

Dr. Percy suggests a reason for this curious failure of modern psychiatry. Since it developed out of nineteenth-century medical science, it has always felt that the phenomena it observes are only symptoms of inner disturbance. Thus it has always attempted to trace overt signs of mental disorder back to their covert sources. But if it investigates the covert sources in the patient's psyche, only to find that all biological and cultural needs are being met, then it is forced by its own rationale to conclude that the patient is suffering from some condition that originated in early childhood. According to its basic premises, it cannot admit that the anxiety could arise from present conditions, that the patient suffers not from improper psychic development but from an inability to find meaning in his present life.

To rectify this failure, Dr. Percy argues, orthodox psychiatry must admit " . . . that there are certain human needs quite impervious to the biological approach. . . . In the language of the existentialists, there are certain traits of human existence which are utterly different from the traits of the world; and not only does the existing self fail to understand itself by objective science, but in so doing it falls into an unauthentic existence."[12] If it will make this admission, psychiatry will discover " . . . that it is possible, entirely apart from religious convictions, to speak of the sickness of Western man."[13]

Since the illness seems primarily spiritual, should psychiatry yield to religion or become itself a secular religion? Dr. Percy supports neither alternative. Yet a third choice, which he does advocate, is for psychiatry to admit within its purview the realization that " . . . transcendence is the one distinguishing mark of human existence,"[14] to acknowledge, as all schools of existentialism have acknowledged, " . . . man's incurable God-directedness."[15] By this admission, he maintains, psychiatry would become more nearly aware that reality includes the transempirical: "If there is such a thing as transcendence in man's nature, it would seem to be the proper function of psychiatry to take due note of it. . . . "[16] The situation can no longer be ignored, Dr. Percy declares in his conclusion, and he utilizes a double echo of Kierkegaard to emphasize his challenge to psychiatry: "Either we have outgrown monotheism, and good riddance; or modern man is estranged from being, from his own being, from the being of other creatures in the world, from transcendent being. He has lost something, what he does not know; he knows only that he is sick unto death with the loss of it."[17]

The allusions to Kierkegaard in "The Coming Crisis in Psychiatry" provide a transition between Dr. Percy's nonfictional concerns and their embodiment in his fiction. For just as the essay ends with an allusion to *The Sickness Unto Death*, so *The*

Moviegoer begins with a quotation from the same "Christian Psychological Exposition": " . . . the specific character of despair is precisely this: it is unaware of being despair." For his motto, Dr. Percy chose a description of the despair that, according to Kierkegaard, is the most common and most dangerous form, because "in unconsciousness of being in despair a man is further from being conscious of himself as a spirit."[18] This kind of despair masquerades as happiness and contentment.

It was exactly such a condition which concerned Dr. Percy in "The Coming Crisis," for in it he asked the question: "Who is mentally healthy? What about the man or woman who lives, say, in the Park Forest development near Chicago, who has a good sexual relation with his or her partner, who feels secure, who is socially adjusted, who has many acquaintances, who consumes all manner of goods and services, participates in 'cultural activities,' enjoys 'recreational facilities,' who is never lonely?"[19] His answer denies that these people enjoy sound mental health: "These people are desperately alienated from themselves. They are in fact without selves. They experience themselves in things, as commodities, or as nothing. They are . . . in the position of the man in the gospel who would gain the whole world and lose his soul."[20] And a little later Dr. Percy adds: "We all know perfectly well that the man who lives out his life as a consumer, a sexual partner, an 'other-directed' executive; who avoids boredom and anxiety by consuming tons of newsprint, miles of movie films, years of TV time; that such a man has somehow betrayed his destiny as a human being."[21] Such a man has become alienated, fallen prey to everydayness, become unauthentic; he has become a thing and is a victim to the other things that he can accumulate.

In "The Coming Crisis" Percy describes two types of sufferers in the modern world: "What shall we make of two individuals, suburbanite A, who is tranquillized in his never-ending consumption of goods, services, entertainment and human intercourse; suburbanite B, who feels himself an alien in Park Forest, who knows not who is and is afraid."[22] Exactly such a person as suburbanite B is The Moviegoer, John Bickerson Bolling, known more familiarly as "Binx." To himself he has been "x," an unknown quality, all his life; to himself he is not real, his world is not real, and the transcendent is not real: "My unbelief," he admits, "was invincible from the beginning. I could never make head or tail of God. The proofs of God's existence may have been true for all I know, but it didn't make the slightest difference. If God himself had appeared to me, it would have changed nothing. In fact, I have only to hear the word God and a curtain comes down in my head" (p. 136).[23]

An admission of this kind is typical of Binx. He is candid, intelligent, and urbane, conscious that, judged by the standards of most of his contemporaries, his life is an unqualified success. He himself knows better; he realizes that he is a desperately wounded animal seeking a place to shelter. His only protection against the world is an ironical detachment about himself,[24] and he outwardly plays the role that others would cast for him. But in the meantime he attempts to place together the fragments of his experience, and he relates his attempts to the reader in his highly idiosyncratic manner of speaking. The characterization of Binx thus is the foremost critical concern of the student of the novel, who must attempt to translate Binx's entirely subjective discourse into a language of wider currency. And the reader's appreciation of the artistry of the novel must rest upon an understanding of Dr. Percy's success in filtering through Binx's consciousness a considerable amount of existentialist (usually Kierkegaardian) statement.

Binx is very much like Kierkegaard's introverted aesthete.[25] Such a man is able to keep anyone from discussing the self and to keep up a pretense of being a whole man. He observes moderation and discretion in all things, and he masters the way of the world. He earns a good living and takes care to be sociable when he cannot avoid intercourse with others. But although he can be a pleasant companion, " . . . he often feels a need of solitude, which for him is a vital necessity—something like breathing, at other times like sleeping."[26] This is because his nature is deeper than that of most people. He dislikes discussing religion, for such discussion strikes him as meaningless and superficial. He lives for successive moments, for the continuum of time means nothing to him, since he cannot believe that it leads anywhere. Such a man can thus mark time for his entire life. But if any change in his condition does occur, it must take one of two courses: somehow he must gain the faith that is the only antidote to despair, or he must seek to forget his despair in sensuality.

Binx has developed for himself a " . . . tidy and ingenious life . . . " (p. 175). He lives in New Orleans, in the middle-class suburb of Gentilly, on the corner of Bons Enfants and Elysian

Fields.   It is particularly appropriate that he lives on Elysian Fields, since the name suggests the Kierkegaardian paradox found in "immediacy," Kierkegaard's term for a condition that is sheer happiness, materially considered, and sheer despair, spiritually considered.[27] To the others living in Gentilly, Dr. Percy's suburbanites-commuters A, "Elysian Fields" would mean a place of paradise; to Binx, it means only a place of death.   Being unaware of or indifferent to any loss of religious significance in in their lives, the suburbanites would live only for their creature comforts; Binx, however, feels these same creature comforts contributing to his feelings of everydayness.[28]   In this average American suburb, Binx has found a basement apartment in the home of a widow, Mrs. Schexnaydre, whose name, Brainard Cheney suggests, could be pronounced "she's nadir."[29] It seems very appropriate, too, that Binx lives in the basement apartment, since Kierkegaard likens anyone who lives only " . . . in the determinants of sensuousness . . . " to the person who " . . . prefers to dwell in the cellar." "And not only does he prefer to dwell in the cellar; no, he loves that to such a degree that he becomes furious if anyone would propose to him to occupy the *bel étage* which stands empty at his disposition—for in fact he is dwelling in his own house."[30]

A successful salesman of the middle-class dream, mutual funds, Binx is himself a middle-class dream. As he portrays himself:

> I am a model tenant and a model citizen and take pleasure in doing all that is expected of me.   My wallet is full of identity cards, library cards, credit cards. Last year I purchased a flat olive-drab strongbox, very smooth and heavily built with double walls for fire protection, in which I placed my birth certificate, college diploma, honorable discharge, G.I. insurance, a few stock certificates, and my inheritance: a deed to ten acres of a defunct duck club down in St. Bernard Parish, the only relic of my father's many enthusiasms. It is a pleasure to carry out the duties of a citizen and to receive in return a receipt or a neat styrene card with one's name on it certifying, so to speak, one's right to exist.[31] What satisfaction I take in appearing the first day to get my auto tag and brake sticker! I subscribe to *Consumer Reports* and as a consequence I own a first-class television set, an all but silent air conditioner and a very long lasting deodorant. My armpits never stink. I pay attention to all spot announcements on the radio about mental health, the seven signs of cancer, and safe driving. . . . (p. 12)

Ordinarily he spends quiet evenings, either viewing television
or going to a movie. A bachelor with a red MG, he has no difficulty finding a pretty girl, usually his current secretary, to share
his weekends on the Gulf Coast.

His only difficulty, in fact, is that for him the fabric of reality
has dissolved. Life has no meaning, and as a result nothing is
significant. For Binx, "everydayness is the enemy" (p. 135).[32]
Most of the time, he can bear his unauthentic existence: "It is
not a bad thing to settle for the Little Way, not the big search for
the big happiness but the sad little happiness of drinks and kiss-
es, a good little car and a warm deep thigh" (p. 127). But there
are times when the malaise tortures him: "What is the malaise?
you ask. The malaise is the pain of loss. The world is lost to
you, the world and the people in it, and there remains only you
and the world and you no more able to be in the world than
Banquo's ghost" (p. 114). When the malaise strikes, Binx can
only hope that in sensuousness will he forget it. His MG " . . . is
immune to the malaise" (p. 115), and when the sickness strikes,
he can only hope that his car and his latest girl can help him
ward it off. But sometimes even these opiates do not work:

> On it way home the MG becomes infested with malaise. It is not
> unexpected, since Sunday afternoon is always the worst time for ma-
> laise. Thousands of cars are strung out along the Gulf Coast, whole
> families, and all with the same vacant headachy look. There is an
> exhaust fume in the air and the sun strikes the water with a malig-
> nant glint. A fine Sunday afternoon, though. A beautiful boule-
> vard, ten thousand handsome cars, fifty thousand handsome, well-
> fed and kind-hearted people, and the malaise settles on us like a
> fall-out.
> Sorrowing, hoping against hope, I put my hand on the thickest
> and innerest part of Sharon's thigh.
> She bats me away with a new vigor.
> 'Son, don't you mess with me.'
> 'Very well, I won't,' I say gloomily, as willing not to mess with
> her, to tell the truth. (pp. 153-154)

The success of Binx's life, then, cannot be determined by the
degree to which he approaches the fantasy dreamed of by the
middle class. Outwardly "well-adjusted," he is inwardly a melancholy stranger, who lives " . . . solitary and in wonder, wondering day and night, never a moment without wonder" (p. 42),
who spends his " . . . entire time working, making money, going
to movies and seeking the company of women" (p. 41).

Kierkegaard knew of such deceptions: "By seeing the multitude of men about it, by getting engaged in all sorts of worldly affairs, by becoming wise about how things go in this world, such a man forgets himself, forgets what his name is (in the divine understanding of it), does not dare believe in himself, finds it too venturesome a thing to be himself, far easier and safer to be like the others, to become an imitation, a number, a cipher in the world."[33]

The movies are not merely a distraction for Binx. They are, on the contrary, the metaphysical attraction of his life. It was in a movie that Binx " . . . first discovered place and time, tasted it like okra." Since then he has made a ritual of going to the movies: "Before I see a movie it is necessary for me to learn something about the theater or the people who operate it, to touch base before going inside. . . . If I did not talk to the theatre owner or the ticket seller, I should be lost, cut loose metaphysically speaking. I should be seeing one copy of a film which might be shown anywhere and at any time. There is a danger of slipping clean out of space and time" (p. 72).

Within the ritual of moviegoing Binx has developed his own peculiar liturgy. There is, first of all, the rite of certification: "Nowadays when a person lives somewhere, in a neighborhood, the place is not certified for him. More than likely he will live there sadly and the emptiness which is inside him will expand until it evacuates the entire neighborhood. But if he sees a movie which shows his very neighborhood, it becomes possible for him to live, for a time at least, as a person who is Somewhere and not Anywhere" (p. 61). Then there is repetition: "A repetition is the re-enactment of past experience toward the end of isolating the time segment which has lapsed in order that it, the lapsed time, can be savored of itself and without the usual adulteration of events that clog time like peanuts in brittle" (p. 77).[34] And finally there is rotation: "A rotation I define as the experiencing of the new beyond the expectation of the experiencing of the new" (p. 134).[35]

In an age of loss of faith in the mana of the old institutions, Percy apparently believes that most people thrill more to the magic of Hollywood than the magic of the holy rood. Movie stars have become Binx's saints, and he imitates them and hopes for their gestural perfection.[36] He often emulates them: "Toward her I keep a Gregory Peckish sort of distance" (p. 66), or "I go home as the old Gable, asweat and with no thought for her and sick to death with desire" (p. 91). Or he invokes them: "Ah, William Holden, we already need you again. Already the fabric is wearing thin without you" (p. 22), or "O Tony. O Rory. You never had it so good with direction. Not even you Bill Holden, my noble Will. O ye morning stars together. Farewell forever, malaise" (p. 119). If we believe in the pantheon of stars, the mere act of seeing one confirms and heightens our own reality. Binx describes one such encounter, which occurs on the street to the French Quarter, not the road to Damascus, when William Holden appears to a despairing honeymooning couple:

> Holden slaps his pockets for a match. He has stopped behind some ladies looking at iron furniture on the sidewalk. They look like housewives from Hattiesburg come down for a day of shopping. He asks for a match; they shake their heads and then recognize him. There follows much blushing and confusion. But nobody can find a match for Holden. By now the couple have caught up with him. The boy holds out a light, nods briefly to Holden's thanks, then passes on without a flicker of recognition. Holden walks along between them for a second; he and the boy talk briefly, look up at the sky, shake their heads. Holden gives them a pat on the shoulder and moves on ahead.
>
> The boy has done it! He has won title to his own existence, as plenary an existence now as Holden's, by refusing to be stampeded like the ladies from Hattiesburg. He is a citizen like Holden; two men of the world are they. All at once the world is open to him. Nobody threatens from patio and alley. His girl is open to him too. He puts his arm around her neck, noodles her head. She feels the difference too. She had not known what was wrong nor how it was righted but she knows now that all is well.
>
> Holden has turned down Toulouse shedding light as he goes. An aura of heightened reality moves with him and all who fall within it feel it. (p. 20)

So Binx is the moviegoer;[37] he knows only that he finds more reality in the movies than on the street, that life is played out against a backdrop of meaningless traditions. He recognizes that most people are unconscious despairers, unreflective aesthetes, suburbanites-commuters A, like his cousin, Nell Lovell, who does indeed love hell: "I don't feel a bit gloomy! . . . Now that Mark and Lance have grown up and flown the coop, I am having the time of my life. I'm taking philosophy courses in the morning and working nights at Le Petite Theatre. Eddie and I have re-examined our values and found them pretty darn enduring. To our utter amazement we discovered that we both have the same lifegoal. . . . To make a contribution, however small, and leave the world just a little better off. . . . we gave the television to the kids and last night we turned on the hi-fi and sat by the fire and read *The Prophet* aloud" (pp. 95-96). Such people have hobbies: "As for hobbies, people with stimulating hobbies suffer from the most noxious of despairs since they are tranquillized in their despair" (p. 82). They are thus unaware even that life should have a fabric, much less worried about the fabric's dissolution. Binx knows, also, that a few still can find meaning in the world, and he admires an aunt for this ability: "For her too the fabric is dissolving, but for her even the dissolving makes sense" (p. 53).[38] But he comes to discover that she is a fatalist and hence a despairer, since she has given up possibility, which is, according to Kierkegaard, God.[39]

Nell Lovell is a Pangloss and the aunt is a Brother Martin, and neither can communicate with Binx, for neither understands his loss. But Binx has one ally: the condition that makes him miserable, his consciousness of his despair, can also prompt him to search for an answer. He had first become aware of the possibility of a search as he lay wounded in Korea, in the presence of eternity: "Perhaps there was a time when everydayness was not too strong and one could break its grip by brute strength. Now nothing breaks it—but disaster. Only once in my life was the grip of everydayness broken; when I lay bleeding in a ditch" (p. 135).[40] At the time Binx had vowed a search, and some years later he attempted one:

> During these years I stood outside of the universe and sought to understand it. I lived in my room as an Anyone living Anywhere and read fundamental books and only for diversion took walks around the neighborhood and saw an occasional movie. Certainly it did not matter to me where I was when I read such a book as *The Expanding Universe*. The greatest success of this enterprise, which I call my vertical search, came one night when I sat in a hotel room in Birmingham and read a book called *The Chemistry of Life*. When I finished it, it seemed to me that the main goals of my my search were reached or were in principle reachable, whereupon I went out and saw a movie called *It Happened One Night* which was itself very good. A memorable night. The only difficulty was that though the universe had been disposed of, I myself was left over. There I lay in the hotel room with my search over yet still obliged to draw one breath and then the next.[41] (p. 68)

Binx's difficulty here illustrates Percy's contention in "The Coming Crisis" that " . . . Western man's sense of homelessness and loss of community is in part due to the fact that he feels himself a stranger to the method and data of his sciences, and especially to himself construed as a datum. . . . "[42] After this frustrating experience, Binx had abandoned his search, finally to move to Gentilly as a stock salesman.

The Moviegoer is the story of the revival in Binx of the possibility of a search. Only seven days are covered by the span of the novel, yet these are seven crucial days, this last week before Binx's thirtieth birthday on Ash Wednesday, because, so far, they constitute Binx's inward existence.[43] The time of year suggests the contrasts that at once parody and emphasize his melancholy solitude.

Binx awakens to the possibility of a new search whenever he discovers that he has become a collection of things:

> . . . this morning when I got up, I dressed as usual and began as usual to put my belongings into my pockets: wallet, notebook (for writing down occasional thoughts), pencil, keys, handkerchief, pocket slide rule (for calculating percentage returns on principal). They looked both unfamiliar and at the same time full of clues. I stood in the center of the room and gazed at the little pile, sighting through a hole made by thumb and forefinger. What was unfamiliar about them was that I could see them. They might have belonged to someone else. A man can look at this little pile on his bureau for thirty years and never once see it. It is as invisible as his own hand. Once I saw it, however, the search became possible.[44] (p. 16)

The search, as Binx defines it, ". . . is what anyone would undertake if he were not sunk in the everydayness of his own life. . . . To become aware of the possibility of the search is to be onto something. Not to be onto something is to be in despair" (pp. 17-18). Or as Kierkegaard has it: "The believer possesses the eternally certain antidote to despair, viz. possibility; for with God all things are possible every instant."[45] What he seeks, Binx admits he cannot define, but he slowly discovers that it is being, an authentic existence, a self. The conclusion of the search, however tentative and precarious and preliminary it may be, is when he discovers that he can accept the absurd and that he can share his discovery with another self.

Chastened by the failure of his "vertical search" some years earlier, Binx now decides upon a "horizontal search" (p. 68). What he means is that he now disbelieves in the search for meaning through objective, scientific methods, that he now believes that he can gain insight into the nature of his condition only through personal observation of how the world affects him specifically. He refuses to accept himself as a datum among data; there is something unique about him, the truth and essence of which he can only learn for himself. He rejects rotation, the lure of the unexpected future, and accepts repetition, the quest returning to the past.

The "first real clue" in the search occurs when Binx becomes aware of Jews:

> When a man is in despair and does not in his heart of hearts allow that a search is possible and when such a man passes a Jew in the street, he notices nothing.
>
> When a man becomes a scientist or an artist, he is open to a different kind of despair. When such a man passes a Jew in the street, he may notice something but it is not a remarkable encounter. To him the Jew can only appear as a scientist or artist like himself or as a specimen to be studied.
>
> But when a man awakes to the possibility of a search and when such a man passes a Jew in the street for the first time, he is like Robinson Crusoe seeing the footprint on the beach.[46] (p. 85)

Here Percy is discussing, as in "The Coming Crisis," the inability of a modern world to recognize alienation. The Philistine, suburbanite-commuter A, the unconscious despairer, would not be aware of the Jew, the very personification of alienation, because such a despairer does not comprehend alienation. The modern scientist recognizes the alienated person but looks for causes of alienation only by merging the individual into the statistical mass or by looking within the individual's psychic history.[47] The conscious despairer not only recognizes the alienated person but also recognizes their brotherhood. He recognizes alienation, or despair, if you will, as a universal condition.

Even with such progress, there comes a dark night of the soul for Binx, when at his mother's fishing camp, he wakes " . . . in the grip of everydayness" (p. 135). But his new awareness strengthens him, and he vows, " . . . I'm a son of a bitch if I'll be defeated by the everydayness." Then in a note to himself he tries to chart his future course:

REMEMBER TOMORROW
Starting point for search:
It no longer avails to start with creatures and prove God.
Yet it is impossible to rule God out.

> The only possible starting point: the strange fact of one's invincible apathy—that if the proofs were proved and God presented himself, nothing would be changed. Here is the strangest fact of all. Abraham saw signs of god and believed. Now the only sign is that all the signs in the world make no difference. Is this God's ironic revenge? But I am onto him.[48] (p. 136)

Here Binx gets one step closer to an understanding. He admits that he cannot be convinced of the existence of God by rational and objective means. Further, he thinks, the actuality of God is not important to a human mind which really cannot conceive of Him; what is important to the human mind is that it can have the faith to believe in something so foreign to itself. Binx concludes that he must still start within his subjectivity, even though his subjectivity reflects an absurd world of dissolving fabric. Nevertheless, Binx recalls, Abraham, according to Kierkegaard's *Fear and Trembling*, faced a new condition, the absurd, and yet he remained a "knight of faith." Then modern absurdity can offer an opportunity for the search, a search built upon faith, not upon rational conviction. And the search for that which has been lost to everydayness can still be Christian, for as Kierkegaard has it, " . . . Christianity takes a prodigious giant-stride. . . . a stride into the absurd—there Christianity begins . . . "[49]

There remains still, however, Binx's most severe test. For years he has felt drawn to Kate Cutrer, his aunt's stepdaughter. Sick though he is, Binx has passed admirably in a world which does not recognize his disease, and it is natural that Kate, who *is* recognized by the world as a sick person, since she is undergoing analysis, should also turn to him. Kate illustrates Percy's contention in "The Coming Crisis" that mental illness today may result from general anxiety, not necessarily from some specific psychic malfunction. Supposedly Kate fell prey to anxiety because she was in an accident in which her fiancé was killed, and this is the condition which her analyst is trying to treat. But Kate is not suffering from anything induced by the accident; on the contrary, the accident was a departure from everydayness for her. Like Binx, she has reverse responses: Binx admits, "What are generally considered to be the best times are for me the worst of times, and that worst of times was one of the best" (p. 15); and Kate once asks Binx, "Have you noticed that only in time of illness or disaster or death are people real? I remember at the time of the wreck—people were so kind and helpful and *solid*" (p. 78).

Only Kate's methods of trying to avert everydayness are different from those that Binx employs; her opiates are alcohol and narcotics, not yet sexual activity. Yet again like Binx, she begins to find herself only through her own subjectivity; as she finally tells her analyst; "How good to think that there are reasons and that if I am silent, it means that I am hiding something. How happy I would be to be hiding something. And how proud I am when I do find secret reasons for you, your own favorite reasons. But what if there is nothing? That is what I've been afraid of until now—being found out to be concealing nothing at all" (p. 108).[50] Her realization confirms what Jung once said: that fully a third of his patients were suffering from an inability to find meaning in their world, not from a neurotic or psychotic disorder. And of course, since Kierkegaard often defines by comparing a condition to its opposite, nothing for him is everything. This dialectic Kate finally understands, for she tells Binx, who does not yet recognize the nature of her anxiety: "You're right. You don't understand. It is not some one thing, as you think. It is everything. It is all so monstrous" (p. 118).[51]

The test begins when Binx is given an unwelcome reward. Since he has been such a successful salesman, his uncle decides to send him to a convention on open-end funds in Chicago. Binx knows that as a Philistine he must appear delighted, yet he is really horrified: "Oh sons of all bitches and great beast of Chicago lying in wait. There goes my life in Gentilly, my Little Way, my secret existence among the happy shades in Elysian Fields." For no part of Chicago will be "certified," and he will be completely anonymous, completely at the mercy of everydayness. He fears that he might find himself " . . . No one and Nowhere" (p. 94).

Kate, too, is at that moment undergoing an unbearable crisis of everydayness, and she asks Binx to take her along, in the hope of running away from her despair. Binx recognizes her motive, as he observes her on the train that is taking them to Chicago: "Kate is shaking like a leaf because she longs to be anyone who is anywhere and she cannot" (p. 175). As the trip progresses, Binx becomes more aware that they are alike deviates from "good" mental health: "We hunch up knee to knee and nose to nose like the two devils on the Rorschach card" (p. 177). Binx proposes to her, but she is suspicious of his intentions. Knowing much more of his condition than he knows of hers, she suspects that marriage would be another of his " . . . ingenious little schemes," another way of attempting to build immunity to

everydayness, of evading despair. She suspects, possibly that he
intends to substitute her for the series of secretaries which has
served as his sex opiate.

Yet despite her refusal to marry him, Kate is so caught up in
despair that she virtually forces Binx to copulate with her. She
seems so anxious to escape the consciousness of her condition
for even the briefest moment that she will breed like a barnyard
animal. She tries to force herself to believe that copulation is a
purely physical act, without moral or emotional ramifications,
and she hopes in the act itself to experience for once the real:
"So—when all is said and done, that is the real thing, isn't it?"
(p. 182).

The copulation is hardly a success. Binx has to admit that he
was by no means a Rhett dispatching a Scarlett into the sweetest
sleep: "The truth is I was frightened half to death by her bold
(not really bold, not whorish bold but theorish bold) carrying on"
(p. 183). He had in fact despaired of reaching a climax: "There is
very little sin in the depths of the malaise. The highest moment
of a malaisian's life can be that moment when he manages to sin
like a proper human . . . " (p. 184). Binx's contrast of himself
with Clark Gable only emphasizes how much Binx had needed
gestural perfection in this act of all acts, and how much he had
failed to attain it, and how deeply he felt the consequent despair.[52]

The rampant everydayness of the convention is enough to
drive Binx and Kate to the nearest bar. But in the bar a step
forward in Binx's search occurs: "There I see her plain, see plain
for the first time since I lay wounded in a ditch and watched an
Oriental finch scratching around in the leaves—a quiet little
body she is, a tough little city Celt; no, more of a Rachel, really, a
dark little Rachel bound home to Brooklyn on the IRT" (p. 189).
He realizes, according to his theory of the recognition of a Jew, in
seeing her as a Jewess he must be a despairing person seeing a
despairing person. For the first time since his wounding, he is
aware of standing in the presence of being; he is celebrating with
someone else a common phenomenon, and this for Percy is "the
constituent act of consciousness."[53]

For a few brief moments, on their way to meet a wartime
companion of Binx's, Kate and Binx share the comradeliness
that exists when two people realize that they share, really share,
something. The companion Harold Graebner, however, is the archetypal suburbanite A, earning " . . . thirty five thou a year . . . "

and living in a suburb " . . . back of Wilmette . . . " (p. 190), a development which must surely be the fictional counterpart of the Park Forest that Dr. Percy cited in "The Coming Crisis." Harold is delighted to see Binx, but the repetition for him is frightening: "It is too much for Harold, not my gratitude, not the beauty of his own heroism, but the sudden confrontation of a time past, a time so terrible and splendid in its arch-reality; and so lost—cut adrift like a great ship in a flood of years. Harold tries to parse it out, that time and the time after, the strange ten years intervening, and it is too much for him" (p. 192). In his frustration, Harold settles upon Binx as the source of his discomfort, as the stimulus which drew him out of his pleasant materialistic existence in everydayness and caused him to have ontological doubts. Playfully (but with great unconscious seriousness of intent) he begins to punch Binx, and Binx and Kate are overjoyed to leave. The meeting has been so deadening that they seem really to expect the summons from Kate's stepmother (Binx's aunt) that hails them back to New Orleans.

With her rigidity and dogmatic rightness and despairing fatalism, the aunt destroys the little freedom from everydayness that Binx had retained from the sense of comradeliness that he and Kate had realized. Using her conventional standards, she views Binx not as a sick, despairing man but as a shameless Lothario; her complete lack of understanding is revealed by her question: "What do you think is the purpose of life—go to the movies and dally with every girl that comes along?" (p. 207). Her rejection drives Binx into a frenzy of despair:

> Now in the thirty-first year of my dark pilgrimage on this earth and knowing less than I ever knew before, having learned only to recognize merde when I see it, having inherited no more from my father than a good nose for merde, for every species of shit that flew—my only talent—smelling merde from every quarter, living in fact in the very century of merde, the great shithouse of scientific humanism where needs are satisfied, everyone becomes an anyone, a warm and creative person, and prospers like a dung beetle, and one hundred percent of people are humanists and ninety-eight percent believe in God,[54] and men are dead, dead, dead; and the malaise has settled like a fall-out and what people really fear is not that the bomb will fall but that the bomb will not fail—on this my thirtieth birthday, I know nothing and there is nothing to do but fall prey to desire. (pp. 208-209)

Believing that Kate has been persuaded to abandon him, Binx is frenetic to secure his secretary, Sharon, to use her body in the

hope of escaping his anxiety. The revelation that she is no longer available seems to Binx the final blow, and from the telephone booth where he had called her, Binx looks out upon a
wasteland: "A watery sunlight breaks through the smoke of the
Chef and turns the sky yellow. Elysian Fields glistens like a vat
of sulphur . . . " (p. 211). Across the way stands a Catholic
church, and Binx is a Catholic, but it does not occur to him to go
in. Finally Kate drives up: "There she sits like a bomber pilot,
resting on her wheel and looking sideways at the children and
not seeing, and she could be I myself, sooty eyed and nowhere"
(p. 211). In a Sartrean sense, Binx looks upon Kate in her
nakedness, in her subjectivity, but the result is not a feeling of
superiority or of aggression; the look, Percy maintains, " . . . can
also be love in the communion of selves. 'L' enfer c'est autrui.'
But so is heaven."[55] Her return prompts a very hesitant renewal
of hope in the possibility of a search: "Is it possible . . . it is not
too late?" (p. 211). Acknowledging to each other their precarious
condition, acknowledging that failure would crush both of them,
they decide to take a most desperate risk, to marry.

In the Epilogue Binx reports upon the first two years of his
marriage. But the report offers only public events; Binx refuses
to comment upon the condition of himself or Kate. But despite
his refusal to discuss the success of his search, several clues suggest that he has leaped from the aesthetic to the ethical sphere of
existence.[56] For one thing, he is able to retain control of himself
at the death of his afflicted half-brother, Lonnie, whom he had
loved deeply. There is not the slightest indication that he will
run away to escape this pathetic event, although Lonnie's death,
after a short life of uninterrupted affliction, would surely be a
most absurd phenomenon to anyone not struggling toward
faith. But Binx, like Kierkegaard's Abraham, seems to know
now the capacity that faith has to confront the absurd. For another thing, the very fact that Binx has been able to transcend his
concern with himself in order to care for Kate indicates his progress, just as marriage, in Kierkegaard's thought, denotes the
ethical sphere. As for the marriage, however, Percy is not roman-
tically suggesting that Binx and Kate will live happily ever after.
Existence will remain precarious for them, and neither of them
is in any sense "cured," but they are conscious now that they
exist, for they see confirmation of their existence in the eyes of
the other. And that last phrase is not a conceit; they literally
depend upon the recognition of themselves they see in each

other's eyes for their feeling of authenticity.[57] Kate's last question in the novel indicates her absolute dependence upon their relationship: "While I am on the streetcar—are you going to be thinking about me?" (p. 222). They realize that they have gained a prize of comradeship and love, and though they know that it is a prize only too often lost, they seem ready to fight desperately for it.

II

Will Barrett: From the Aesthetic to the Religious

In "The Man on the Train," Dr. Percy at once implies a dichotomy that is integral to his thinking. Contrary to the assumptions of the objective empiricists, all reality is not revealed through their scheme of universalizing all of man's experiences and abstracting all of man's needs and aspirations. There is the infinitely more important reality of the subjectivity, that reality which is the concern of the existentialists. It is in discussing this second or higher reality that Dr. Percy introduces the three existential modes which distinguish the topography of his fiction.

Some men, of course, may be tranquil in the objective empirical mode; they may feel that they are anyone existing anywhere and that all their needs have been met through science. But is should go without saying that these men are alienated, whether or not they know it, just as those who do not despair are nevertheless in despair, the most dangerous form of despair, according to Kierkegaard. Other men, however, live in the mode which is reversal of the objective empirical. This mode is alienation, and such men feel alienated, estranged from being, precisely to the degree that they feel restricted to the rewards/limitations of the objective empirical mode. Inhabited by an orientation toward transcendence, which is not accounted for by the objective empirical world in which they live, they feel victimized and threatened by the "everydayness" which surrounds them. They thus attempt to escape this "everydayness," to get deliverance from alienation.

If the present is alienation, there remain the alternatives of future and past. Perhaps invariably the victim of a meaningless present first attempts to seek meaning in the future. This search

for meaning is rotation, " . . . the quest of the new as new, the re-
posing of all hope in what may lie around the bend. . . . "[58] On
the other hand, the victim may learn to distrust the lure of the
future and turn instead to the past. This conversion of rotation
is repetition. Such a conversion necessarily involves turning inward, in the hope of discovering within the self where it was
that "everydayness" became triumphant.

Dr. Percy is interested not only in these modes in reality but
also in their representation in fiction. The very fact that literature stands as a symbolic construct between writer and reader
frustrates the attempt of the writer to present the three existential modes in fiction. Relying upon the important role for intersubjectivity which he develops in "Symbol as Hermeneutic in
Existentialism" and "Symbol, Consciousness, and Intersubjectivity," Dr. Percy demonstrates that in fiction, re-presenting is not
nearly synonymous with presenting.

One cannot really, for example, re-present alienation in literature. If a reader unaware of his alienation reads about an alienated character, he simply will not understand the nature of the
character or be able to apply the derived experience to his own
condition. A reader whose needs are satisfied by the objective
empirical will hardly understand a character who real needs are
denied by the same category. But even if a reader aware of his
alienation reads about an alienated character, the result will only
be " . . . the speakability of his alienation, and the new triple
alliance of himself, the alienated character, and the author."
Thus there is created a sense of comradeliness, the very reversal
of alienation, and there can be, therefore, no experience of alienation to derive. "The only literature of alienation is an alienated
literature, that is, a bad art, which is no art at all. An Erle Stanley
Gardner novel is a true exercise in alienation. A man who finishes his twentieth Perry Mason is that much nearer total despair than when he started."[59]

Since rotation is the quest for the new, " . . . the coming upon
the Real Thing among the ruins . . . ,"[60] the attempt to find
meaning outside the subjectivity, then the sense of novelty
which one hopes to experience is the same, more or less, for both
character and reader. Thus rotation can be re-presented in literature without appreciable change. The reader, as well as the character, can be diverted from "everydayness" by a trip down the
mighty Mississippi or a baptismal plunge into the river at Capor-
etto. Both will thrill to the chance encounter with others (or

"meeting cute," as Dr. Percy says they call such events in Holly-wood)[61] and to the fortuitous escapes from any self-commitment that might develop from the chance encounter. And this is the strategy of rotation—chance encounter, exultance over the new, and fortuituous escape without any memory of the encounter. Indeed, so essential is the escape without remembering that Dr. Percy terms amnesia the supreme rotation. "Perfect rotation could only be achieved by a progressive amnesia in which the forgetting kept pace with time so that every corner turned, every face seen, is a rotation."[62] But it must be understood that only for the character does the rotation satisfy and heal; there is no experi-ence which the reader can derive for himself here that would combat his own "everydayness." For the reader who thinks that such encounters will happen to him, the ultimate conclusion will be either suicide or total self-loss, either of which, it need hardly be added, is a condition of despair or alienation.

Unlike rotation, repetition in literature requires that the read-er make a radical identification with the character. Whereas he can enjoy the trip down the Mississippi without imagining him-self as Huck, the reader cannot go home with Tom Wolfe with-out casting for himself Tom Wolfe's background. But even with the greatest empathy, the reader cannot really gain anything of significance from the repetition, for,

> unlike rotation, it is of two kinds, the aesthetic and the existential, which literature accordingly polarizes. The aesthetic repetition captures the savor of repetition without surrendering the self as a locus of experience and possibility. When Proust tastes the piece of cake or Captain Ryder finds himself in Brideshead, the incident may serve as an occasion for either kind: an excursion into the inter-esting, a savoring of the past as experience; or two, the passionate quest in which the incident serves as a thread in the labyrinth to be followed at any cost. This latter, however, however serious, cannot fail to be polarized by art, transmitting as the interesting. The ques-tion: what does it mean to stand before the house of one's child-hood?, is thus received in two different ways, one, as an occasion for the connoisseur sampling of a rare emotion, the other literally and seriously: what does it really mean?[63]

Such interior states as alienation, rotation, and repetition are exactly what Dr. Percy wishes to create in his characterization of Williston Bibb Barrett, the young protagonist of *The Last Gentle-man*. Indeed, one of the mottoes of the novel, "If a man cannot forget, he will never amount to much," is derived from Kierke-

gaard's "The Rotation Method."[64] Here Kierkegaard is being brilliantly ironical, for he is permitting the aesthetic man to reveal
his own limitations: if a man residing in the aesthetic sphere
cannot counter "everydayness" by rotation, then his life will be
unpleasant.   The aesthete cannot grasp that, either pleasant or
unpleasant, the aesthetic life is one of alienated incompleteness.
Just as clearly, Percy is also being ironical in his choice of this
motto. For the novel is "about" Barrett's attempts to amount to
something by coping with his forgetting.

Admittedly resembling Dostoevsky's "Idiot," Prince Myshkin,[65] Will Barrett, unlike Binx Bolling, exhibits symptoms that
enable the world to recognize him as a sick man.   Like Myshkin
he suffers from a type of epileptic condition, probably, in Barrett's case, best called "psychic seizures," rather than "*petit mal*"
attacks. Most of the time his condition is quiescent, with only an
occasional *déjà vu* to suggest what Barrett terms his "nervous
condition."   But there come those moments when Will feels
most intensely a part of the conventional world, when he develops a " . . . great thirst for the 'answer,' the key which will unlock
everything . . . " (p. 38), when he buys some expensive machine,
as if to acknowledge his capture by the objective empirical
culture which surrounds him.   Then he lapses into a fugue state,
a condition of cloudy or completely obscured consciousness.
When he recovers, usually after a considerable period of time
and in some totally strange place, he suffers from amnesia.

Will has suffered such attacks from childhood, but his condition seems to have been very much aggravated by the suicide of
his father.   The various generations of male Barretts described in
the novel reflect a growing alienation and cultural degeneration:

> The great grandfather knew what was what and said so and acted
> accordingly and did not care what anyone thought. He even wore a
> pistol in a holster like a Western hero and once met the Grand Wiz-
> ard of the Ku Klux Klan in a barbershop and invited him then and
> there to shoot it out in the street. The next generation, the grand-
> father, seemed to know what was what but he was not really so
> sure. He was brave but he gave much thought to the business of be-
> ing brave. He too would have shot it out with the Grand Wizard
> if only he could have made certain it was the thing to do. The
> father was a brave man too and he said he didn't care what others
> thought, but he did care. More than anything else, he wished to
> act with honor and to be thought well of by other men. So living for
> him was a strain. He became ironical. For him it was not a small
> thing to walk down the street on an ordinary September morning.

In the end he was killed by his own irony and sadness and by the strain of living out an ordinary day in a perfect dance of honor.[66] (pp. 9-10)

Will's great-grandfather had been a Southern gentleman who could still act without any self-doubt to enforce his principles upon the unprincipled people of the community. But his father, though he had the same principles, could only enforce them at the cost of his alienation from the community, since the whole community has lost its principles; as he says of the unprincipled people: "Once they were the fornicators and the bribers and the takers of bribes and we were not and that was why they hated us. Now we are like them . . . (p. 330). Will's father is very much like Percy's Southern stoic, and when he finally decides that the cost of enforcing his principles is too great, he admits his despair, his lack of belief in possibility, by self-destruction. Since the South is, in a way, responsible for his father's death, Will, the last gentleman, has fled the South, though he still figuratively carries the wound which he received there. He suffers from deafness in one ear, and one soon conjectures that its origin is not organic, but hysterical, that it resulted from hearing the shotgun blast which took his father's life. The frequently mentioned impairment, then, seems symbolic both of Will's loss of and quest for a father and of his alienation from his sense of Southern community.

After his father's death, Will had been a recluse until he was drafted. Being in the army was not for Will a hardship, however, for it permitted him to live away from the South in the objective empirical world—until he was discovered wandering, in a state of amnesia, in " . . . the Shenandoah Valley, between Cross Keys and Port Republic, sites of notable victories of General Stonewall Jackson" (p. 18). According to medical theory, amnesia occurs when the victim cannot face the present, so that Will must have been fleeing from the "everydayness" which he had thought preferable to his life of loss in the South. But his point of destination seems evidence of a compulsion to confront the community from which he felt alienated; he himself admits that his " . . . nationalistic feelings . . . " are strongest before an onset of amnesia (p. 267). To the army, however, his wandering had seemed unaccountably irrational, and he was therefore given a medical discharge. Thereafter he took up residence at a Y.M.C.A., in New York City, submitted himself to a psychiatrist for a period of five years, and, in order to help pay for the treatment, became a humidification engineer at Macy's, three floors below street level.

Will's behavior has existential as well as psychological implications, of course. Like Binx Bolling, he spends his time underground, " . . . in the determinants of sensuousness. . . . "[67] As he later admits, he has had for a long time " . . . a consuming desire for girls, for the coarsest possible relations with them, without knowing how to treat them as human beings" (p. 385). He has attempted to live happily in the aesthetic sphere of existence, satisfying social and sexual needs, convinced that his inward difficulty would be resolved through his mastery of "life adjustment" goals established by mental health specialists. But his fugue states and consequent bouts of amnesia reflect his attempts to employ the rotation method to avoid his boredom: "He had a way of turning up at unlikely places such as a bakery in Cincinnati or a greenhouse in Memphis, where he might work for several weeks assaulted by the *déjà vus* of hot growing green plants" (p. 12). Occasionally his rotations offer the chance for a repetition, a reintegration of self, when he could discover his orientation toward the South, where his loss occurred, but he has not understood or grasped these opportunities.

The action of *The Last Gentleman* concerns yet another attempt by Will Barrett to collect the pieces of time and space that constitute his life. He is first seen in the midst of a euphoric state that has always signaled, as his analyst points out, the coming of a fugue. But Will refuses to accept such a warning; rather he bids farewell to Dr. Gamow, " . . . a father of sorts, and from his alma mater, sweet mother psychoanalysis . . . " (p. 41). At the same time he exhausts his money in order to buy an expensive German telescope, in the hope that a scientific instrument will recover for him the density of the outside world (a loss caused by "science" in the first place, according to Dr. Percy). Then he decides to become the master of his own fate: "I am indeed an engineer, he thought, if only a humidification engineer, which is no great shakes of a profession. But I am also an engineer in a deeper sense: I shall engineer the future of my life according to the scientific principles and the self-knowledge I have so arduously gained from five years of analysis" (p. 42).

With the telescope Dr. Percy engineers a classic example of "meeting cute." In Central Park one day, after having left his "alma mater," Will happens to see a beautiful young girl, with whom he immediately falls in love, through his telescope. Like the complete believer in possibility that he is, he immediately abandons everything in the hope that this rotation will hold meaning for him. After an interval of observances of the girl, he finally chances to meet her and her family. The Vaught family, of Atlanta, could hardly be more heterogeneous: "Poppy," the father, owner of the second-largest Chevrolet agency in the world, completely happy/despairing; "Dolly," the mother, devotee of every kooky rightist cause imaginable; Sutter, the elder son, brilliant failure of a doctor; Rita, Sutter's ex-wife, cold-blooded humanist; Valentine, the elder daughter, embittered nun; Kitty, Will's beloved, twenty-one and the very picture of Kierkegaardian immediacy; and Jamie, the younger son, sixteen and hopelessly ill with leukemia.

Even though Will loves Kitty and agrees to become a paid companion for Jamie, it is Sutter who most affects Will's life and thus plays the most crucial role in the novel. For it is Sutter, the despairing intellectual, who understands his own spiritual malady and the alternatives to it chosen by the other members of the family and who analyzes these various modes in a casebook which Will finds and is drawn more and more to study. Will first learns of Sutter's observations in New York City, in Jamie's hospital room, when he reads Sutter's article, entitled " . . . *The incidence of Post-orgasmic Suicide in Male University Graduate Students,* and divided into two sections, the first subtitled 'Genital Sexuality as the Sole Surviving Communication Channel between Transcending-Immanent Subjects,' and the second, 'The Failure of Coitus as a Mode of Reentry into the Sphere of Immanence from the Sphere of Transcendence' " (p. 65). As befitting an engineer, Will understands only the technique, not the motivation, involved, and it is only much later that he begins to grasp the significance of Sutter's use of "immanence" and "transcendence."

Sutter Vaught accepts Kierkegaard's contention that *"in the end all corruption will come from the natural sciences."*[68] According to Sutter, science is responsible for the objective empirical world in which we live, where the universal has replaced the individual and where abstraction has displaced the concrete. And thus we have lost the feeling of a particular place and a particular time, so that the world no longer seems "real." "Things, persons, relations emptied out, not by theory but by lay reading of theory" (p. 279).

In consequence, we are alienated; we feel above and apart from and against the world which surrounds us. We have fallen victim to transcendence, while the world has been " . . . demoted to immanence and seen as examplar and specimen and coordinate . . . " (p. 345). But, "science, which (in layman's view) dissolves concrete things and relations, leaves intact touch of skin to skin" (p. 280). Thus, "lewdness=sole concrete metaphysic of layman in age of science—sacrament of the dispossessed. . . . there remains only relation of skin to skin and hand under dress" (pp. 279-280). "Relation of genital sexuality reinforced twice: once because it is touch, therefore physical, therefore 'real'; again because it corresponds with theoretical (i.e., sexual) substrata of all other relations. Therefore genital sexuality=twice 'real' " (p. 280). "Hotel room=site of intersection of transcendence and immanence; room itself, a tri-axial coordinate ten floors above street; whore who comes up=pure immanence to be entered" (p. 345).

With this situation prevailing, Sutter refuses to be hypocritical like most Americans. With Kierkegaard, he deals with the either/or. *Either* be a Christian and seek the juncture of transcendence and immanence through faith *or* be a fornicator and seek the juncture through genital sexuality. Most Americans overtly profess Christianity and covertly practice lewdness: "Main Street, U.S.A.=a million-dollar segregated church on one corner, a drugstore with dirty magazines on the other, a lewd movie on the third, and on the fourth a B-girl bar with condom dispensers in the gents' room" (p. 292). But Sutter has openly rejected Christianity and accepted its alternative: "I am overtly heterosexual and overtly lewd. I am therefore the only sincere American" (p. 293). And he makes sure that his practice scandalizes "decent" Americans; he schedules his couplings so that he will be observed. "We are doomed to the transcendence of abstraction and I choose the only reentry into the world which remains to us. What is better then than the beauty and the exaltation of the practice of transcendence (science and art) and of the delectation of immanence, the beauty and the exaltation of lewd love" (p. 354).

There is only one trouble with his choice of fornication as " . . . the sole channel to the real" (p. 372): " . . . since reentry coterminus c orgasm, post-orgasmic despair without remedy" (p. 345). "Suicide considered as consequence of the spirit of abstraction and of transcendence; lewdness as sole portal of reentry into world demoted to immanence; reentry into immanance via orgasm; but post-orgasmic transcendence 7 devils worse than first" (p. 345). Couplings in Percy's novels are fraught with anxiety (e.g., that between Binx and Kate or that between Will and Kitty), ending unsuccessfully or, if successfully, in greater despair. It was after such an experience that Sutter had attempted suicide and, having failed, had done the research which resulted in his article.

It is in light of Sutter's distinction between fornicators and nonfornicators that much of the extraneous action of the novel can best be understood. While the novel is primarily concerned with Will's quest, it contains a background that very effectively dramatizes the post-Christian culture of the United States of the early sixties. Here Percy has great fun with his immense satiric gifts, working with humor in a way that constantly reminds the reader that, according to Kierkegaard, the humorous state immediately precedes the religious state. Indeed, Percy's humor is perhaps his best utilization of indirect communication: "Religiosity with humor as its incognito is therefore a synthesis of absolute religious passion (the inwardness being dialectically produced) with a maturity of spirit, which withdraws the religiosity away from all externality back into inwardness, where again it is absolute religious passion."[69] In this humorous background, it should be stressed, however, that a fornicator is not necessarily an evil person; rather, he is simply one whose highest feeling of awe and reverence is reserved for the fleshly contact. The fornicators against whom Will's father rails before his suicide, for example, are evil not because of their fornication but because of their hypocrisy. They profess Christianity, yet their practice of fornication reveals its priority as a metaphysic for them.

After Will's happenstance involvement with the Vaught family, he is given the opportunity to return to the South, to live in the Vaught home and be a companion to the dying Jamie while he courts Kitty. He somewhat dimly knows that the answer to his ailments lies in the South, that a repetition might occur if he returned to stand before the home of his youth. Even his analyst had offered that suggestion: "Moreover, suggestible as he was, he began to think it mightn't be a bad idea to return to the South and discover his identity, to use Dr. Gamow's expression" (p. 79). Of course, the very fact that science could make a generalization about the phenomenon of repetition would render it that much harder to achieve.

The South to which Will returns is a composite South, bearing resemblance, as Dr. Percy says, variously to Alabama, Mississippi, and, Louisiana (p. 2). On the surface this is a new South: " . . . happy, victorious, Christian, rich, patriotic and Republican" (p. 185). Under the surface it is a place where little Negro girls are killed in the bombing of a Birmingham church (p. 307), where open rebellion occurs when Meredith is brought to the University of Mississippi campus (pp. 287-289), and where civil rights workers are ever in danger (pp. 323-326). Only in rare, isolated cases does the old, innocent relationship between servile Negro and superior white man exist, as a Shut Off, Louisiana, where Will's Uncle Fannin and his retainer Merriam share a delight over Captain Kangaroo and Mr. Greenjeans.

Dr. Percy draws none of the usual distinctions between Northerners and Southerners. For there no longer is any distinction to be drawn: both groups believe in the metaphysics of fornication. On his way South Will meets Forney Aiken, whose name suggests his membership in the faith-in-flesh religion. Forney is a black white, a liberal, a humanist, a Northerner who believes in all the right causes. Yet for Dr. Percy he is a caricature because he has no transcendent orientation. Let me be emphatic here: Dr. Percy does not make him a caricature; he *is*, as most of us are, a caricature because he is overdeveloped in one way and undeveloped in another. His limitation is more clearly seen when his colleague Morton Prince is introduced. Prince is a novelist of the Norman Mailer School; his novels are " . . . deeply religious . . . " studies of "——ing" (p. 137). Will reads the latest result of Prince's fertile brain: "*Love* was about orgasms, good and bad, some forty-six. But it ended, as Forney had said, on a religious note. 'And so I humbly ask of life,' said the hero to his last partner with whose assistance he had managed to coincide with his best expectations, 'that it grant us the only salvation, that of one human being discovering himself through another and through the miracle of love" (p. 138). The Southerners whom Will meets on his return may be divided into two groups: the romantic fornicators and the practical fornicators. Rita Vaught is a romantic; although she does not now practice fornication, she is still limited to the human and she still reads such books as Erich Fromm's *The Art of Loving*. Son Junior Thigpen is typical of the practical fornicators; he believes only in sex and makes no bones about it.

When he returns to the South, Will is determined to live the life of an engineer. He will care for Jamie, whom he recognizes as being like himself, filled with possibility but having no actuality. At the same time he will marry Kitty and become a model of middle-class respectability. The only trouble is that in his new objective empirical paradise, his anxiety, amnesia, and dislocation become increasingly worse. Desperately he pursues the life of immediacy promised by Kitty Vaught, seeing himself in a split-level, as personnel manager of Confederate Chevrolet; but just as desperately he finds himself drawn to Sutter Vaught, seeing in Sutter a father who might have answers for him.

As a doctor, Sutter recognizes that Jamie is very soon to die, and he finally kidnaps his brother and takes him to New Mexico. There he may die, Sutter intends, not as a drugged "thing," from whom death is hidden, as it is in middle-class America, but as a conscious being, with the opportunity to "leap" if he likes. Although Sutter lacks the ability to believe that his sister Val possesses, he apparently wishes Jamie to have that option. Will is commissioned by the family to retrieve Jamie, but as he follows the pair he reads the casebook, which, the reader begins to think, Sutter had planted for him.

For, as Will approaches Jamie and Sutter, so the casebook begins to approach Will's dilemma—only to break off just as Will reaches them. Although Will at once wishes to learn from Sutter, the next few days are devoted to their ministrations to Jamie as he dies. Bowing to Val's request, Will arranges for a Catholic baptism for Jamie, although, according to Percy, failing to understand its significance.[70] But, so shaken has he been by the presence of death, Will now demands that Sutter help him if he can. Having reserved the significance of Will's name for the entire novel, Dr. Percy now uses it:

> 'Dr. Vaught, I need you. I, Will Barrett—' and he actually pointed to himself lest there be a mistake, '—need you and want you to come back. I need you more than Jamie needed you. Jamie had Val too.' (p. 409)

In willing to bear the kind of world seen by Sutter, a world where one must either be fornicator or be Christian, Will creates freedom for himself. For by exercising will, he becomes a self. Dr. Percy emphasizes this point: " 'I, Will Barrett—' and he actually pointed to himself . . . " And in willing one thing, Will, according to Kierkegaard, is showing purity of heart. In so identifying himself and the purity of his intentions, Will Barrett has leaped from Kierkegaard's Religion A, the religion of immanence, to Religion B, the religion of transcendence. And it may be that he can take Sutter Vaught with him. For though earlier Sutter had refused to tell Will whether or not to be a fornicator and had implied that he would not outlive Jamie by an hour or two, at the very last he recognizes Will's need of him and halts his car to wait for him.

A good many of the reviewers of *The Last Gentleman* transparently dodged any attempt to comment upon the meaning of the conclusion of the novel. And a few expressed disappointment that Will would apparently return to become personnel manager of Confederate Chevrolet. Some even implied that Will and Sutter would commit suicide together. All of these responses testify to the success of Dr. Percy's intended ambiguity, which allows the reader to see Will as sane or insane, sick or healthy, despairing or recovering, according to his own bent.[71] Certainly, though, Dr. Percy has brilliantly employed indirect communication: he has showed us how it is with Will and through aesthetic captivation obliged us to reflect upon the most decisive definitions of Christianity.

Notes

[1] Walker Percy, "From Facts to Fiction," The Washington Post *Book Week*, December 25, 1966, p. 5.

[2] *Ibid.*

[3] *Ibid.*

[4] Percy's bibliography during these years includes (in chronological order):

"Symbol as Need," *Thought*, 29(Autumn 1954), 381-390.

"Symbol as Hermeneutic in Existentialism," *Philosophy and Phenomenological Research*, 16 (June 1956), 522-530.

"Stoicism in the South," *Commonweal*, 44 (July 6, 1956), 342-344.

"The Man on the Train: Three Existential Modes," *Partisan Review*, 23 (Fall 1956), 478-494.

"The Coming Crisis in Psychiatry," *America*, 96 (January 5, 1957), 391-393; (January 12, 1957), 415-418.

"The American War," *Commonweal*, 45 (March 29, 1957), 655-657.

"Semiotic and a Theory of Knowledge," *Modern Schoolman*, 23 (May 1957), 225-246.

"Truth, or Pavlov's Dogs?" *America*, 97 (June 8, 1957), 306-307. [Review of *The Battle for the Mind*, by William Sargant.]

"The Southern View," *America*, 97 (July 20, 1957), 428-429.

"A Southern Moderate," *Commonweal*, 47 (December 13, 1957), 279-282.

"Decline of the Western," *Commonweal*, 48 (May 16, 1958), 181-183.

"Symbol, Consciousness, and Intersubjectivity," *Journal of Philosophy*, 55 (July 17, 1958), 631-641.

"Culture: The Antimony of the Scientific Method," *New Scholasticism*, 32 (October 1958), 443-475.

"The Loss of the Creature," *Forum* [University of Houston], 2 (Fall 1958), 6-14.

"Metaphor as Mistake," *Sewanee Review*, 66 (Winter 1958), 79-99.

"Culture Critics," *Commonweal*, 70 (June 5, 1959), 247-250. [Review of *The Waist-High Culture*, by Thomas Griffith, and *The Lonely Crowd*, by David Riesman.]

"The Message in the Bottle," *Thought*, 34 (Fall 1959), 405-433.

"Naming and Being," *Personalist*, 41 (Spring 1960), 148-157.

"Seven Laymen Discuss Morality," *America*, 104 (October 1, 1960), 12-13.

"The Symbolic Structure of Interpersonal Process," *Psychiatry*, 24 (February 1961), 39-52.

[5] Walker Percy, "From Facts to Fiction," p. 9.

[6] Ashley Brown, "An Interview with Walker Percy," *Shenandoah*, 18 (Spring 1967), 7.

[7] Walker Percy, *The Moviegoer* (New York, 1962), p. 218. Hereafter page references to *The Moviegoer* will be incorporated in the text.

[8] Sören Kierkegaard, *The Point of View for My Work as An Author*, trans. Walter Lowrie (New York, 1962). Although it was written in 1848, *The Point of View* was not published until 1859, after Kierkegaard's death. In this short work Kierkegaard discussed the products of his amazingly prolific pen during the years 1843-1847. It would appear, Kierkegaard begins, that his writing would divide into two discrete camps, the "aesthetic" and the "religious." The "aesthetic" works would include *Either/Or*, *Fear and Trembling*, *Repetition*, *Philosophical Fragments*, *The Concept of Dread*, *Stages on the Road to Life*, and *Final Unscientific Postscript*, all of which Kierkegaard published pseudonymously. The "religious" works were generally entitled *Edifying Discourses*, with Kierkegaard acknowledging himself as the author.

[9] "The Coming Crisis," p. 391.

[10] *Ibid.*, p. 392.

[11] *Ibid.*

[12] *Ibid.*, p. 415.

[13] *Ibid.* Percy further amplifies this point in "Culture: The Antinomy," pp. 474-475: "Scientists of man must accept as their 'datum' that strange creature who, like themselves, is given to making assertions about the world and, like themselves, now drawing near, now falling short of the truth. It is high time for social scientists in general to take seriously the chief article of faith upon which their function is based: that there is a metascientific, metacultural reality, an order of being apart from the scientific and cultural symbols with which it is grasped and expressed. The need for a more radically scientific method de-

rives not merely from metaphysical and religious argument, but also from the antimony into which a nonradical science falls in dealing with man."

[14] "The Coming Crisis," p. 417.

[15] *Ibid.*, p. 418.

[16] *Ibid.*

[17] *Ibid.*

[18] Sören Kierkegaard, *Fear and Trembling and The Sickness Unto Death*, trans. Walter Lowrie (New York, 1954), p. 178.

[19] "The Coming Crisis," p. 392.

[20] *Ibid.*

[21] *Ibid.*, p. 415.

[22] *Ibid.*, p. 392. Earlier, in "The Man on the Train," Percy had distinguished between commuter A and commuter B: "I mean that whereas one commuter may sit on the train and feel himself quite at home, seeing the passing scene as a series of meaningful projects full of signs which he reads without difficulty, another commuter, although he has no empirical reason for being so, although he has satisfied the same empirical needs as commuter A, is alienated. To say the least, he is bored; to say the most, he is in pure anxiety; he is horrified at his surroundings—he might as well be passing through a lunar landscape and the signs he sees are absurd or at least ambiguous. (It will not be necessary at this point to consider the further possibility that commuter A's tranquillity is no guarantee against alienation, that in fact he may be more desperately lost to himself than B in the sense of being anonymous . . .)" (p. 478). Percy allows Binx to describe, in *The Moviegoer*, the very picture of commuter A, pp. 173-175, as Binx and Kate travel by train to Chicago. Binx observes his fellow traveler reading a newspaper counseling column, an action that Percy, in "The Man on the Train," warns against: "It is just when the alienated commuter reads books on mental hygiene which abstract immanent goals that he comes closest to despair. One has only to let the mental-health savants set forth their own ideal of sane living, the composite reader who reads their books seriously and devotes every ounce of his strength to the pursuit of the goals erected: emotional maturity, inclusiveness, productivity, creativity, belongingness—there will emerge, far more faithfully than I could portray him, the candidate for suicide" (p. 480).

[23] Binx is very much a product of what Percy, following Marcel, calls the " . . . 'ontophobic' [fearful of authentic existence] age . . . " (See "Culture: The Antinomy," p. 453.)

[24] Since Binx is attempting to lift himself from the aesthetic to the ethical sphere, his nature, according to Kierkegaard, *would* be ironical. See Sören Kierkegaard, *Kierkegaard's Concluding Unscientific Postscript*, trans. David F. Swenson (Princeton, 1944), pp. 448 ff.

[25] *Fear and Trembling and The Sickness Unto Death*, pp. 196-200. Along the way to his existential insight, Binx successively echoes Kierkegaard's personifications of the various aesthetic subspheres. At first he is the Don Juan of simple sensuousness, then he is the bored Faust who seeks relief from "everydayness" in the unexpected, and then he is Ahasuerus, recognizing his despair and seeing in other Jews the reflection of his own alienation.

[26] *Ibid.*, pp. 197-198.

[27] *Ibid.*, pp. 184-194.

[28] In "Symbol as Hermeneutic," Percy discusses the ambiguous nature of

things for modern Americans: "A new product, an automobile, resplendent in its autonomous form (and endowed, we shall see later, with certain magic properties by virtue of the mystery and remotion of its manufacture) is loved for the sake of its form—what characterizes an idolatrous desire for a new car is not the need of a means of getting from one place to another, but a prime desire to *have* the car itself. If I can have that car, my life will be different, for my nothingness will be informed by the having of it. But possession turns out to be a gradual neutralization. Once it enters the zone of my naught, the car is emptied out, and instead of informing me, only participates in my nothingness" (p. 528).

[29] "To Restore a Fragmented Image," *Sewanee Review*, 69 (Autumn 1961), 693.

[30] *Fear and Trembling and The Sickness Unto Death*, p. 176.

[31] Binx is very much like Ellison's invisible man, who keeps in a briefcase all of the papers that impose objective identification on him. But whereas the invisible man learns only in the conclusion of his story about the duplicity of such identification, Binx knows from the very beginning that such papers deny, rather than confirm, his individuality.

[32] Percy first uses the term "everydayness" in "The Man on the Train."

[33] *Fear and Trembling and The Sickness Unto Death*, pp. 166-167.

[34] This concept of the reintegration of the self Percy derives from Kierkegaard, especially from the short book entitled *Repetition*.

[35] "Rotation" is also derived from Kierkegaard. See "The Rotation Method," *Either/Or*, Vol. I, trans. David F. Swenson and Lillian Marvin Swenson (New York, 1959), pp. 279-296, for Kierkegaard's fullest description of this mode.

[36] "Gestural perfection" seems to be Percy's label for the complete achievement of all the possibilities of a situation. He utilizes it in both "The Man on the Train" and "Decline of the Western."

[37] Percy first makes use of the concept of the moviegoer in "The Man on the Train."

[38] In "Stoicism in the South," Percy offers a very accurate description of the aunt, Emily Bolling Cutrer: "Yet, like the Stoa of the Empire, the Stoa of the South was based on a particular hierarchical structure and could not survive the change. Nor did it wish to survive. Its most characteristic mood was a poetic pessimism which took a grim satisfaction in the dissolution of its values—because social decay confirmed one in his original choice of the wintery kingdom of self" (p. 343). Such a mood can be seen in the novel, in Aunt Emily's climactic statement to Binx: "Perhaps we are a biological sport. I am not sure. But one thing I am sure of: we live by our lights, we die by our lights, and whoever the high gods may be, we'll look them in the eye without apology. . . . I did my best for you, son. I gave you all I had. More than anything I wanted to pass on to you the one heritage of the men of our family, a certain quality of spirit, a gaiety, a sense of duty, a nobility worn lightly, a sweetness, a gentleness with women—the only good things the South ever had and the only things that really matter in this life" (p. 205).

[39] *Fear and Trembling and The Sickness Unto Death*, p. 174.

[40] In "The Man on the Train," Percy writes that " . . . Prince Andrey [in *War and Peace*] transcended everydayness and came to himself for the first time only when he lay wounded on the field of Borodino" (p. 493). It is only at such moments, as Percy points out in "Naming and Being," that the aesthete can re-

capture being: "If one sees a movement in a tree and recognizes it and says it is
only a sparrow,' one is disposing of the creature through its symbolic formulation. The sparrow is no longer available to me. Being is elusive; it tends to escape, leaving only a simulacrum of symbol. Only under the condition of ordeal
may I recover the sparrow. If I am lying wounded or in exile or in prison and a
sparrow builds his nest at my window, then I may see the sparrow" (p. 154).

41 In "The Symbolic Structure of Interpersonal Process," Percy closely anticipates Binx's realization of the failure of his search by means of objective data,
when he writes:

This patient is in his world in a way wholly different from that of his therapist, yet it is in a way which is heavily influenced by the presence of science
in the world. The patient, let me postulate, is the sort of person who has adopted the objective point of view but has adopted it secondhand. He is convinced
that the scientific world view is the right way of looking at things, but since he
is not a scientist and does not spend his time practising the objective method,
his objective-mindedness raises some problems. Deprived of the firsthand encounter with the subject matter which the scientist enjoys, he is even more apt
than the scientist to fall prey to what Whitehead called the 'fallacy of misplaced concreteness' and so to bestow upon theory, or what he imagines to be
theory, a superior reality at the expense of the reality of the very world he
lives in. His problem is not, as is the scientist's, *What sense can I make of the
data?* but is instead, *How can I live in a world which I have disposed
theoretically?* . . . Such a misplacement of the concrete is a serious matter
because, although one may dispose of the world through theory, one is not thereby excused from the necessity of living in this same world. (p. 51)

42 "The Coming Crisis," p. 392.

43 Camus seems to have been on Percy's mind when he created Binx. Certainly the famous description of a life of everydayness in *The Myth of Sisyphus*
would apply to Binx's life in Gentilly: "Rising, streetcar, four hours in the
office or the factory, meal, streetcar, four hours of work, meal, sleep, and Mon-
day Tuesday Wednesday Thursday Friday and Saturday according to the same
rhythm— . . . " So, too, would Camus's description of the awakening apply:
"Yet a day comes when a man notices or says that he is thirty. Thus he asserts
his youth. But simultaneously he situates himself in relation to time. He takes
his place in it. He admits that he stands at a certain point on a curve that he
acknowledges having to travel to its end. He belongs to time, and by the horror
that seizes him, he recognizes his worst enemy." And Percy's recollection, in
"From Facts to Fiction," suggests that Binx's journey, like that of Camus's
Mersault, in *The Stranger*, was to be toward self-awareness: "When I sat down
to write *The Moviegoer*, I was very much aware of discarding the conventional
notions of a plot and a set of characters, discarded because the traditional concept of plot-and-character itself reflects a view of reality which has been
called into question. Rather would I begin with a *man* who finds himself in a
world, a very concrete place and time. Such a man might be represented as *coming to himself* in somewhat the same sense as Robinson Crusoe came to himself
on his island after his shipwreck, with the same wonder and curiosity" (p. 9).

44 Like Sartre's Roquentin, in *Nausea*, Binx notices for the first time in
years his own hand and is shaken to the depths of anxiety to discover that it is
a part of the *It*, that one is separated even from one's own body.

45 *Fear and Trembling and The Sickness Unto Death*, p. 173.

[46] Robinson Crusoe is a favorite reference for Percy. He may have been struck by Kierkegaard's use of it, in *Repetition*, trans. Walter Lowrie (New York, 1964), p. 71: "This in itself was blissful, and yet I sensed the lack of something. Then in the desert which I beheld about me I discovered a figure which gladdened me more than the sight of Friday gladdened the heart of Robinson."

[47] In "The Loss of the Creature" Percy discusses the manner in which a person loses his "sovereignty" by becoming a scientific specimen.

[48] In "Culture Critics," Percy comments upon those who are beset with such apathy that if the proofs were proved, nothing would be changed: "There is something wrong with The Ethical Secularist's Speech. . . . the latter usually considers himself to be as commendably motivated as those with faith, and often is. To these good folk, who live so securely on the accumulated capital of the Christian faith, the core of faith itself is apt to appear as an anomaly, easily dispensable and in fact dispensed with one or two standard objections. It seems pertinent here to raise a question, not about the objections, but about the posture from which the objections are mounted. The point is that even though the objections be answered, nothing is really changed for the objector. All that business about God, the Jews, Christ, the Church seems no less dispensable—queer—whether it is true or not. Yet our ethical friend who is aware of the sickness might do well to consider the possibility that the dislocation of his times is related to this very incapacity to attach significance to the sacramental and historical-incarnational nature of Christianity. Instead of chewing over the same old objections, that is, he should consider the more pressing problem: how is it that even if these things were all true, could be proved, it would make no difference to me?" (p. 250).

[49] *Fear and Trembling and The Sickness Unto Death*, p. 173.

[50] In "The Symbolic Structure of Interpersonal Process," Percy speaks of the patient who " . . . is pleased when the dream he offers to the therapist turns out to be a recognized piece of pathology" (p. 51).

[51] If one despairs over everything in his life, then he really suffers from Nothingness; if, when asked over what he despairs, he replies, "Nothing," then he really despairs over the fact that everything fails to make sense.

[52] In "The Man on the Train," Percy discusses the dangers which can befall the reader or the moviegoer who attempts to imitate the gestural perfection of the fictional or movie hero (p. 487).

[53] See "Symbol, Consciousness, and Intersubjectivity," especially p. 641.

[54] See "Seven Laymen Discuss Morality," where Percy cites the same statistics to illustrate the falsity of evaluating the quality of religious experience objectively (p. 13).

[55] See "Symbol as Hermeneutic in Existentialism," p. 528.

[56] Certainly the provisional quality of the conclusion is consistent with Dr. Percy's theories of existentialistic possibilities in fiction, which he presents in "The Man on the Train." To present Binx as having come to an overpoweringly successful conclusion to his quest would be untrue to the way life really is, for life is always becoming. Binx himself ridicules the pilgrim who is just in from Sambuco or Guanajuato " . . . where he has found the Real Right Thing. . . . " William Styron's Cass Kinsolving, in *Set This House on Fire*, had returned from Sambuco; the pilgrim from Guanajuato is a reference to Dr. Percy's "The Loss of the Creature." Further, to present such fictional success would only further alienate the reader, who cannot achieve any such realistic achievements. Rather,

argues Percy in "The Man on the Train," the writer may " . . . simply affirm alienation for what it is and as the supreme intersubjective achievement of art set forth the truth of it: how it stands with both of us" (p. 491). We may intuit Binx's progress, but he would destroy it if he were to make an explicit statement about it.

57 See "Symbol as Need," especially p. 388.

58 "The Man on the Train," p. 481.

59 *Ibid.*, p. 478.

60 *Ibid.*, p. 493.

61 *Ibid.*, p. 485.

62 *Ibid.*, p. 487.

63 *Ibid.*, pp. 489-490.

64 *Either/Or*, I, 290.

65 Brown, p. 6.

66 See "The Man on the Train" for Percy's conception of the anxiety which results when one attempts to perform selfconsciously what others had performed unselfconsciously.

67 *Fear and Trembling and The Sickness Unto Death*, p. 176.

68 Alexander Dru, *The Journals of Sören Kierkegaard* (London, 1951), p. 181.

69 *Concluding Unscientific Postscript*, p. 452.

70 Brown, p. 8.

71 *Ibid.*, p. 7.

Walker Percy's Southern Stoic

After the death of his widowed mother, when he was four-teen, Walker Percy, along with his brothers Leroy and Phinizy, went to live in the home of William Alexander Percy, in Green-ville, Mississippi.[1] Walker Percy thus lived for about a decade in the household of one of the most admired men of the modern South. Descendant of a family prominent in the Mississippi Delta for a hundred years,[2] William Alexander Percy was virtual-ly a Renaissance man: teacher, decorated military officer, lawyer, poet, and plantation owner.[3] And, although he did not aspire to elective office, he was a politician in the older sense of the word—a citizen competent in the art of government. He was Chairman of the Greenville Flood Relief Committee and the lo-cal Red Cross during the disastrous months-long 1927 flood and thus responsible for feeding and either housing or evacuating six-ty thousand people. He felt so strongly that the Delta needed a progressive newspaper that he persuaded Hodding Carter to set-tle in Greenville and found the *Delta Star* (now the highly re-spected *Delta Democrat-Times*), to which he and other promi-nent citizens whom he enlisted contributed financial and moral support.[4] Frank Smith, the moderate Congressman from the Del-ta, credited his success in getting elected and reelected to the rational and humane climate of opinion inspired by the civic leadership provided in great part by William Alexander Percy.[5]

Although Walker Percy and his brothers were rather distant relatives of William Alexander Percy—they were sons of his first cousin—he nevertheless adopted them as his sons. Then he dis-covered that he had taken on a new role, as father, to which he had never given any thought. What he attempted to teach his sons, over a ten-year period, by example and instruction, is sum-marized in "For the Younger Generation," the climactic chapter of *Lanterns on the Levee.* Although he had doubts that his experience would interest others, he had long thought of writing an autobiography. Finally, in the late Thirties, in poor health, he began to write an account of himself and his ancestors. When

several of his friends were asked to read chapters of it, they dis-
couraged his efforts, and he gave up the project. It was only after
David Cohn returned to Greenville and convinced him of the
artistry of what he had written that he was willing to finish the
work.[6] Dedicated, appropriately enough, to "Walker, Roy, &
Phin," in addition to some other members of his family, the
work was published March 10, 1941, less than a year before his
death.

Had he intended only to relate the events of his life, William
Alexander Percy probably would not have written the book. For
the last page offers his confession of failure: "at law undistinguished, at teaching unprepared, at soldiering average, at citizen-
ship unimportant, at love second-best, at poetry forgotten before
remembered . . . " (LL, 348). But the structure of the book suggests that he had a much larger intent in mind. Although the
style is informal and the content is highly anecdotal, a plan gradually becomes apparent. There is, first of all, a historical sketch
of the Delta. Then a light, frequently humorous genealogy of the
Percy family is given; the conclusion of this section is a statement of what has been learned from the past that will be vital to
the present:

> Perhaps it is all contained in a remark of Father's when he was
> thinking aloud one night and I sat at his feet eavesdropping eager-
> ly:
> "I guess a man's job is to make the world a better place to live
> in, so far as he is able—always remembering the results will be in-
> finitesimal—and to attend to his own soul."
> I've found in those words directions enough for any life. Maybe
> they contain the steady simple wisdom of the South. (LL, 74-75)

The middle chapters of the work are devoted to William
Alexander Percy's efforts to follow his father's advice. Then
comes the account of the arrival in his household of his three
young charges. Percy seems to realize that the fortuitous event is
profoundly symbolic when viewed as a part of his life's continuum. Just as his maturity had begun when he had learned from
the past generation, so now he is obligated to become the past
generation for his sons and provide them with the philosophy
that will insure their successful maturity. But the only precepts
he can honestly offer will provide small comfort:

> Should . . . I teach deceit, dishonor, ruthlessness, bestial force
> to the children in order that they survive? Better that they per-

ish. It is sophistry to speak of two sets of virtues, there is but one: virtue is an end in itself; the survival virtues are means, not ends. Honor and decency, compassion and truth are good even if they kill you, for they alone give life its dignity and worth. Yet probably . . . all the good and the noble and the true of all the world will die and obscenity will triumph. Probably those that practiced virtue will be destroyed, but it is better for men to die than to call evil good, and virtue itself will never die.

We of my generation have lost one line of fortifications after another, the old South, the old ideals, the old strengths. We are now watching the followers of Jesus and Buddha and Socrates being driven from the face of the earth. But there's time ahead, thousands of years: there is but one good life and men yearn for it and will again practice it, though of my contemporaries only the stars will see. Love and compassion, beauty and innocence will return. It is better to have breathed them an instant that to have supported iniquity a millennium. Perhaps only flames can rouse man from his apathy to his destiny.

There is left to each of us, no matter how far defeat pierces, the unassailable wintry kingdom of Marcus Aurelius, which some more gently call the Kingdom of Heaven. However it be called, it is not outside, but within, and when all is lost, it stands fast. To this remaining fastness I knew I should help the children find their way.... (LL, 313)

After giving his life's perception, Percy has little else to say, nor does he need to say much. There is a chapter, "A Bit of Diary," which describes the succession of frequently trivial events that account for most of one's impression of living. It is followed by a chapter that is ostensibly about his garden, "Jackdaw in the Garden," which is really about his garden of memories, those few really memorable, perhaps even epiphantic moments that are the peaks of one's impression of living. Taken together the two kinds of experience are the sum of one's existence, all that one is, all that one loses, in Percy's belief, at death. Thus it is appropriate that he has summarized himself before he offers the last chapter, which is "Home," the cemetery where his ancestors lie buried. Having been born in a certain class, having learned its philosophy, having lived by that philosophy, and having done all that he could to transmit that philosophy to his children, William Alexander Percy indicates his readiness to be no more.

If a single utterance can speak for a man, then William Alexander Percy is captured here: "There is left to each of us, no matter how far defeat pierces, the unassailable wintry kingdom of Marcus Aurelius, which some more gently call the Kingdom of

Heaven." In one of the few critical discussions of Percy, Phinizy Spalding has pointed to the "Stoic trend" that pervades Percy's thought, not just in *Lanterns on the Levee*, which is modeled on the Emperor's *Meditations*, but in his poetry as well. As described by Spalding, Percy's intensely personal appropriation of classical Stoicism thoroughly determined the uses that he made of his life:

> According to the poet Seneca, man's path on earth was one strewn with heartbreak and defeat. Hemmed in by fate, virtually helpless to help himself, and if not opposed by the Supreme Maker certainly not aided by Him, man staggered guidelessly through life. However, unlike Seneca, Percy did not believe in a kind of stoical resignation, but in accord with Aurelius, he felt that convictions should be molded into something practical, possible, and above all, workable. Percy observed as well as felt the pain and suffering in the path of humanity, and concluded that much of the sorrow and frustration was caused by human institutions which, with much effort, could be eventually righted. He considered the American system of democracy a valid, yet in many ways impotent, form of government which invited extremists and dishonesty. Fearful of the consequences which might ensue if unscrupulous men were allowed to come to power in his home town, he made strong efforts to ferret out and elect men of integrity and courage to local office. He worked entirely on the local level, following the precedent handed down to him by his father, but observing as well the outstanding example set by Aurelius. The Emperor clearly construed man's duty to be one of continuing and never resting action, even in the unsmiling face of fate. Aurelius, in line with the classical beliefs, saw that man should attempt by gradual stages to improve humanity's lot in the world—the great strides toward perfection were destined to fail because by attempting overpowering reforms man opposes not only his own fate, but also interferes with the will of God and the destiny of others. Man's all enveloping aspirations will be met by opposition and hatred which he will be incapable of overcoming.[7]

Using the characterization of Percy as a believer in the necessity of continually fighting small skirmishes, even though the war will probably be lost, Spalding is able to give an enlightened reading of "Enzio's Kingdom," longest and Percy's favorite of his own poems. The poem seems at first to be a celebration of the heroic Frederick II, King of Sicily, who dreams of warring against the world "and after peace . . . . enchant[ing] the world / Into a universal Sicily / And prove life even can be livable. . . . "[8] Frederick's kingdom would thus become "the only godlike, all-inclusive scheme / Of hope and betterment. . . . " (*CP*, 317).

But the title of the poem is not "Frederick's Kingdom," nor is Frederick the speaker in the poem. The reader must, therefore, appreciate the form of the poem, the dramatic monologue, and focus upon the figure of the speaker, Enzio, son of Frederick. Through Enzio's eyes, the reader sees Frederick fail in his grandiose "all-inclusive scheme," suffer the betrayal of his chief lieutenant, Pietro da Vigna, and the forced separation from his son, and finally die in despair: " . . . all his heart was homesick for had gone, / Vanished in cloud-dust, dust of death, or prison: / His kingdom was a boundary, bounding nothing. / He died because he had no heart to live . . . " (*CP*, 339).

Enzio perceives his father's failure; his father had overevaluated the potentiality for nobleness in mankind and had believed that it would want his ideal state, "His kingdom of the spirit for the few, / His fancied freedom for the falcon-souled . . . " (*CP*, 327). Enzio concludes that his father's philosophy, his "kingdom of the spirit," was noble, but that his father had tragically erred in thinking that he could will it into being. All that remain from the carnage of his dream are Enzio and the trusted old friend, Berard, whom Enzio tells: "Ah, you and I are all that now remain / Of his heart's Kingdom, so we must keep worthy. . . . / Go now, Berard. The waiting's empty, but / The end is sure, and we have much to dream on" (*CP*, 342). Enzio's kingdom thus is finally seen as the "unassailable wintry kingdom of Marcus Aurelius," a kingdom not of "universal Sicily," but of personal integrity surrounded on all borders by ever victorious tribes of base men.

Spalding relates that Percy wrote to John Chapman that many of Frederick's traits of character reminded him of his father.[9] But the resemblance is wisely qualified immediately. Percy may have seen his father as the high-minded ruler defeated finally by base men, as when Senator Percy was defeated by James K. Vardaman for renomination in the primary election of 1911; indeed Percy may have developed his "Stoic trend" from this experience, for he later wrote: "Father was not only defeated, but overwhelmingly. Thus at twenty-seven I became inured to defeat: I have never since expected victory" (*LL*, 151). But he would not have seen his father believing in anything except the accomplishment of the possible, or dying of a broken heart, for he remembered these words to a dejected supporter written by his father soon after his defeat: "A good deal has been written about 'shooting at the stars.' I have never thought much of that kind of marksmanship. It may be characterized by imagination, it is lacking in common sense. I rather think it is best to draw a bead on something that you have a chance to hit. To keep any part of Mississippi clean and decent in these days, is a job that no man may deem too small" (*LL*, 152).

If he saw his father as a model for at least a part of Frederick's character, then it is plausible that he saw himself as the model for the character of Enzio. Thus Spalding is justified in arguing that Enzio speaks for Percy himself and in ignoring the possibility that Enzio is merely a persona who might simply be expressing his own view. There can be no doubt at all, however, about the authenticity of Percy's voice in his short poem, "That Kingdom," presented here as his most representative poetic statement of belief:

> Fingerless cactus hands heal in the sun
> And tortured olive trees grope up the hills;
> A lizard feigns to sleep but flinching kills
> The busy spider in her web half done.
>
> The gaunt Sicilian pastures burn blue-white,
> The sunlight rains its blue perpetual rain;
> The south is still the south, but not again
> Shall I find there my kingdom, Heart's Delight.
>
> Oh, not on hills of blue eternal lustre
> Build we the kingdom of our heart's delight,
> But on love's shale, that quakes above a night
> Where ocean yawns and screaming storm-birds cluster.
>   (*CP*, 229)

The concluding stanza seems heavily indebted to the last stanza of Arnold's "Dover Beach," the poem which awakened Percy's love of poetry (*LL*, 135), where also love shared by kindred spirits is the only refuge, precarious though it be, against a hostile, at best an indifferent universe. The concluding stanza is also an anticipation of the resolution in "Enzio's Kingdom" to hold fast against that Sicily that lies outside of the self. Restricted only to a lofty philosophical level, "That Kingdom" is yet another expression of Percy's reliance upon the Aurelian conviction that the self is the only kingdom known to human existence which has the possibility of both freedom and control. Moreover, it seems possible that the "south" of the poem is also the intensely personal "South" of Percy's birth. For, though the "south is still the south," Percy grew to be more and more estranged from it, as it scorned his father's kind of patrician leadership to succumb to such leaders as Vardaman and Bilbo.

Offered with such obvious earnestness and eloquence as William Alexander Percy gave it, the Stoic attitude must have been vivid and enticing to his adoptive sons, who would have had an intimate opportunity to observe the attitude embodied in the daily behavior of a good man. The one of his sons who followed him into the profession of letters, Walker, was certainly impressed by the attitude, for one of his first public utterances was an analysis of Southern Stoicism. Without ever mentioning his deceased guardian's name, in "Stoicism in the South"[10] Walker Percy seems to have him in his mind's eye as he creates a representative Southern Stoic. Until the present generation, Percy says, the best friend of the Negro in the South has been the white upper class. Since the reader has read of the efforts of William Alexander Percy in behalf on the Negro, the reader is prepared for a warm, filial salute to such men. Then the realization crashes into the reader's understanding: the thesis of the article is a gentle, but uncompromising rejection of the validity of the Southern Stoic's belief, a refusal to accept that which had been specifically dedicated in the pages of a stirring autobiography to the Southern Stoic's sons.

Percy acknowledges that the Stoic way was "remarkably suited to the agrarian South of the last century" ("Stoicism in the South," 343). The white patrician was noble who heeded "the stern inner summons to man's full estate, to duty, to honor, to generosity toward his fellowmen and above all to his inferiors— not because they were made in the image of God and were therefore lovable in themselves, but because to do them an injustice would be to defile the inner fortress which was oneself" ("Stoicism in the South," 343). "The greatness of the South, like the greatness of the English squirearchy, had always a stronger Greek flavor than it ever had a Christian. Its nobility and graciousness was the nobility and graciousness of the old Stoa. How immediately we recognize the best of the South in the words of the Emperor: 'Every moment think steadily, as a Roman and a man, to do what thou hast in hand with perfect and simple dignity, and a feeling of affection, and freedom, and justice' " ("Stoicism in the South," 343). "Yet, like the Stoa of the Empire, the Stoa of the South was based on a particular hierarchical structure and could not survive . . . change. Nor did it wish to survive. Its most characteristic mood was a poetic pessimism which took a grim satisfaction in the dissolution of its values—because social decay confirmed one in his original choice on the wintry kingdom of self" ("Stoicism in the South," 343).

The emotional cost of rejecting his guardian's proffered advice as "poetic pessimism" and viewing the "unassailable wintry kingdom of Marcus Aurelius" as the "wintry kingdom of self" must have been dear. Only by recognizing how personal and how painful Walker Percy's rejection of Southern Stoicism had to be, however, can one really understand how fully committed he is to its alternative. In the South that alternative, the Church, has always coexisted with the Stoa. Now, though, that the winds of change have blown over the South, there is no longer any chance of selectively relying on both philosophies. The Negro, once the appreciative recipient of aid from his former master, the white aristocrat, against his present master, the white lower class, has lost his sense of deference and now makes demands upon *all* whites. Thus, since there is no target for what little *noblesse oblige* he has left, the white aristocrat is less and less drawn to the plight of the Negro and more and more drawn to the redneck outlook of the numerically superior white lower class. Thoroughly discredited, the Stoic attitude has fled, leaving the Christian attitude in the field against the barbarians.

The Christian attitude is admirably suited to the conditions of the times, Percy says in summation. For "the Christian is optimistic precisely where the Stoic is pessimistic" ("Stoicism in the South," 344). The Stoic cherished his *view* of another; the Christian cherishes the *self* of another. Thus the Christian, unlike the Stoic, can adapt to the frenzied change so characteristic of these times. But, if Christianity is to flourish in the South, it must die as it is practiced and be reborn as it once was. Its adherents must cease viewing it merely as a legalistic code against sexual misconduct, drinking, and gambling, and accept it as the revolutionary creed that it is.

This is not to say that in abjuring the Stoic attitude himself, Walker Percy rejects the tradition which utilized it so effectively. Just a year after his article, "Stoicism in the South," he felt it necessary to refute certain allegations made against himself and other "backsliding Southern liberals who have betrayed the cause by affirming certain values of the South, while continuing to oppose segregation."[11] To that end he contributed "A Southern View" to the journal that had published the article by his critic. That man had confessed himself unable to understand how a Southerner could oppose segregation and at the same time honor the Southern tradition, which he described as "the Old South of slavery, of mocking birds, hominy grits and Bourbon whiskey . . . " ("A Southern View," 428). Percy replies that *he* fails to see how a Southerner could oppose segregation without honoring the Southern tradition. His definition of the traditions is, of course, completely opposed to that of his critic: "There *is* a Southern heritage, and it has nothing to do with the colonel in the whiskey ad. It has to do with the conservative tradition of a predominantly agrarian society, a tradition which at its best enshrined the humane aspects of living for rich and poor, black and white. It gave first place to a stable family life, sensitivity and good manners between men, chivalry toward women, an honor code, and individual integrity" ("A Southern View," 428).

The dialectic revealed in these two articles, admiration of the Stoic attitude as it was embodied in William Alexander Percy and his class, but rejection of the attitude as being irrelevant to the present generation, has remained with Walker Percy. Such a dialectic provides the essence of the relationship between the protagonist and the representative of the past, the father figure, in both of his novels.

The earlier of his two published novels, *The Moviegoer*, appeared in 1961, dedicated, with an appropriateness that cannot escape a tinge of the ironic, to "W.A.P." Although the representative of the past is an aunt, rather than an uncle, which is usually the degree of relation that William Alexander Percy is said to be to Walker Percy, the character is still based on William Alexander Percy. There is a similarity, to begin with, in the establishment of the two relationships; after the death of his father, John Bickerson "Binx" Bolling had spent fifteen years in the home of his great-aunt, Mrs. Emily Bolling Cutrer (M, 26). But more important than the similarity is the philosophy shared by William Alexander Percy and Mrs. Cutrer. Feeling the responsibility of forming his character, Mrs. Cutrer had always attempted to transmit the values of the Bollings to Binx; late in the novel, when she believes that she has completely failed as father, she attempts, in an outburst of despair and scorn, to summarize the attitude that she has been advocating:

> All these years I have been assuming that between us words mean roughly the same thing, that among certain people, gentle-

folk I don't mind calling them, there exists a set of meanings held in common, that a certain manner and a certain grace come as naturally as breathing. At the great moments of life—success, failure, marriage, death—our kind of folks have always possessed a native instinct for behavior, a natural piety or grace, I don't mind calling it. Whatever else we did or failed to do, we always had that, I'll make you a little confession. I am not ashamed to use the word class. I will also plead guilty to another charge. The charge is that people belonging to my class think they're better than other people. You're damn right we're better. We're better because we do not shirk our obligations either to ourselves or to others. We do not whine. We do not organize a minority group and blackmail the government. We do not prize mediocrity for mediocrity's sake. Oh I am aware that we hear a great many flattering things nowadays about your great common man—you know, it has always been revealing to me that he is perfectly content so to be called, because that is exactly what he is: the common man and when I say common I mean common as hell. Our civilization has achieved a distinction of sorts. It will be remembered not for its technology nor even its wars but for its novel ethos. Ours is the only civilization in history which has enshrined mediocrity as its national ideal. Others have been corrupt, but leave it to us to invent the most undistinguished of corruptions. No orgies, no blood running in the street, no babies thrown off cliffs. No, we're a sentimental people and we horrify easily. True, our moral fibre is rotten. Our national character stinks to high heaven. But we are kinder than ever. No prostitute ever responded with a quicker spasm of sentiment when our hearts are touched. Nor is there anything new about thievery, lewdness, lying, adultery. What is new is that in our time liars and thieves and whores and adulterers wish also to be congratulated and are congratulated by the great public, if their confession is sufficiently psychological or strikes a sufficiently heartfelt and authentic note of sincerity. Oh, we are sincere. I do not deny it. I don't know anybody nowadays who is not sincere. . . . We are the most sincere Laodiceans who ever got flushed down the sinkhole of history. No, my young friend, I am not ashamed to use the word class. . . . Perhaps we are a biological sport. I am not sure. But one thing I am sure of: we live by our lights, we die by our lights, and whoever the high gods may be, we'll look them in the eye without apology. . . . I did my best for you, son. I gave you all I had. More than anything else I wanted to pass on to you the one heritage of the men of our family, a certain quality of spirit, a gaiety, a sense of duty, a nobility worn lightly, a sweetness, a gentleness with women—the only good things the South ever had and the only things that really matter in this life. (M, 222-224)

There is a clear resemblance between Aunt Emily's philosophy and that creed posited for the Southern Stoic in the two articles that Percy had published a few years before the novel. Especially striking is the similarity of Aunt Emily's final statement to Percy's definition of the authentic Southern tradition, in "A Southern View," as "a tradition which at its best enshrined the humane aspects of living for rich and poor, black and white. It gave first place to a stable family life, sensitivity and good manners between men, chivalry toward women, an honor code, and individual integrity" ("A Southern View," 428).

But the more significant indebtedness of Aunt Emily's portrait is to the self-portrait of William Alexander Percy in *Lanterns on the Levee.* His love of the great moral teachers, Jesus, Socrates, and the Buddha (*LL,* 313) is utilized in Binx's reference to his aunt: "My aunt likes to say she is an Episcopalian by emotion, a Greek by nature and a Buddhist by choice" (*M,* 23). There is also the grim satisfaction that both Mrs. Cutrer and William Alexander Percy possess at the coming of the chaos of social decay that they have predicted, the most characteristic mood of the Stoic, according to Percy ("Stoicism in the South," 342). Mrs. Cutrer reveals her contempt in this fashion: "I no longer pretend to understand the world. . . . The world I knew has come crashing down around my ears. The things we hold dear are reviled and spat upon. . . . It's an interesting age you live in—though I can't say I'm sorry to miss it." All the while, Binx observes, "she is shaking her head yet smiling her sweet menacing smile" (*M,* 54). William Alexander Percy employs virtually the identical tone: "Watching the flames mount, we, scattered remnants of the old dispensation, smile scornfully, but grieve in our hearts" (*LL,* 63).

The most salient resemblance between William Alexander Percy and Aunt Emily, though, is their reliance upon Marcus Aurelius as the supreme guide to the conduct of life. When Aunt Emily sends the following note to Binx, she is the very personification of the tradition of the Southern Stoic that William Alexander Percy had so ably represented and advocated: "Every moment think steadily as a Roman and a man, to do what thou hast in hand with perfect and simple dignity, and a feeling of affection and freedom and justice. These words of the Emperor Marcus Aurelius Antoninus strike me as pretty good advice, for even the orneriest young scamp" (*M,* 78).

The only trouble is that such advice has never helped Binx find his way through the world. For ten years he has looked at the portrait of his father and his uncles that sits on his aunt's mantelpiece, trying without success to understand it (*M,* 24). He can appreciate the past validity of the tradition, and he obviously loves his aunt, the spokesman for the tradition in the present. But he simply cannot gain sustenance from the past; the gap between his aunt and himself is made painfully clear on the occasion when his aunt cries out against what she considers as his deliberate, feckless knavery. As she speaks so eloquently, quite without thinking about it, she draws the letter opener-sword held by a helmeted figure on the desk at which she sits. Looking "as erect and handsome as the Black Prince" (M, 221), personifying in her mind's eye the Cavalier of the old tradition, she even waves the sword as she confronts one she now views as a traitor to her kingdom. Binx, for his part, can only wonder if she has seen the bend in the sword that he caused years before using it to open a drawer.

His adult life began with a quest for a creed by which he could live. But after repeated failure, he gave up to settle for what he calls the "Little Way," the life of fornication. The only luxury that he did not allow himself was hope. Now, though, he has exposed himself to hope (which brings anxiety with it) in thinking that perhaps there is the slightest possibility that he and Kate, Aunt Emily's step-daughter, a recognized sufferer, might be able to aid each other. Thus he takes Kate with him on a trip that terrifies him, and they begin to blunder their way toward confessions of weakness and need for the understanding that only a fellow sufferer can offer.

But when Aunt Emily learns of their trip, her response is chilling; viewing the human self from her austere, wintry kingdom, she cannot understand selves that feel incomplete, so incomplete as to seek fulfillment in an unsanctioned fleshly encounter. She thus condemns her nephew's motives out of hand, with the summation of her philosophy previously quoted. Her sense of opposing styles of life is quite evocative of William Alexander Percy's mutually exclusive categories:

> One last question to satisfy my idle curiosity. What has been going on in your mind during all the years when we listened to music together, read the *Crito*, and spoke together—or was it only I who spoke—good Lord, I can't remember—of goodness and truth and beauty and nobility?

When Binx is forced to admit that her code does not reach him, her response is scornful: "What do you think is the purpose of life—to go to the movies and dally with every girl that comes along?" (*M*, 226).

An encounter with his aunt such as this has always left Binx in such a state of anxiety that he fairly lunges into fornication in an attempt to escape his consciousness of anxiety (*M*, 228). At the conclusion of his interview with his aunt, Kate had told him to wait for her. But when she does not arrive for some time, he concludes that she has accepted the view of his aunt and has abandoned him. Desperately he telephones his last girl friend, only to learn that she is unavailable and that the very effort of even attempting to talk with her roommate is exhausting and dispiriting. Then Kate arrives, in demonstration of her faith in him, and they agree to take the chance involved in marrying. In the Epilogue, after a year has passed, Binx reports on the marriage. He is going to medical school, as his aunt has always wanted him to do. Thus he is now acceptable in her eyes, for his actions fit her prefigurations. But it should not be assumed that he has accepted her Stoic attitude; rather the valid assessment of his state of mind lies in appreciating his ability to abandon fornication in order to accept the responsibility for another self's well-being. He has thus become an ethical man, in Kierkegaardian terms, and its beginning to grope toward the Christianity that can cope with chaos.

William Alexander Percy, of Percy Street, Greenville, Mississippi, is an even more identifiable ghost in Walker Percy's second novel, *The Last Gentleman*. Again the protagonist is a young man who comes from an old Southern family:

> Over the years his family had turned ironical and lost its gift for action. It was an honorable and violent family, but gradually the violence had been deflected and turned inward. The great grandfather knew what was what and said so and acted accordingly and did not care what anyone thought. He even wore a pistol in a holster like a Western hero and once met the Grand Wizard of the Ku Klux Klan in a barbershop and invited him then and there to shoot it out in the street. The next generation, the grandfather, seemed to know what was what but he was not really so sure. He was brave but he gave much thought to the business of being brave. He too would have shot it out with the Grand Wizard if only he could have made certain it was the thing to do. The father was a brave man too and he said he didn't care what others thought, but he did care. More than anything else, he wished to act with honor and to be thought well of by other men. So living for him was a strain. He became ironical. For him it was not a small thing to walk down the street on an ordinary September morning. In the end he was killed by his own irony and sadness and by the strain of living out an

ordinary day in a perfect dance of honor. (*LG*, 9-10).

The family of this young man, Williston Bibb Barrett, is quite similar to the family of John Bickerson Bolling. The portrait of his father and his uncles that Binx studies reveals that his uncles "are serene in their identities," but that his father "is not one of them." The difference is apparent in his father's eyes: "beyond a doubt they are ironical" (*M*, 25). Binx's father had been one of Percy's Southern Stoics: "For the Stoic there is no real hope. His finest hour is to sit tight-lipped and ironic while the world comes crashing down around him" ("Stoicism in the South," 344). Thus, imprisoned in a world without meaning, he had eagerly volunteered for a perilous position where the sense of really living might dwell and had been killed in the RCAF in World War II. Since Will's father also suffers from the ironic awareness of the Stoic who has outlived his creed, the reader anticipates that he too will be revealed as a fatal casualty in World War II.

Like John Bickerson Bolling, Williston Bibb Barrett feels cut off from his tradition and lost in the modern world. But unlike Bolling, Barrett decides to seek help from modern psychological science. Somehow his heritage has failed him, so he spends his inheritance on analysis—but once he learns that analysis is a game and that he can master its rules, he is willing to be the kind of patient he thinks his analyst would like and accordingly displays the proper symptoms. After five years of this coy game, he suddenly buys himself an expensive telescope, convinces himself that the telescope can enable him to recover the reality of things, so that he can be an engineer in an engineer's world. He is an engineer after all, if only a humidification engineer who works three floors below street level at Macy's. Thus, like Bolling, he dwells in the cellar and not in the house, as anyone does, Kierkegaard says, who lives in sensuousness and nothing else.

The first thing of value the telescope discovers for him is the innocent Kitty Vaught, who immediately personifies all the untold hopes of the future. Once Barrett has seen her, he is ready to cast all else to the winds and follow her. Thus he bids farewell to Dr. Gamow, who has been a "father of sorts" (*LG*, 39), even though Dr. Gamow protests that no resolution of his problem has been accomplished. Which is certainly true, for Barrett has symptoms of both physical and psychological malfunction. His physical malfunction, the partial loss of hearing, is at first insignificant when compared with his sporadic loss of memory preceded by attacks of *déjà vu* and fugue states. Although Barrett has fled the South, he keeps finding himself after his psychological seizures as a wandering amnesiac on some Civil War battlefield. Most cases of amnesia are caused by an unwillingness to face the present, but to face the present is often to face the past, and the particular homing pattern that Barrett evinces suggests that his primary problem is in accepting something that occurred in his past. Hence the apparent appropriateness of one of the novel's mottoes, this one from Kierkegaard: "If a man cannot forget, he will never amount to much."

Casting all else aside involves becoming captive of the wackiest menage below the Mason Dixon Line. The Vaughts in their several ways display just about every kooky trait presently associated with the South of the Sixties. Even Jamie Vaught, suffering from an incurable illness and for whom Barrett becomes a paid nurse, seems to participate in the frantic activities of a household that can only be described as vintage Marx Brothers, say like *Coconuts*. Collectively the Vaughts alternately entice and abandon Barrett, drawing him all the while deeper and deeper into the South, both geographical and psychological.

And all the while Barrett's memory hovers from time to time around the outskirts of a crucial scene from his past. The scene contains a large house close by a levee in the summer time. Barrett sits on the steps, tending a record player, from which "the Great Horn Theme [goes] abroad, the very sound of the ruined gorgeousness of the nineteenth century, the worst of times" (*LG*, 96). On the sidewalk in front of the house, his lawyer father paces, now quoting Montaigne (*LG*, 96) or "Dover Beach" (*LG*, 297), waiting for his scared clients, both black and white, both Jew and Catholic, railing against any kind of priesthood (*LG*, 214), railing against the Snopesian fornicators, who go to prayer meeting and then creep up to the levee to park (*LG*, 96).

The activities performed by Barrett's father in this recurrent scene constitute some of the most memorable aspects of William Alexander Percy's life style. David Cohn remembered him as, above all else, a lonely man: "Often on summer nights, as though keeping a lover's tryst with loneliness, he would pace up and down on the sidewalk before his house, his small figure dwarfed into tinyness by the huge oaks under which he walked; pace with head bowed, lost in thought or dreams, while sometimes lightning flickered, thunder growled, and an evening thrush sang an evening song from blue-entangled wisteria."[12] And, of course, all the mannerisms captured in Barrett's father may be observed in Percy's self-portrait in *Lanterns on the Levee*, especially in "For the Younger Generation."

As a gentleman, William Alexander Percy had an undisguised animus for the Snopesian intruders into his society after the turn of the century, when the exodus of large numbers of blacks left a vacuum in the labor market: "Unbeknownst, strangers had drifted in since the war—from the hills, from the North, from all sorts of odd places where they hadn't succeeded or hadn't been wanted. . . . The newcomers weren't foreigners or Jews, they were an alien breed of Anglo-Saxon" (*LL*, 230). Although he recognizes that their present condition is at least in part due to poverty, malnutrition, and other non-moral causes, he finally has to confess a hostility toward them: "I can forgive them as the Lord God forgives, but admire them, trust them, love them—never. Intellectually and spiritually they are inferior to the Negro, whom they hate. Suspecting secretly they are inferior to him, they must do something to him to prove to themselves their superiority. At their door must be laid the disgraceful riots and lynchings gloated over and exaggerated by Negrophiles the world over" (*LL*, 19-20). They are, he says on another occasion, "the sort of people that lynch Negroes, that mistake hoodlumism for wit, and cunning for intelligence, that attend revivals and fight and fornicate in the bushes afterwards. They [are] undiluted Anglo-Saxons" (*LL*, 149).

Although the setting of the recurrent scenes remains static, there develops a rising line of action which involves a battle between Barrett's father and some nameless group, the consequences of which are so painful that Barrett does not want to remember them. He recalls the occasion when his father had begun to warn him against the fornicators, but the memory is blocked finally with his cryptic, shocked thought: *"Then what happened after that? After he—"* (*LG*, 97). The next remembered segment reveals that his father's enemies plan to kill him:

> Father, I know that the police said those people had sworn to kill you and that you should stay in the house.
> They're not going to kill me, son.
> Father, I heard them on the phone. They said you loved niggers and helped the Jews and Catholics and betrayed your own people. (*LG*, 228).

At this point the reader suspects that "they" eventually made good their threat and that Barrett's physical fleeing of, but psychic obsession with, the South results from the horrible memory of his father's murder.

All the time that Barrett is suffering from his attacks of compulsive memory, he is actually traveling rather slowly and unpurposively toward the house of his father. When he arrives, on a summer evening, he observes his many aunts blithely watching television in the house and is overcome by the actual setting of his tortured memory. This time he recalls that his father had apparently won his victory against the faceless enemies, recalls that a policeman had come by to say that "they" had left town. Then he recalls that he had congratulated his father, but that his father had replied:

> We haven't won, son. We've lost
> But they've gone, Father.
> Why shouldn't they leave? They've won.
> How have they won, Father?
> They don't have to stay. Because they found out that we are like them after all and so there was no reason for them to stay.
> How are we like them, Father?
> Once they were the fornicators and the bribers and the takers of bribes and we were not and that was why they hated us. Now we are like them, so why should they stay? They know they don't have to kill me.
> How do they know that, Father?
> Because we've lost it all, son.
> Lost what?
> But there's one thing they don't know.
> What's that, Father?
> They may have won, but I don't have to choose that.
> Choose what?
> Choose them. (LG, 316-317).

Barrett's father begins once again his pacing, but Barrett is terrified and cries "Wait." And his further conversation with his father is punctuated with his pleas—"Don't leave," *"Don't leave."* But his father had not waited; rather he "went on without saying anything: went into the house, on through the old closed-in dogtrot hall to the back porch, opened the country food press which had been converted to a gun cabinet, took down the double-barrel twelve-gauge Greener, loaded it, went up the back stairs into the attic, and, fitting the muzzle of the Greener into the notch of his breastbone, could still reach both triggers with his thumbs" (*LG*, 318).

Standing there before his father's house, clutching one of the oaks for support, Williston Barrett is able to visualize the scene of his father's choice of the noble Roman way:

> *Wait.* While his fingers explored the juncture of iron and bark, his eyes narrowed as if he caught a glimmer of light on the cold iron skull. *Wait.* I think he was wrong and that he was looking in the wrong place. No, not he but the times. The times were wrong and one looked in the wrong place. It wasn't even his fault because that was the way he was and the way the times were, and there was no other place a man could look. It was the worst of times, a time of fake beauty and fake victory. *Wait.* He had missed it! It was not in the Brahms that one looked and not in solitariness and not in the sad old poetry but—he wrung out his ear—but here, under your nose, here in the very curiousness and drollness and extraness of the iron and the bark that—he shook his head—that . . . (*LG*, 318-19).

The conflict between the Anglo-Saxon fornicators and Barrett's father seems to rely upon the conflict between the Percys and the Ku Klux Klan in 1922. Former Senator LeRoy Percy spoke out forcefully against the Klan in "The Modern Ku Klux Klan"[13] to a national audience and served as head of the anti-Klan forces in the South (*LL*, 234). And William Alexander Percy served the cause of his father, on one occasion telling the local Cyclops: "I want to let you know one thing: if anything happens to my Father or to any of our friends you will be killed. We won't hunt for the guilty party. So far as we are concerned the guilty party will be you" (*LL*, 236). The decisive battle of the campaign was won by the Percy faction when it was able to elect its candidate for the office of sheriff, but in William Alexander Percy's view such a battle only delayed the total victory of the Anglo-Saxons for a few years.

Of course William Alexander Percy did not actually commit suicide in recognition of the Snopesian occupation of his homeland. But, then, neither did he feel that there was really any cause for joy in the victory against the Klan. As he said, "My generation, inured to doom, wears extinction with a certain wry bravado, but it is just as well the older ones we loved are gone. They had lived, for the most part, through tragedy into poverty, which can be and usually is accomplished with dignity and a certain fine disdain. But when the last act is vulgarity, it is as hateful and confused a show as *Troilus and Cressida*" (*LL*, 63). The only response to such chaos available to him was reliance upon Aurelius: "The self-communings of the Emperor, though often cold to clamminess, convince a man he never need be less than tight-lipped, courteous, and proud, though all is pain" (*LL*, 316). For as Walker Percy generalizes from the personal: "For the Stoic there is no real hope. His finest hour is to sit tight-lipped and ironic while the world comes crashing down around him" ("Stoicism in the South," 344).

As he stands there in front of his father's house, Will Barrett touches a "tiny iron horsehead" of a hitching post. As he feels the cold iron he must think of another piece of cold metal, for "his eyes narrowed as if he caught a glimmer of light on the cold iron skull" (*LG*, 318). The "glimmer of light" may be a new truth occurring to him as he envisions the "skull," the death of his father. His father had gone to the "attic to his house," the wintry kingdom of self, to indicate his broken heart—his choice of an abode to die in is as Kierkegaardian as Barrett's choice of a cellar to work in.

The new truth supplants the old truth derived from Brahms, and solitariness, and "the old sad poetry." Such a truth is a refutation of the "poetic pessimism" of the Southern Stoic that must apply to the poet of such poems as "Enzio's Kingdom." The false serenity of the Great Horn Theme will never be heard again, nor will the crashing of the shotgun blast of his father's suicide that must have accounted for his hysteric deafness. For at the moment he concludes that his father's philosophy was useless, he wrings out his ear, as if to fling off his malady and his loss of father. One must look, he decides, into the "very curiousness and drollness and extraness" of the past in order to recover it. Accordingly he leaves his father's house to visit his Uncle Fannin, who continues to live the old life. In the author's preface, Walker Percy acknowledges that he has moved the town of Shut Off, Louisiana, so that it would be opposite the town he calls Vicksburg (though in reality he is describing Greenville): what would be a better name for a locality where the old tradition still obtains? And what kind of tradition would it be but the hilarious plantation antics of Uncle Fannin, and his faithful black servant, Merriam, whose deference is straight out of Thomas Nelson Page? Their perpetuation of the old order consists of locating coveys for New Orleans hunters—when they're not watching *Captain Kangaroo* or *Gunsmoke*.

In another of his non-fiction articles, "The Man on the Train:

Three Existential Modes,"[14] Walker Percy discusses the strategies of rotation and repetition as deliverances from alienation. The man unaware of his alienation will not be aware that his life could be other than it is, hence he will ordinarily be "happy," or so he thinks. But the man who becomes aware of his alienation will attempt to escape it. Since he thinks that his condition is produced by the present, he will attempt to go forward or backward to discover that news which will bring meaning to his life.

Rotation seems to offer the better possibility of escape, for the human being is a forward-looking animal: around the next bend will be the answer! But one can only keep banking on the next bend, if he can forget that the present bend has not given a satisfactory answer. In Percy's words, "Perfect rotation could only be achieved by a progressive amnesia in which the forgetting kept pace with time so that every corner turned, every face seen, is a rotation" ("The Man on the Train," 487). It need hardly be said that perfect rotation as a treatment is worse than the illness to which it is applied. For even if a person could achieve perfect rotation all his life, he would always be missing the present; if the rotation ever ceased to be a lure, then the person would once again be immersed in the present and thus a candidate for suicide.

Repetition, the turning to the past, then, is paradoxically the more valuable strategy. "What's done is done," our folk wisdom says, and the statement is true to a point: we cannot restore the past. But existentially speaking, "What's done is still doing." If the present is alienation, one must return to the past, which is to say, the self, to discover at what point the alienation erupted. The alienated person must, in Percy's words, return to "stand before the house of one's childhood" ("The Man on the Train," 490).

Will Barrett certainly manifests the Kierkegaardian strategies of rotation and repetition that Percy has modified for his own literary uses. Barrett comes upon the lure of the new, Kitty Vaught, by the miraculous chance encounter so dear, Percy says, to writers of simple rotatory literature. But his movement also takes him into contact with the repetitional possibility, Sutter Vaught, Kitty's mysterious brother. First, though, he must go back to accept finally the fact that his Stoic father had abandoned him, would not wait for him, did not prepare him for the chaos that is life. And he must accept the fact that the past in the present, Uncle Fannin, offers no solution to his problems. Only then can he follow Sutter into the desert to seek an answer for himself.

All along Barrett had read the strange journal that Sutter Vaught seems purposefully to have left for him. His readings of this journal begin to counterpoint with his memories of his father after a while in the novel, and he must see that Sutter tends to make the same basic discrimination of humanity that his father had made: one must believe in the kingdom or fornicate. But where his father had despaired over defeat by the fornicators and destroyed himself, Sutter Vaught has accepted a world where there is no kingdom and has become the complete fornicator. In a world without faith there is no reality except that provided by genital friction—Sutter will have no truck with ethical humanists like his former wife, or such liberals as Forney Aiken, the far-out devotee of fornication-as-religionist, "or such religionists" as his sister Val who have swallowed Christianity but managed to spit out the Offense, the Scandal.

Like Barrett's father, too, Sutter has attempted suicide. Although he shot away half his face, he survived, and the reader reaches the conclusion that Sutter belongs to that group of attempted suicides who do not succeed because they really do not need to succeed. He has the message of salvation, if he will allow himself to accept it; the Stoic act has failed him, leaving only the strife of a life of anxiety. When Barrett finally catches up with him, Sutter is ironically aware of their relationship, for he asks Barrett, "Are you Philip and is this the Gaza Desert?" (LG, 345). Actually the roles, he well knows, are reversed: Barrett is not Philip running to join the sincere eunuch in his chariot and explain the text that he pores over; rather it is Barrett who runs to get into Sutter's rattly Edsel, vaguely knowing that somehow Sutter has the message for him, that Sutter's "passionate eloquence" has not been silenced because the journal has been burned.

Together they must face the trial of Jamie Vaught's death. But the death seems so inevitable that it seems to lose its fearsomeness for them; it becomes, in fact, quite instructive. For a priest is brought in to conduct the rites of baptism, and in the accomplishment of the ritual he solicits the grace of God for Jamie, so that Jamie receives the faith necessary to believe at the moment of his death. Both Barrett and Sutter seem to be aware that this miracle has occurred as they walk out of the hospital.

Barrett, though, wants confirmation of his intuition from Sutter, just as he has wanted information from Sutter throughout their association.   Sutter knows, though, that he cannot *give* information to Barrett; Barrett must *gain* his own news.   Thus Sutter walks off to get in his flatulent car, while Barrett, thinking that Sutter intends to commit suicide, begins to call back over the years to his father, "Wait," "Where are you going?" Making the appeal as personal as he can, he implores, "Dr. Vaught, I need you. I, Will Barrett—" (*LG*, 393). Thus he not only identifies himself for the first time, but he characterizes himself as one who must transcend Stoicism, as one who will bear it. " 'Wait,' he shouted in a dead run" (*LG*, 393). This time the Edsel stops, and Will Barrett has finally found a father.

And it may be that Walker Percy, in a psychological sense, has become his own father. Throughout his writing—both nonfiction and fiction—there has appeared that haunting figure of William Alexander Percy. It may be that the vision of such a noble man's failure has been the single most powerful stimulus to Walker Percy's continued writing. If so, each individual work must represent a desire to achieve repetition. Walker Percy thus has often stood before the house of his father. In the beginning he could only speak of that man's now irrelevant creed. Then in *The Moviegoer* he was able to describe the abandoned son who gives at the novel's conclusion only the slightest hint that he may be able to survive the loss of his heritage. Finally in *The Last Gentleman* he imagines a man who is compelled to look unblinkingly at his father's failure, but who then is able to pick himself up, struggle, and find another father, the only true creed. Walker Percy should not again have to return to that house on Percy Street in Greenville.

Notes

1 William Alexander Percy, *Lanterns on the Levee* (New York, 1941), p. 310. Hereafter references to *Lanterns on the Levee* will be incorporated into the text as (*LL*).

[2] William Alexander Percy's father was Senator LeRoy Percy; his grandfather was Colonel William Alexander Percy, known as the Gray Eagle of the Delta because of his leadership after the Civil War. Further information about the family may be found in John Hereford Percy, *The Percy Family of Mississippi and Louisiana, 1776-1943* (Baton Rouge, 1943).

[3] David L. Cohn offers a friend's evaluation of Percy in "Eighteenth-Century Chevalier," *Virginia Quarterly Review*, 31 (Autumn 1955), 561-575.

[4] Hodding Carter, *Where Main Street Meets the River* (New York, 1953), pp. 67-78, 90-91.

[5] Frank E. Smith, *Congressman from Mississippi* (New York, 1964), p. 247.

[6] Cohn, 575.

[7] Phinizy Spalding, "A Stoic Trend in William Alexander Percy's Thought," *Georgia Review*, 12 (Fall 1958), 246. Spalding has also written of Percy's poetic use of his homeland in "Mississippi and the Poet: William Alexander Percy," *Journal of Mississippi History*, 27 (February 1965), 63-73.

[8] William Alexander Percy, *The Collected Poems of William Alexander Percy* (New York, 1943), p. 311. Hereafter references to *The Collected Poems of William Alexander Percy* will be incorporated into the text as (CP).

[9] Spalding, "A Stoic Trend," 248.

[10] Walker Percy, "Stoicism in the South," *Commonweal*, 64 (July 6, 1956), 342-344.

[11] Walker Percy, "A Southern View," *America*, 97 (July 20, 1957), 428-429.

[12] Cohn, 562-563.

[13] LeRoy Percy, "The Modern Ku Klux Klan," *Atlantic Monthly*, 130 (July 1922), 122-128.

[14] Walker Percy, "The Man on the Train: Three Existential Modes," *Partisan Review*, 23 (Fall 1956), 478-494.

The Moviegoer and the Stoic Heritage

Early in Walker Percy's *The Moviegoer* (1961) the patrician Aunt Emily sends her nephew, John Bickerson Bolling, the following note: "Every moment think steadily as a Roman and a man, to do what thou has in hand with perfect and simple dignity, and a feeling of affection and freedom and justice. These words of the Emperor Marcus Aurelius Antoninus strike me as pretty good advice, for even the orneriest young scamp."[1] Despite the forced levity of her application, the adjuration remains: Aunt Emily is proclaiming that the stoic way, after a three-hundred-year history in the South, still offers its aristocratic sons a sufficient philosophy.

It cannot be said that a reliance upon stoic texts to temper the prevailing Christian ecclesiastical structure was a telling distinction between North and South from the very beginning of the American colonies. Indeed, perhaps the earliest mention of the stoics is in John Harvard's will, in 1638, which left, among other books, a copy of Epictetus to the young college at New Towne,[2] in Massachusetts, which was happy enough to adopt the name of its benefactor. But the evidence does suggest that the stoic view did soon become a part of the set of ideas which motivated Southern patricians—such ideas as deism, squirearchy, and rationalism.[3]

A focus for the stoic view in the oldest colony was found in the College of William and Mary, which was begun in 1693, the second college in the colonies. Then, as now, one fruitful source of books for libraries was the benevolence of wealthy men, and the administration at Middle Plantation, shortly to become Williamsburg, made its appeal. The first to respond was Colonel Francis Nicholson, who left, in his bequest of 30 May 1695, a collection of books that included Meric Casaubon's *Marcus Aurelius*.[4] Such public support continued, for in 1739 the Reverend Emanuel Jones, rector of Petsworth Parish in Gloucester County, left at least part of his library to the college, including the only book to survive the library fires of 1859 and 1862, Arrian's *Enchir-*

idion, which Jones had acquired as a student at Oriel College, Oxford, in 1687.[5] With its Anglican tolerance for the tenets of stoicism,[6] William and Mary continued as the Southern locus of that philosophy in the eighteenth century. There were, of course, the basic texts in the growing library. There is also evidence that members of the college board of visitors—those wealthy and influential men who set the tone of the intellectual community[7]—possessed such books in their private libraries. Ralph Wormeley, of Middlesex, had a copy of Seneca's *Morals* among the items of his estate in 1703,[8] while the library of the great Carter family included the *Enchiridion*.[9] The most distinguished man of letters in colonial Virginia, Colonel William Byrd, left Seneca, Aurelius, and Epictetus to his heirs.[10] The no less distinguished Richard Lee II, of Mount Pleasant, left both Epictetus and Seneca in his library when it was inventoried in 1714.[11] Indeed, London booksellers seem to have recognized the Virginian inclination to the stoic view, for Robert Beverley's *The History and Present State of Virginia* (1705) contained an advertisement for Seneca's *Morals* on one of its back pages.[12]

In time the Williamsburg book trade employed a much wider form of advertisement—*The Virginia Gazette*. To judge from the frequency with which they were offered, Seneca's works were perhaps the most popular books available during the period 1770-5.[13] But Marcus Aurelius was also so well known that certain public responses to the use of his name could reasonably be expected, for it was used as a newspaper pseudonym in 1768-9.[14] And, as would be expected, wills and inventories for the period reveal yet more private libraries which contained the key stoic texts.[15] The 1759 will of Daniel Parke Custis, whose widow married George Washington, listed two copies of Seneca's *Morals*.[16] Fittingly, in this time of wide stoic influence, the governor, Norborne Berkeley, Baron de Botetourt, was a reader of Aurelius and Epictetus, the latter in the popular new translation by Mrs Elizabeth Carter.[17]

It was during this period of widespread recourse to the stoics that Thomas Jefferson attended the College of William and Mary, where he graduated in 1762. When he first became acquainted with the stoic works is unknown, but once he had discovered them, he never ceased thinking that they provided a body of guiding principles that every educated person ought to possess. For that reason he on several occasions included them on reading lists that he provided for young people. In 1771, when he was twenty-eight, Jefferson drew up such a list for his friend and relative John Skipwith: among the fourteen titles under "religion" were both Mrs Carter's *Epictetus* and Collin's *Antoninus*.[18] His advice to his nephew Peter Carr, in 1785, is much the same: "In morality, read Epictetus, Xenophontis Memorabilia, Plato's Socratic dialogues, Cicero's philosophies, Antoninus, and Seneca."[19] Forty years later he still possessed his respect for the Stoa, for he included Schweighauser's *Epictetus*, in six volumes, among the starting collection he was ordering for his creation, the University of Virginia.[20] Epictetus seems to have been his lifelong favourite of the school, for he wrote William Short, in 1819, that Epictetus had "given us what was good of the Stoics; all beyond, of their dogmas, being hypocrisy and grimace."[21] At the same time he stressed his dedication to Epictetus by implying that he had never been given the felicitous translation that would have won him a wider audience among those citizens who did not have the good fortune of a classical education: "I have sometimes thought of translating Epictetus (for he has never been tolerably translated into English)."[22]

Through Jefferson the stoic bequest to the American experience was fully realized. Had stoicism provided only the concept of natural law that permeates Jefferson's *Declaration of Independence*, it would have left an indelible mark on American history.[23] But Seneca, Aurelius, and Epictetus are credited with an even greater effect on Jefferson and the other founders: "From them came some thoughts and ideals that became part of the higher thought of Western civilization: nobility of character, high ethical purpose, the ideal of self-sacrifice, belief in God and His divine providence, emphasis on virtue as the highest good and on action to make it effective, the need of bringing conduct into conformity with the law of Nature, and the realization of a high and stern sense of duty in public and private life."[24]

It should be understood, though, that the claim is not being advanced that Jefferson was entirely and only a stoic. On the contrary, in the same letter to William Short he acknowledged: "As you say of yourself, I too am an Epicurian. I consider the genuine (not imputed) doctrines of Epicurus as containing everything rational in moral philosophy which Greece and Rome have left us." Then he appended his appreciation of Epictetus. But even then he had not sketched in the fullness of his conception of the moral faculty and role. For he continued: "the greatest of all the reformers of the depraved religion of His own country, was Jesus of Nazareth. Abstracting what is really His from the rubbish in which it is buried, easily distinguished by its lustre from the dross of His biographers, and as separable from that as the diamond from the dunghill, we have the outlines of a system of the most sublime morality which has ever fallen from the lips of man; outlines which it is lamentable He did not live to fill up. Epictetus and Epicurus give laws for governing ourselves, Jesus a supplement of the duties and charities we owe to others."[25]

Jefferson's distinction between the stoics and Jesus supports Adrienne Koch's conclusion about his religious philosophy: "if one speculates on the historic function of Epicureanism and Stoicism and also upon their reintroduction into Europe in the sixteenth and seventeenth centuries, Jefferson's attitude may be better understood. In brief, they both functioned as systems of independent morality, needing no sanction from Church or State. This alone would have been sufficient to evoke some interest on Jefferson's part, since authoritarian religious morality was clearly repugnant to him at this period, as always."[26] His opposition is clearly displayed in his feeling that one of his three most important accomplishments was authorship of "The Bill for Establishing Religious Freedom" in Virginia, even though that action disestablished his own denomination, the Anglican Church. Jefferson, in sum, balanced the pagans and Jesus to develop a view that honoured both the self and the other.

Later Southern patricians failed to maintain such a fine distribution of restraints. Rather, they remained in the church with their Jesus, a Jesus who was a focus for personal piety, rarely a goad to action that would shake the foundations of society. And when they came out of the church and into the workaday world, they lived as stoics, observing their world's steady decline: "In the nineteenth century the Virginian, even more than other Southerners, was a deteriorationist. He believed in the inevitable superiority of former times."[27]

For many Southerners, then, the year 1861 brought no surprise. The fire-eaters, conceiving themselves as Cavaliers, may have viewed the outbreak of the war as the long-sought opportunity not merely to separate from the base Puritans, but to administer a deeply deserved drubbing as they took their leave. But many others, of a fatalistic cast of mind, seemed to see the hostilities as only the latest calamity visited upon the South. Such men may even have felt that defeat was certain; but such knowledge would have made them even more energetic in their participation in the Southern effort, once the war started: stripped of any opportunity for sordid success, Southern participation became the perfect vehicle for the display of unadulterated virtue. Such psychology may explain, as readily as any other, the fact that so many men fought on, long after the outcome was evident.

It is fitting that during the war the noblest Southerner of them all sought consolation in that other general's *Meditations*.[28] A devotion to Aurelius had been a part of Robert E. Lee's inheritance from his father, a devotion revealed in behaviour more than in direct reference. Such behaviour is apparent in his practice of committing evening thoughts to paper when there was a moment to spare in camp. One of the meditations which survived the dismal day at Appomattox, found in Lee's effects after his death, stated his Aurelian vision as starkly as it might be presented: "Private and public life are subject to the same rules; and truth and manliness are two qualities that will carry you through this world much better than *policy*, or *tact*, or *expediency*, or any other word that was ever devised to conceal or mystify a deviation from a straight line."[29]

Nor did Lee deviate from the straight line after the worst had come. Rather than accept a titular position in business that would advertise his name or retire to write a defence of it, he accepted the presidency of Washington College, there to serve the last five years of his life. His statement to Valentine, the sculptor, as he sat for him, sums up, as well as a single sentence could, Lee's sense of duty after the war: "Misfortune nobly borne is good fortune."[30] Only later, when he was reading the *Meditations*, did Valentine discover the source of Lee's comment. The transcendent indifference to the external world in Lee's code is in sharp contrast to Jefferson Davis's response to the postwar world. His *Short History of the Confederate States of America* (1890) possesses a motto from Seneca which herald the ironic vision that the stoic heritage has provided for the twentieth-century Southerner: *"Prosperum et felix scelus virtus vocatur."*[31]

From Davis's mordant farewell it is but a step to the sundered world of the twentieth-century South. With separate spheres of high thinking and low acting, modern Southern literature offers few depictions of the man who combines the inner restraint fostered by stoicism and the will to selfless action derived from an imitation of Jesus. Jefferson and Lee fade from a commanding position in the foreground of the Southern imagination, to be replaced by the Snopeses. And against these invaders the patrician remnant offers a futile rear-guard defence. There seem to be no warriors among the band, but, rather, flaccid fathers too often given to the sententious, and thewless sons too often unwilling to pass through the rites of maturity in order to face the external world. Faulkner, in *The Sound and the Fury* (1929), offers the most widely known example of these types: Mr Compson, hiding his impotent virtue behind drunkenness and cynicism, and Quentin, cloaking his desperation to remain a child behind an exaggerated regard for his sister's chastity.

But there are other examples easily available. In Robert Penn Warren's *All the King's Men* (1946) these two: the aristocratic Judge Irwin, who plays at being the noble Roman as he constructs his models of catapults and battering rams and reads his Tacitus, until he achieves a semblance of Roman nobility by committing suicide at the revelation of his acceptance of a bribe; his son, Jack Burden, who self-consciously employs flight to the womb, until through the agency of his father's death he is enabled to enter the world of moral consequence. William Styron's *Lie Down in Darkness* (1951) presents Milton Loftis and his father. As Milton reveals the wreckage of his life on the day that he must bury the daughter who killed herself at least in part because of his failure to guide her, he often recalls the advice offered by his father, in preparation for the shock of maturity: *"Your first duty remember, son, is always to yourself"*[32]; *"My son, never let passion be a guide"* (LDD, p. 41); *"My son, most people, whether they know it or not . . . get on through life by sopho-moric fatalism. Only poets and thieves can exercise free will, and most of them die young"* (LDD, p. 91); *"My son, pure frustration can lead to the highest understanding"* (LDD, p. 151). However valid the advice may be, it is tinged with weariness and paltriness, and hence never becomes a vital presence in Milton's character. Nor does the curriculum at Jefferson's university set the concept of self-descipline, so Milton becomes a self-worshipping—rather than a self-respecting—man, in contrast to the old man he meets in Charlottesville who has come up 'to die near Mr. Jefferson' (LDD, p. 181). Thus, Milton can never really recognize the needs of any other person. The most generous appraisal of his actions would be that they are thoughtless and immature.

In decisive contrast to the fictional picture of toothless heri-

itage and triumphant materialism is the vision sketched in
William Alexander Percy's autobiography *Lanterns on the Levee*
(1941).[33] Perhaps in the realization of mortality brought on by
declining health, Percy, after years of demanding from his frail
body an active life (teaching, the law, military duty, and community obligation), offers, through his memoir, a meditation
which will convey the values of the past to the future—his
adopted sons and their generation.   Descended from an aristocratic family which had been influential in community life in
Louisiana and Mississippi since the eighteenth century, Percy
(1885-1941) seems in many ways to be a remarkable conservator
of the classic Southern stoic values.   For, like Jefferson and Lee,
he draws his strength from a dual tradition: "I think if one
would sit in the Greek theater above Taormina with the wine-
dark sea below and AEtna against the sunset, and if there he
would meditate on Jesus and the Emperor, he would be assured
a god had made earth and man.   And this is all we need to
know" (LL, p. 320).

Still like Jefferson, who created his own "bible" by retaining
the statements of Jesus while discarding the divine actions attrib-
uted to Him by the writers of the Gospels, Percy carefully win-
nows that which is unacceptable from the Christian heritage:
"The Gospels were written by simple men who earnestly and
with a miraculous eloquence tried to report events which they
themselves had never witnessed but of which they had been
told.   Even what these writers of hearsay set down we have
never seen in the words they used, but only in later Greek translations.   Consequently the narratives of the four Evangelists as
we read them are full of misunderstandings and contradictions
and inaccuracies—as every lawyer knows any human testimony
aiming at truth is sure to be—yet they throw more light than
darkness on the heart-shaking story they tell.   They are pitifully
human and misleading, but drenched in a supernal light and
their contagion changed the dreaming world" (LL, p. 316).   Those
"misunderstandings and contradictions and inaccuracies" have
been used by the churches, Percy feels, to pervert the genuine
message offered by Jesus: "I think of what is being offered to our
young people in their need by the churches, and my heart is
filled with anger and sorrow. I asked a clergyman recently why it
was that so many prominent church-goers were crooks in business and hypocrites in private life. He replied: 'They have been
born again."   This clarified nothing for me and I told him as

much. He explained sadly: 'When they are born again, they are certain of salvation, and when you are certain of salvation you may do what you like.' But I urged, horrified: 'People don't really believe that!' 'Hundreds of thousands of them,' he rejoined, obviously as grieved as I. 'The ethics of Jesus do not interest them when their rebirth guarantees them salvation.' " (LL, p. 314).

Rejecting the abandonment of manners and morals that others justify by their acceptance of a religion preoccupied with eternal life, Percy looks elsewhere for his salvation: "There is left to each of us, no matter how far defeat pierces, the unassailable wintry kingdom of Marcus Aurelius, which some more gently call the Kingdom of Heaven" (LL, p. 313). With this orientation, one can face the world, where "Nothing is so sad as defeat, except victory" (LL, p. 145). From the *Meditations* can be extracted a sufficient belief: "The self-communings of the Emperor, though often cold to clamminess, convince a man he never need be less than tight-lipped, courteous, and proud, though all is pain" (LL, p. 316). Armed with such traits of behaviour, Percy can face the inevitable disappointments of his life like his grandfather: "he never spoke of the war, it hurt so much, as besides, silence was General Lee's example" (LL, p. 115).

But though silent, Percy cannot avoid the ironic, Davis-like vision inherent in the possession of a heritage: "In Russia, Germany, and Italy, Demos, having slain its aristocrats and intellectuals and realizing its own incompetence to guide or protect itself, had submitted to tyrants who laughed at the security virtues and practiced the most vile of survival virtues with gangster cynicism. In the democracies Demos had been so busy providing itself with leisure and luxury it had forgotten that hardihood and discipline are not ornaments but weapons. Everywhere the security virtues appeared as weaknesses and the survival virtues as strength and foresight" (LL, p. 312). To such transmogrification Percy will not assent; rather, there is an eloquent appeal to his sons to cleave by the old truth: "It is sophistry to speak of two sets of virtues, there is but one: virtue is an end in itself; the survival virtues are means, not ends. Honor and honesty, compassion and truth are good even if they kill you, for they alone give life its dignity and worth" (LL, p. 313).

If *Lanterns on the Levee* is but the distillate of the living presence of William Alexander Percy, then how much more captivating would have been his creed embodied in action, especially upon someone during his impressionable adolescence? After the death of his parents Walker Percy discovered the charm of the man: "to have lived in Will Percy's house, with 'Uncle Will' as we called him, as a raw youth from age fourteen to twenty-six, a youth whose only talent was a knack for looking and listening, for tuning in and soaking up, was nothing less than to be informed in the deepest sense of the word. What was to be listened to, dwelled on, pondered over for the next thirty years was of course the man himself, the unique human being, and when I say unique I mean it in its most literal sense: he was one of a kind: I never met anyone remotely like him. It was to encounter a complete, articulated view of the world as tragic as it was noble" (LL, "Introduction," p x).

Writing over forty years after his first encounter with his 'Uncle Will,' Percy has tried to recapture his first impression: "I can only suppose that he must have been, for me at least, a personage, a presence, radiating that mysterious quality we call charm, for lack of a better word, in such high degree that what comes to mind is not that usual assemblage of features and habits which make up our memories of people but rather a quality, a temper, a set of mouth, a look through the eyes." Then the expansion upon the image: "For his eyes were most memorable, a piercing gray-blue and strangely light in my memory, as changeable as shadows over water, capable of passing in an instant, we were soon to learn, from merriment—he told the funniest stories we'd ever heard—to a level gray gaze cold with reproof. They were beautiful and terrible eyes, eyes to be careful around. Yet now, when I try to remember them, I cannot see them otherwise than as shadowed by sadness" (LL, "Introduction," p. viii).

Walker Percy must have felt those eyes following him as he went away, first to the University of North Carolina for undergraduate work, then to Columbia University for medical school. They must have reminded him not only of the sole parent, conduit to a family past, but also of a personification of the best of the Southern tradition. Their "level gray gaze" must have provided a constant beacon, even during the years when he was away in the North, suffering from the debility of tuberculosis. And they must have seemed to grow larger when he acted upon his decision to return to Louisiana to live.

Once there, although his health denied him the career for which he had prepared himself, he discovered that he was not without resources. Writing later about the effect that rearing

three boys may have had upon his Uncle Will's creation of poetry, Walker Percy said: "At any rate, whatever he lost or gained
in the transaction, I know what I gained: a vocation and in a real
sense a second self, that is, the work and the self which, for better
or worse, would not otherwise have been open to me' (LL,
"Introduction," pp ix-x). That is to say, the example of a man
sensitive to ideas and capable of conveying them through words
was offered to him. Thus, Walker Percy devoted himself to
reading, especially in those areas, such as existentialism, which
had been ignored by his scientific education. In time he began a
series of articles on language, that medium which seems most
promising as a relief to the isolation celebrated by the existential
philoso-phers.

But those eyes must have remained fixed on him, for an early essay was entitled "Stoicism in the South."[34] Having returned
to the South to live, Percy may have been deciding how he
could, or would, live there. For the essay is like so much of his
writing, both non-fiction and fiction, in that it seems in a way to
be a thinking out loud. The first style of life to come to mind
could easily have been that of his adoptive father. The essay
thus becomes a testing of the tradition of Southern stoicism
against the demands of a new era. Percy's presentation of the
Southern stoic heritage is an admirable realization: "The greatness of the South, like the greatness of the English squirearchy,
had always a stronger Greek flavor than it ever had a Christian.
Its nobility and graciousness was the nobility and graciousness of
the old Stoa. How immediately we recognize the best of the
South in the words of the Emperor: 'Every moment think steadily, as a Roman and a man, to do what thou hast in hand with
perfect and simple dignity, and a feeling of affection, and freedom, and justice.' And how curiously foreign to the South
sound the Decalogue, the Beatitudes, the doctrine of the Mystical
Body . . . When [the Southerner] named a city Corinth, he did
not mean Paul's community. How like him to go into Chancel-
lorsville or the Argonne with Epictetus in his pocket; how unlike him to have had the Psalms" (SS, p. 343).

Stoicism may have been the best practicable philosophy for
patricians in the old South, given the primacy of the reality of slavery, Percy implies. Of course, if there had been a widespread,
genuine, radical Christianity, slavery could not have existed.
But it did, so that "hierarchical structure" was the predominant
factor in establishing human relations. That being the case, stoi-

cism, with its emphasis upon "the stern inner summons," ensured that Southern slave-holding was at least leavened by restraint.

The war swept away the legality of absolute hierarchy. And the hundred-odd years since have witnessed social change, at an ever increasing tempo, as the black has claimed what is justly his. Such achievement does not depend upon the granting of favours by the patrician; hence the patrician has found himself ever more irrelevant and defensive. His mentality has thus developed a definite cast: "Its most characteristic mood was a poe-tic pessimism which took a grim satisfaction in the dissolution of its values—because social decay confirmed one in his original choice of the wintry kingdom of self" (SS, p. 343). And there the patrician waits for the *Götterdämmerung*: "For the Stoic there is no real hope. His finest hour is to sit tight-lipped and ironic while the world comes crashing down around him" (SS, p. 344).

The personality sketched in "Stoicism in the South" vividly anticipates Emily Bolling Cutrer in *The Moviegoer*. Although she has a surviving older brother, Oscar, Emily seems to be the venerable figure of the family; not merely formidable in her own right, she acts as the repository of the past. Her nephew Jack, the protagonist, seems to see her as the still-living member of a series of larger-than-life figures that stretches back into history. As he stands in her living room, early in the novel, he faces the mantelpiece in an effort to address the household gods: "One picture I never tire looking at. For ten years I have looked at it on this mantelpiece and tried to understand it. Now I take it down and hold it against the light from the darkening sky. Here are the two brothers, Dr. Wills and Judge Anse with their arms about each other's shoulders, and my father in front, the three standing on a mountain trail against a dark forest. It is the Schwarzwald. A few years after the first war they had gotten together for once and made the grand tour. Only Alex Bolling is missing—he is in the third frame: an astonishingly handsome young man with the Rupert Brooke-Galahad sort of face you see so often in pictures of World War I soldiers. His death in the Argonne (five years before) was held to be fitting since the original Alex Bolling was killed with Roberdaux Wheat in the Hood breakthrough at Gaines Mill in 1862" (M, pp. 24-5).

The crowning demonstration of a vital family virtue has been the death of a warrior in each generation. There had been Captain Alex Bolling in the Civil War, then his namesake in the

First World War. By then the tradition was so well established that Dr Will's son John lived a life of disquiet, apparently fearing that if he had no opportunity to live (and die) up to the family model, he would be condemned to live a life of everydayness. He thus regarded the outbreak of the Second World War as his opportunity to break out of personal insignificance; so he volunteered for the Canadian armed service, before the American entry into the war, thus to fulfill the ideal role, as his son Jack perceives: "He had found a way to do both: to please them and please himself. To leave. To do what he wanted to do and save old England doing it. And perhaps even carry off the grandest coup of all: to die. To win the big prize for them and for himself (but not even he dreamed he would succeed not only in dying but in dying in Crete in the wine dark sea)" (M, p. 157). Because of her sex Emily had been unable to engage in combat; she had achieved an honourable alternative, though, as a Red Cross volunteer during the Spanish Civil War. Thus, Jack sees that his Aunt Emily, despite the handicap of being a woman, has participated in ritualized family behaviour and in so doing become an eloquent voice in its behalf: "It is as if, with her illustrious brothers dead and gone, she might now at last become what they had been and what as a woman had been denied her: soldierly both in look and outlook. With her blue-white hair and keen quick face and terrible gray eyes, she is somehow at sixty-five still the young prince" (M, p. 27).

With an outlook formed by such military rectitude, she would rely upon Marcus Aurelius for inspiration, as her note to her nephew indicates. Even small actions, such as her fondling of the lion's head carved on her chair arm (M, pp. 176, 182), become symbolic of her imperial assertion. Her brisk confidence evokes martial allusions, as when Jack imagines that she is telling him to "hold the fort" (M, p. 29). And she is prone to such imagery herself: "The barbarians at the inner gate and who defends the West? Don John of Austria? No, Mr Bolling the stockbroker and Mr Wade the Lawyer" (M, p. 33).

Indeed, Jack recalls, one of his earliest memories of his aunt is that when his brother Scott died, his aunt told him: "I've got bad news for you, son . . . Scotty is dead. Now it's all up to you. It's going to be difficult for you but I know that you're going to act like a soldier" (M, p. 4). Such an injunction could be derived from Epictetus, who quotes Socrates about the duty of remaining at one's post like a soldier, or simply from family ethos; whatever its origin, Jack recalls that as an eight-year-old he felt it would be a simple order to carry out. And he had apparently grown up accepting his aunt's example, for he had, in his turn, become an army officer during the Korean War. Attempting to meet family expectation, he had written such sentiments to his aunt: "Japan is lovely this time of year. How strange to think of going into combat! Not so much fear—since my chances are very good—as wonder, wonder that everything should be so full of expectancy, every tick of the watch, every rhododendron blossom. Tolstoy and St Exupery were right about war, etc"(M, p. 87).

But Jack, when wounded, makes the mistake of experiencing fear—and surviving. Which, it should be stressed, is not saying that he acts in a cowardly way; rather, he discovers, through the intrusion of fear, that he is condemned to be an individual, not an idealized manikin in a gallant historical series. According to Martin Heidegger, whose ideas Percy utilizes in the novel, fear is one of those states of mind which discloses to the individual his actuality and its vulnerability—he is something which he did not create, even though he is responsible for his actions nevertheless, and those actions may result in his loss of life itself.[35] No longer will Jack be able to accept himself as an object, albeit glamorous with the achievement of ideal behaviour; no longer will he be able to conceive of himself as a self-contained consciousness isolated through proud aloofness from a tawdry world. Fear teaches the individual that the world can penetrate the strongest fort; hence the individual, rather than attempting to withdraw from the world, must thrust himself into it, confront it, quest for the fullness of being that it can yield.

Fear, then, is not negative, but positive. Through its agency the individual discovers possibility; he is what he is, but he is also what he can become. Jack thus returns from the war committed to a search. But the character of the search he performs is self-defeating, literally. Seduced by the promises of the highly praised and widely employed objective—empirical point of view, he conducts a search for larger and larger generalizations, thinking that in understanding the world of matter and mass man, he will at some point arrive at an understanding of himself among them. Quite the opposite is accomplished: as he accepts the concept that all significant knowledge is based upon generalization, so he experiences less and less understanding of himself as a datum identified by generalization. It does him no good to learn how he is like matter, or other forms of life, or even other men, when his quest has been to learn how he is unique (such as when he discovered himself as the I who am experiencing fear). In time, out of frustration he abandons his search, to fall into everydayness, that type of behaviour where all standards are developed by the mass. When the fall occurs, Jack acquiesces to the imposition of Heidegger's "they-self," the totally inauthentic self as commuter, as consumer, as moviegoer.

The world makes no sense, and throughout the novel Jack founders in it. Cut off from the sustenance provided by a myth, he cannot organize his world to resemble his aunt's: "All the stray bits and pieces of the past, all that is feckless and gray about people, she pulls together with an unmistakable visage of the heroic or the craven, the noble or the ignoble" (M, p. 49). For her, as well, although they lack the bold relief of the past, the present and the future still have a meaning, her admission to the contrary notwithstanding: " 'I no longer pretend to understand the world.' She is shaking her head yet still smiling her sweet menacing smile. 'The world I knew has come crashing down around my ears. The things we hold dear are reviled and spat upon . . . It's an interesting age you will live in—though I can't say I'm sorry to miss it. But it should be quite a sight, the going under of the evening land. That's us all right. And I can tell you, my young friend, it is evening. It is very late.' " But Jack senses the difference between them: "For her too the fabric is dissolving, but for her even the dissolving makes sense" (M, p. 54).

When Aunt Emily speaks of the unfathomable world, she is of course addressing her irony at Jack, for his actions are especially mystifying in their failure to conform to the mould which she has cast for them. Already in this passage she is separating Jack from his status as a family member—"my young friend." But the absolute rupture of their relationship occurs when, in her eyes, Jack violates the chivalric code in his behaviour with her stepdaughter Kate: utterly overwhelmed with his own problems (which are of a type his aunt cannot apprehend), he allows Kate, who has a medically recognized history of mental instability, to accompany him on a trip to Chicago.

Jack is ordered to return to New Orleans, there to approach his aunt as if she were a military superior: "There is nothing to do but go directly in to her and stand at ease until she takes notice of me. Now she looks over, as erect and handsome as the Black Prince' (M, pp. 220-1). As she begins to upbraid him, she withdraws a metal letter opener in the shape of a sword from "the grasp of the helmeted figure on the inkstand." Thus armed, she is ready to speak of the stoic tradition: "At the great moments of life—success, failure, marriage, death—our kind of folks have always possessed a native instinct for behavior, a natural piety or grace, I don't mind calling it" (M, p. 222).

Then, waving the sword to the street, as if to defend Jack in his weakness from the corruption of the "barbarians at the inner gate," she makes clear what the traditional behaviour is: "I did my best for you, son. I gave you all I had. More than anything I wanted to pass on to you the one heritage of the men of our family, a certain quality of spirit, a gaiety, a sense of duty, a nobility worn lightly, a sweetness, a gentleness with women—the only good things the South ever had and the only things that really matter in this life" (M, p. 224). When she cannot understand his reasons for the behaviour which she regards as errant, she will not suffer his foolishness. Having been working in her account book when he entered, she now closes it, as she is closing the book on him: "Smiling, she gives me her hand, head to one side, in her old party style. But it is her withholding my name that assigns me my new status" (M, pp. 226-7). " 'I do thank you so much for coming by,' says my aunt, fingering her necklace and looking past me at the Vaudrieul house." Immediately afterward Kate calls Jack a "poor stupid bastard" (M, p. 227), and in a sense he is—now without family in a society that places family before all other institutions and forms of identification.

In another generation thus to be disowned would be a staggering blow to a Southerner. But it is precisely Jack's predicament that he had not flourished within a calcified tradition; hence to be bereaved of it actually frees him to struggle for self-identity. The first small, but absolutely necessary, skirmish is Jack's ability to say that his aunt suffers from rightness and despair (M, p. 228), unimaginative attitudes that preclude any possibility of openness and change. He, though, is at least stumbling towards a new form of confirmation of self: he will be that self which sacrifices itself in nurturing Kate's self. It is a small irony that when Kate meets Jack, after his dismissal by his aunt, she misunderstands what has occurred: "She is certain that I have carried off a grand stoic gesture, like a magazine hero" (M, p. 232). In reality Jack had himself despaired, concluding that Kate had abandoned him, and he is therefore trying to pick up a girl, any girl. When Kate does arrive, so great is Jack's relief that his action towards her has its source in that other Jeffersonian principle—"Jesus a supplement of the duties and charities we owe to others." To encourage such inference Percy has Kate and Jack make their first tentative commitment to one another as, in the background, a man enters the church to receive the ritual of imposition on Ash Wednesday.

If Jack is intended to be a representative character, then he would seem to personify Percy's contention, in "Stoicism in the South," that his countrymen must stop standing on the porch and go on into the church. Certainly Jack's action reflects one modern Southerner's decision, for Walker Percy converted to Catholicism about the time he returned to the South. But it should not be concluded that Percy, through the disguise of a novel, has thus rejected the totality of his uncle's example. Of Will Percy he has said: "even when I did not follow him, it was usually in *relation* to him, whether with him or against him, that I defined myself and my own direction. Perhaps he would not have had it differently. Surely it is the highest tribute to the best people we know to use them as best we can, to become, not their disciples, but ourselves" (LL, "Introduction," p. xi). *The Moviegoer* exists, then, because there was a force so impressive to inspire it; its dedication to "W.A.P." stands as testimony to the continuing vitality of stoicism in the South.

Notes

[1] Walker Percy, *The Moviegoer* (New York: Noonday Press 1967), p. 78; hereafter cited as M.

[2] Thomas E. Keys, 'The Colonial Library and the Development of Sectional Differences in the American Colonies,' *Library Quarterly*, 8 (1938), 374.

[3] See Thomas Franklin Mayo, *Epicurus in England (1650-1725)* (Dallas: Southwestern Press 1934), pp. 110-11, for the alliance of stoicism with the Platonic idealists, the Royal Society, and the Cartesian rationalists.

[4] John Melville Jennings, 'Notes on the Original Library of the College of William and Mary,' *Papers of the Bibliographical Society of America*, 41 (1947), 265.

[5] John Melville Jennings, *The Library of the College of William and Mary in Virginia, 1693-1793* (Charlottesville: University Press of Virginia, 1968),

pp. 47-8.

[6] Mayo, pp. 110-11, argues that Anglican Christianity had little difficulty in accepting nearly all stoic beliefs as relatively harmless departures from orthodoxy.

[7] Jennings, *The Library*, p. 30, points out that 'Three of the six private book collections analysed by Louis B. Wright in his *First Gentlemen of Virginia* were owned by members of the college board of visitors [of the College of William and Mary]—Ralph Wormeley II, Robert ("King") Carter, and William Byrd, II." If Wright can generalize broadly upon the reading and other tastes of a class from six examples, then it seems not entirely out of line to suggest here that the thinking of that class was coloured by particular books found in its libraries.

[8] George K. Smart, "Private Libraries in Colonial Virginia," *American Literature*, 10 (1938), 51.

[9] John Rogers Williams, "A Catalogue of Books in the Library of 'Councillor' Robert Carter," *William and Mary College Quarterly*, 11, 1st series (1902), 23.

[10] John Spencer Bassett, *The Writings of Colonel William Byrd* (New York: Doubleday, Page, 1901), appendix A, pp. 413-43.

[11] Louis B. Wright, *The First Gentlemen of Virginia* (San Marino, Calif.: Huntington Library 1940), p. 233.

[12] William D. Houlette, "Sources of Books for the Old South," *Library Quarterly*, 38 (1958), 195.

[13] Lester J. Cappon and Stella F. Duff, *Virginia Gazette Index* (Williamsburg: Institute of Early American History and Culture 1950), 11, 1022.

[14] See *Virginia Gazette*, 13 November 1768; 21 November 1768; 11 April 1769.

[15] The stoics were being read in other Southern colonies as well. For Maryland see Joseph T. Wheeler, "Reading Interests of the Professional Classes in Colonial Maryland, 1700-1776," *Maryland Magazine of History*, 36 (1941), 201; for North Carolina see J. B. Grimes, *North Carolina Wills and Inventories* (Raleigh: Edwards and Braughton 1912), pp. 559, 562-4; and S. B. Weeks, "Libraries and Literature in North Carolina in the Eighteenth Century," *Annual Report of the American Historical Association* (1895), p. 205.

[16] "Catalogue of the Library of Daniel Parke Custis," *Virginia Magazine of History and Biography*, 17 (1903), 404-12, esp p. 409.

[17] Genevieve Yost, "The Reconstruction of the Library of Norborne Berkeley, Baron de Botetourt, Governor of Virginia, 1768-1770," *Papers of the Bibliographical Society of America*. 36 (1942), 119.

[18] Eleanor Davidson Berman, *Thomas Jefferson Among the Arts* (New York: Philosophical Library 1947), p. 271.

[19] Andrew A. Lipscomb, ed, *The Writings of Thomas Jefferson*, Memorial ed (Washington 1903), v, 85.

[20] Elizabeth Cometti, *Jefferson's Ideas on a University Library* (Charlottesville: University Press of Virginia 1950), p. 30.

[21] Lipscomb, XV, 219.

[22] Lipscomb, XV, 221.

[23] Anson Phelps Stokes, *Church and State in the United States* (New York: Harper 1950), I, 136.

[24] Stokes, I, 82-3.

[25] Lipscomb, XV, 220. Nor was Jefferson's classification to William Short merely one of those statements so influenced by friendship that it is tailored to please the person for whom it is intended. Over fifteen years before Jefferson had employed the same assignment of values in writing to Dr Benjamin Rush. The purpose of the letter was to urge Dr Rush to write a book that Jefferson would have written himself had his life not been given over to public service. He had gone so far as to prepare a "Syllabus of an Estimate of the Merit of the Doctrines of Jesus, compared with those others." In the letter he announced: "To the corruptions of Christianity I am, indeed, opposed; but not to the genuine pre-cepts of Jesus himself. I am a Christian, in the only sense in which he wished any one to be; sincerely attached to his doctrines, in preference to all others; ascribing to himself every *human* excellence; and believing he never claimed any other." Then he explained why, despite the nobility of classical philoso-phy, the doctrines of Jesus were essential:

"Let a just view be taken of the moral principles inculcated by the most esteemed of the sects of ancient philosophy, or of their individuals; particularly Pythagoras, Socrates, Epicurus, Cicero, Epictetus, Seneca, Antoninus.

1. Philosophers. 1. Their precepts related chiefly to ourselves, and the government of those passions which, unrestrained, would disturb our tranquility of mind. In this branch of philosophy they were really great.

2. In developing our duties to others, they were short and defective."
See Lipscomb, X, 380-2.

[26] Adrienne Koch, *The Philosophy of Thomas Jefferson* (Gloucester: Peter Smith 1957), p. 4.

[27] Jay B. Hubbell, *South and Southwest* (Durham: Duke University Press 1965), p. 235. James McBride Dabbs, *Who Speaks for the South?* (New York: Funk and Wagnalls 1964), p. 127, expands on the reasons for the popularity of stoicism in the South during the nineteenth century: "For several reasons, Stoicism found a rich soil in the ante-bellum South. First, because of the rising individualism of the Western World, of which the South was a part, an individualism which coincided with and was in part the cause of the decay of the inclusive community life of the Middle Ages. Second, because of the existence of slavery, increasingly under moral attack, impossible to defend in the humanitarian air of the nineteenth century and within a Christianity increasingly concerned about life in the world, but easy to defend by the Stoic doctrine that a man's worldly condition does not matter. Third, because of the growing doubt within the minds of Southern leaders, a sense of the coming eclipse of the nation, a fear of the possible breakdown of the social and economic order of the South. In such a mood a man, if he were a Stoic, could retire to the inviolable castle of his own soul and watch with stern composure the playing out of the game."

[28] Douglas Southall Freeman, *R. E. Lee* (New York: Scribner's 1935), IV, 464.

[29] Freeman, III, 237.

[30] Freeman, IV, 464.

[31] "Fortunate and prosperous wickedness is called virtue" (New York: Belford Company 1890), frontispiece.

[32] William Styron, *Lie Down in Darkness* (New York: New American Library 1951), p. 12; hereafter cited as LDD.

[33] William Alexander Percy, *Lanterns on the Levee* (Baton Rouge: Louisi-

ana State University Press 1973); hereafter cited as L. L.

34 *The Commonweal*, 44 (6 July 1956), 342-4; hereafter cited as SS.

35 *Being and Time*, trans John Macquarrie and Edward Robinson (New York: Harper and Row 1962), pp. 179-82.

Walker Percy's *The Moviegoer:*
The Cinema as Cave

After graduating from the University of North Carolina with a major in chemistry, in 1937, Walker Percy entered the College of Physicians and Surgeons of Columbia University. He was an excellent medical student, though he lacked the singleness of purpose that sometimes characterizes a student in a professional school. "I had a misspent youth while going to medical school," he has said. "My uncle would try to get me to come downtown to the opera house, but I spent four years in the movies in Washington Heights."[1]

Percy's description of his medical school years represents, in his own terms, an aesthetic repetition, a condensation of the past into a sequence of meaningful moments. He may have gone to the movies often, but he graduated in 1941 with high honors. He may have gone to the movies often and also studied with great success, but still his past is not adquately represented. For during the same years, he was the patient of a psychiatrist five days a week.

In the fall of 1941 Percy began his residency at Bellevue Hospital, as a member of the pathology staff. He soon contracted tuberculosis. He has never discussed the onset of his illness, but it seems at least possible that the stresses of consciousness had some role in the affliction of his body. He was forced into convalescence at Saranac Lake with very little but reading to occupy his mind. For the first time in his life, thanks to the illness which might take his life, he could devote himself to non-scientific writers—the nineteenth-century Russian novelists, Kierkegaard, Marcel, Heidegger, Jaspers, Sartre, Camus, Buber, among others.

When Percy was able to leave the hospital, he returned to the South, became a Catholic, and married. He decided not to begin an active practice of medicine; having inherited some money, he continued to devote himself to reading. In the Fifties he began to publish essays that continue the strain of thought in which he had been reading; in the Sixties he began to publish novels that make specific the same concerns.

Over the years, as interest in Percy's writing has grown, a good deal of critical attention has been paid to those writers—existentialists, for want of a better label—who provided much of his sickbed reading. Then, in time, his response to his personal, family/class, and Southern backgrounds was noticed. Lately, his reading of the "universal" historian Eric Voegelin has been noted. In this essay I argue that Percy draws upon Henri Bergson, another thinker often identified as an existentialist, and upon Arnold Toynbee, another "universal" historian, in developing the image of moviegoing, the basic image of *The Moviegoer* (1961), Percy's first novel.

It should be immediately noted that Voegelin and Toynbee are linked only by a conjunction, for they differ in their basic philosophy of history. As Karl Löwith points out, an historian must come down on one foot or the other: he must see the historical process as a linear movement which has a definite conception and a definite consummation or as a circular movement which eternally changes, yet eternally recurs.[2] An historian must, in other words, have either a Christian or a non-Christian understanding of the unfolding of human events. Voegelin has "an unconditional faith in God's redemptive purpose," as Löwith characterizes "the Christian hope."[3] But Toynbee (although he professes himself a Christian) does not let go of reason when he reaches for faith; the result, according to Löwith, is disastrous: " . . . Toynbee is neither an empirical historian nor a good theologian. Instead of arguing with Augustine and all the Church Fathers that Christianity is the latest news because it is *the* good news and because God revealed himself in history only once and for all, he argues on astronomical grounds!"[4] Inspired by a lingering received faith, Toynbee *wants* to see as a Christian, yet captivated as he is by his fertile imagination and prodigious learning, he ultimately presents a scheme of history that attempts to reconcile the unique with the universal.

Walker Percy has indicated his awareness of Toynbee's well-meaning, but obtuse attempt to crash the secular historians' party with Christianity as his date. In "The Message in the Bottle" (1959), Percy speaks of the offense taken by "modern eclectics like Whitehead, Huxley, and Toynbee" at the assertion that Christianity is unique.[5] In "The Loss of the Creature" (1958), he ridicules Toynbee's effort to treat a particularity of the Judeo-Christian experience as just one more vegetable for his mulligan. Speaking of the tendency to shift from the concrete to the abstract that

Whitehead defines as "the fallacy of misplaced concreteness," Percy scoffs that the "*reductio ad absurdum* of Whitehead's shift is Toynbee's employment of it in his historical method": " . . . when the Jews and the Jewish religion are understood as—in Toynbee's favorite phrase—a 'classical example of' such and such a kind of *Voelkerwanderung,* we begin to suspect that something is being left out."[6] In "Notes for a Novel about the End of the World" (1967), Percy could be mocking Toynbee when he says: "All issues are ultimately religious, said Toynbee."[7] The statement is undoubtedly true, but it is only a platitude, given Toynbee's understanding of religion.

Yet, even though he objects to Toynbee's fundamental vision, Percy has found uses for one of Toynbee's best known catch phrases, "Withdrawal-and-Return."[8] This movement is a key concept in the structure of Volume III, *The Growths of Civilizations,* in which Toynbee finds that a civilization grows when there is a great leader who, defeated or frustrated in his project, withdraws psychologically (and often physically), communes with himself, then returns, to gain victory over the conditions that had originally defeated him. The universality of that movement is not to be denied; but that is not to say that its existence was first noticed by Toynbee or even that he analyzes it very well.[9]

Percy has from time to time referred to "the Return," most extensively in "The Man on the Train" (1956), an essay essential to any response to his fiction.[10] There he links "the Return" to another idea that recurs in his thought, "Repetition." "The Man on the Train" discusses the alienation, or "everydayness," that is experienced if one understands his world only objectively—empirically, and the available deliverances from alienation, "rotation" and "repetition." All too simply put: since the present is the locus of alienation, then one anticipates a radically better future or attempts to identify that point in the past at which one became alienated. "Rotation," the orientation toward the future, is treated in the second part of the essay, but since it is not central to my concern, it will not be discussed. "Repetition," the third part of the essay, is Percy's main subject. For, whereas one can never run far enough into the future to keep his present from catching up with him, he can return to the past to take the road not taken. Repetition, or the Return, "is thus in the nature of a conversion."[11] There is a crucial distinction in repetition, though: "the aesthetic repetition," or nostalgia, "captures the

savor of repetition without surrendering the self as a locus of experience and possibility"; the existential repetition is a "passionate quest" for the "thread in the labyrinth to be followed at any
cost." If successfully pursued, this Return is, inescapably, a "religious conversion," in the sense that all ultimate, existential decisions are religious "turnings."

The Return has provided Percy with a theme which he has
employed in all of his novels to date. He told an interviewer
that *The Last Gentleman* (1966) was "a novel of the return":[12] a
proof of his intention to use the theme is the action of Will Barrett's standing before his father's house, then to change his mind
about his father's suicide. Will's behavior answers the question
asked, years before, in "The Man on the Train," "what does it
mean to stand before the house of one's childhood?"[13] From
that point, Will's present is no longer dominated by the past.
Percy follows Will's decisive scene with the scene of his visit to
Uncle Fannin's, at Shut Off; Fannin persists in acting the past in
the present, but can only be a parody. The figure of the father, in
the form of the uncle, has deteriorated. Will can go on, then, to
confront his own present and make the ultimate Return or religious conversion. In *Love in the Ruins* (1971), the protagonist,
Tom More, very early says: "Toynbee, I believe, speaks of the Return, of the man who fails and goes away, is exiled, takes counsel
with himself, hits on something, sees daylight—and returns to
triumph" (LR, 25). This reference is a crucial revelation of Tom
More's image of himself and provides a key to his actions in the
novel. More sees himself as on of those "Individuals" who further "Growing Civilizations," in the Toynbee scheme. Having
been in despair since the death of his daughter (since the failure
of medical science), he has now hit upon the invention that will
save humanity, the lapsometer. Modern technology will resolve
the Cartesian split, reunite immanent man with his world.
Tom's intended triumphant Return fails, though, as technology
only further separates. He is defeated, hence his Return becomes
yet another Withdrawal, out of which issues the genuine
Return, his confession at the conclusion that he is again
dependent upon God.

There is no reference or allusion to the Return in *Lancelot*
(1977), yet some sensitivity to the theme in Percy's work alerts
the reader to its presence. The obvious Return is that Lance
Lamar, who has apparently been defeated, been in eclipse for the
last year or so. He has been in a hospital for the criminally in-

sane, after having been responsible for the death of four people. During that year he has devised a scheme of universal history which "proves" that he will be the Saviour of the World. There were reviewers who sympathize with his sense of affront and his plans for the future—which suggests how far afield from any community of understanding we have wandered. Conscious of it or not, they believe, as does Lance, in a progressive scheme of history: the inherent movement insures that change, whatever change, drives toward the millennium that, purely by himself, man will accomplish. Yet, to anyone with any attachment to the Christian truth, Lance's fantasy of a Southern broadsword tradition is utterly insane: it is inconceivable that Percy would offer such a program as his genuine statement to his readers. On the contrary, the real message is carried by Father John, the other character, the one who says nothing until the very end of Lance's tirade. John, too, has been away, to Africa as a missionary physician-priest. Perhaps his mission was not successful, or perhaps he had suffered some sort of collapse. Or perhaps he had felt that he was dodging the real challenge, dealing with the citizens of Christendom. As far back as Kierkegaard, there has been an awareness that the strongest opponent of Christianity is Christendom. John has returned, in other words, to face up to his life's responsibility, ministering to those most hardened to and thus most in need of his help. By his patient silence he has said what he can say to Lance: it is up to Lance to accept the grace to listen, to make his genuine Return.

The Second Coming (1980) is a Return from the title on. Even that gorgeous flake, Kitty Vaught Huger, turns out to be Toynbeean: "Oh, I could have told you twenty years ago if you'd asked me, that you would have to undergo trial and exile before you finally won, . . . Your destiny is the Return" (SC, 286). She has no conception, though, of the real Return that Will Barrett makes: he achieves the fullness of consciousness that is available only through intersubjectivity, thus returning to an Edenic world in which a transcendent Father is present.

It is *The Moviegoer* that reveals Percy's most imaginative response to, most complex use of a Toynbee idea. A consideration of that usage will necessarily be more detailed than the earlier assertions that the Return is part of the narrative plan for each of the four subsequent novels. For that reason, discussion of *The Moviegoer* has been deferred, even though it was Percy's first published novel.

In *The Growths of Civilizations* Toynbee attends first to "civilization" as a history-concept. First the concept is asserted to be a legitimate historical problem; then the nature of civilization growth is described; and finally the process of civilization growth is analyzed. With all his pieces in place, Toynbee is ready to commence play; pursuing the theme of "Withdrawal-and-Return," he is ready to introduce his first Individual who radically affected a growing civilization. Before an extended treatment of an Individual, though, there is a discussion of some examples of "Withdrawal-and-Return" that establishes the universality of the motif. First cited is " . . . the Syriac myth of Moses' solitary ascent of Mount Sinai."[14] Then a short paragraph from the Arabic philosopher Ibn Khaldūn is quoted. Short—but enough to suggest to Toynbee that it contains " . . . an echo of a famous passage of Hellenic philosophy: the Platonic simile of the Cave."

The Simile, in the *Republic*, VII, 514A-521C, is quoted in part:

> "And now," he said . . . , "Picture to yourself people in a kind of cave-like underground dwelling. The place has its entrance open to the light, and this entrance stretches along the whole length of the cave. Picture these people living in this place from their infancy with their limbs fettered and likewise their necks, so that they cannot change their positions and can only see in front of them, because the fetters make it impossible for them to turn their heads. And then imagine firelight coming to them, from behind their backs, from a fire which is burning at a higher level and at a long distance off, with a raised road running between this fire and the prisoners. And now picture a parapet built along the side of the road, like the screens in front of the performers in a Punch and Judy show—the screens over the top of which they display their puppets."
>
> "I see the picture," he said.
>
> "Well, now imagine people carrying past this parapet all kinds of material objects which show up over the top of it—particularly models of living creatures: figures of human beings and figures of animals made of stone and of wood and of all kinds of materials. And imagine that some of the people will be talking—as they naturally will—and others keeping silence as they carry the objects by."
>
> "A strange simile," he said, "and strange prisoners!"
>
> "The prisoners are ourselves," said I.

Toynbee outlines the sequel: a prisoner is brought to the surface; dizzied, he learns to see by the light of the sun; then he is returned to his imprisonment. While specialists in Platonic thought doubt Toynbee's grasp of its complexities, Toynbee reveals here the leaping mind that impressed so many general readers. For one thing, Toynbee sees how the experience of the prisoner is similar, but not identical to the experience of the Christian mystic. For a second thing, Toynbee himself develops, in a footnote, a most happy simile for the Simile of the Cave:

> The simile is more strange to a reader of Plato's generation in Plato's world than to one of our generation in ours; for Plato is really picturing, by a brilliant effort of imagination, the situation of an audience in a cinematograph theatre with its eyes glued to the screen on which a lantern at their backs projects the lights and shadows of a moving film. Plato even anticipates the distinction between silent films and 'talkies'. If Plato had happened to live in this Western World in this twentieth century, he would assuredly have taken the simile which he requires at this point in the *Republic* from real life, instead of resorting to an elaborate and inevitably somewhat bizarre fantasy.[15]

Percy's familiarity with Toynbee's concept of "Withdrawal-and-Return" argues that he read that section of *The Growths of Civilations* very closely and that, in a brilliant response to Toynbee's footnote, conceived of the use of moviegoing as an extended simile for the exploration of visible reality.[16] Both wall-watching and moviegoing, though, must be placed in their context before they yield thematic meaning.

Raven has recently had to remind readers of the *Republic* that Plato links the Analogy of the Sun, the Description of the Divided Line, and the Simile of the Cave: " . . . it is on the basis of the three together, and not one only, that Plato proceeds to expound first his general theory of education and then the actual course that is to lead up to the actual apprehension of the Good."[17] Raven's summary of the function of each part and of the movement as a whole is admirably succinct:

> The analogy of the Sun, I believe, being intended primarily to single out the Idea of the Good from the other Ideas and to show in what relation it stands both to those other Ideas and to the mind that attempts to comprehend it, gives us what is deliberately, owing to its deliberate omission of everything irrelevant, a fragmentary picture of both the visible and the intelligible worlds. Next the Divided Line, by its subdivision of the contents of each world, presses a stage farther the analogy already drawn between visible and intelligible and gives us what is perhaps a total picture of the latter but what is certainly still a partial picture of the former.

The Divided Line has in fact—and herein lies difficulty—a dual function to perform. It sets out not only, as Plato tells us, to complete the analogy between the two worlds, visible and intelligible, but also to prepare us for the return, effected by the time we come to the Cave, to the old contrast between opinion and knowledge. And finally the Cave, no longer singling out sight from the other senses but regarding it now as representative of every form of perception, gives us what is unquestionably intended as a total and all-embracing picture of both worlds alike. Just as, therefore, the Divided Line continues and expands the analogy of the Sun, so the allegory of the Cave continues and expands the Divided Line. And to perfect the essential cohesion of the three figures, the sun itself, which played no part in the Divided Line, reappears, as Plato himself makes abundantly clear at 517 b 3, in the Cave.

Thus Plato's strategy is to begin with a specific, vivid assertion, expand the assertion by general analysis, and conclude with a specific, vivid exemplification of that analysis. First there is the striking image that, figuratively, man stands in relation to ultimate knowledge as, actually, he stands in relation to the sun. Then Plato develops an abstraction—the Divided Line—which analyzes the gradations within the relationship that exists between man and ultimate knowledge. Cornford[18] provides a clear representation of Plato's description:

OBJECTS		STATES OF MIND
	The Good	
		Intelligence (*noesis*)
	Forms	or
		D Knowledge (*Episteme*)
INTEL-LIGIBLE WORLD	Mathematical objects	C Thinking (*dianoia*)
	Visible Things	B Belief (*pistis*)
WORLD OF APPEAR-ANCES	Images	A Imagining (*eikasia*)

Raven makes the obvious point—" . . . the line presents a vertical scale of reality and should therefore be drawn vertically rather than horizontally"[19]—although he does not say why.

Might it not be that Plato's intention to develop a consequent abstract idea governs his creation of the Analogy of the Sun? As a transcendent image, the sun should determine the direction of the subsequent Line. Otherwise, a reader (or auditor) might wonder why a horizontal line might not just as well be used to illustrate man's progress. The point is, that ultimate knowledge must be conceived not as attainable through ungraded diligence, but finally as an ascent. The abstraction of the Line must prepare for the concreteness of the Cave, the culmination of Plato's strategy. People in the Cave, in Heidegger's commentary on the Simile,[20] feel "at home" in the "everyday life" that they conduct by *their sight alone.* If they should be freed of such a prison, they climb through the various states of mind, individually ceasing when they have reached the level of their ability. Ultimately, some perceive the "Form of Good," which, according to A. E. Taylor, crowns Plato's vision of the hierarchy of the sciences.[21] Those who persist in study become the philosophers; those who can be induced to return to the Cave, against their personal wishes, become the better rulers, for they rule out of a sense of duty, not a desire for power, wealth, adulation, and they therefore make disinterested decisions. Having glimpsed the Sun, they will never be "at home" in the Cave and will be misunderstood, even hated, by the people who never left the Cave, yet they must, in order to further public things, transcend their private wishes.

Thus the Platonic movement is from an actuality of fallible sensation and consensus, through education, to a reality established by the apprehension of the Ideal. No one would ever desire to descend from his level of attainment, for he would be abandoning communion with Truth. Only the dutiful return to live among the wall-watchers, and they only to instruct. It is otherwise with the Percy movement. The everyday condition is that of moviegoing, whether or not an individual literally goes to the movies. If an uneducated individual accepts the objective—empirical view provided by the proponents of the Divided Line, or the "vertical search," as it is called in *The Moviegoer,* then that individual is a moviegoer. If an individual masters the education provided by the "vertical search," he too is a moviegoer. Unlike Plato's movement, Percy's does not culminate with a communion that can be attained by the mastery of an abstract scheme. An individual remains a moviegoer, or a wall-watcher, as long as he distances himself from his ultimate world by the very way in which he looks at it.

Early in the novel Binx Bolling discusses his movement in mastering the "vertical search" and in becoming a self-conscious moviegoer:

> Until recent years, I read only "fundamental" books, that is, key books on key subjects, such as *War and Peace*, the novel of novels; *A Study of History*, the solution of the problem of time; Schroedinger's *What is Life?*, Einstein's *The Universe as I See It*, and such. During those years I stood outside the universe and sought to understand it. I lived in my room as an Anyone living Anywhere and read fundamental books and only for diversion took walks around the neighborhood and saw an occasional movie. Certainly it did not matter to me where I was when I read such a book as *The Expanding Universe*. The great success of this enterprise, which I call my vertical search, came one night when I sat in a hotel room in Birmingham and read a book called *The Chemistry of Life*. When I finished it, it seemed to me that the main goals of my search were reached or were in principle reachable, whereupon I went out and saw a movie called *It Happened One Night* which was itself very good. A memorable night. The only difficulty was that though the universe had been disposed of, I myself was left over. There I lay in my hotel room with my search over yet still obliged to draw one breath and then the next. But now I have undertaken a different kind of search, a horizontal search. As a consequence, what takes place in my room is less important. What is important is what I shall find when I leave my room and wander in the neighborhood. Before, I wandered as a diversion. Now I wander seriously and sit and read as a diversion.[22]

The methodology employed in the vertical search depends upon an understanding of education as a process of creating a pyramid composed of layers of generalization. One collects all the immediate data in a single category, then draws generalizations from the data; one then collects generalizations from all related categories, then draws generalizations from the generalizations; and so on, until one has constructed a *Weltansicht*. Thus Binx describes the process: " . . . as you get deeper into the search, you unify. You understand more and more specimens by fewer and fewer formulae. There is the excitement. Of course you are always after the big one, the new key, the secret leverage point, and that is the best of it" (M, 82). But that "secret leverage point," the Archimedean fulcrum to use in moving the world,[23] is far, far outside the world, so that one must look at the world as if it were a movie.

Individuals whom Binx happens upon in his wanderings are representative of various types of moviegoing, or, to put it another way, are at various places in the Cave. Walter Wade, Kate Cutrer's fiancé, is totally "at home" in the immanent, everyday world, utterly content to watch the wall:

> Walter seems to spy something on the table. He leans over and runs a thumb along the grain. "Just look at that wood. It's all one piece, by God." Since his engagement . . . Walter has begun to take a proprietary interest in the house, tapping on walls, measuring floorboards, hefting vases. (M, 38)

Walter is one of Percy's *en soi*-graspers: "Walter gives my shoulder a hard squeeze" (M, 39), Binx notes, but then he returns to more profitable business; "Squatting down on his heels, he runs an eye along the baseboard calculating the angle of settle" (M, 39). When Walter visits Kate in the basement, her retreat from thinking, he must really feel "at home": she notes that "[he] measures the walls. He carries a little steel tape in his pocket. He can't get over how thick the walls are" (M, 58).

Others have made some progress out of the Cave, have the dimmest comprehension of the difference between what is and what could be. There is, for example, the honeymooning couple on Canal Street. The novelty has already worn off their own experience, and the boy, especially, seems to be fearful that his honeymoon is not measuring up to what a honeymoon is supposed to be. He feels that his existence is "shadowy and precarious." He is seeing no more than any other wall-watcher sees. Then the boy and girl spot William Holden, a "resplendent reality," who turns "down Toulouse shedding light as he goes. An aura of heightened reality moves with him and all who fall within it feel it" (M, 16). Having unquestioningly accepted an education which teaches that the highest reality can be perceived only through science and technology, they feel that the camera presents a Person, something more real than they. The boy and girl have ascended out of the "shadowy and precarious" Cave to the Sun! have attained the Platonic Idea of Honeymoon, have enjoyed the perfect moment in which the actual becomes the Ideal. The couple speak to Holden, and for that instant they escape time. They illustrate a process of moviegoing that Binx calls "certification":

> Nowadays when a person lives somewhere in a neighborhood, the place is not certified for him. More than likely he will live there sadly and the emptiness which is inside him will expand until it

> evacuates the entire neighborhood. But if he sees a movie which
> shows his very neighborhood, it becomes possible for him to live,
> for a time at least, as a person who is Somewhere and not Any-
> where. (M, 63)

But there will be no "heightened reality" back in their subdivision, and the malaise will suffocate them until they become a sta-
tistic, the more prevalent modern Platonic Form (as in a statistical profile, sociological median, mean, mode, norm, average,
whatever). Moviegoing, unconsciously questing for perfect moments, in other words, guarantees our dissatisfaction with our
incarnate lives.

On the bus, as he and Kate return from Chicago, Binx
observes such discomfort in a collegian, who, he immediately
discerns, is a romantic:

> The poor fellow. He has just begun to suffer from it, this miserable
> trick the romantic plays upon himself: of setting just beyond his
> reach the very thing he prizes. For he prizes just such a meeting,
> the chance meeting with a chance friend on a chance bus, a friend
> he can talk to, unburden himself of some of his terrible longings.
> Now having encountered such a one, me, the rare bus friend, of
> course he strikes himself dumb. (M, 215)

Binx imagines the collegian's dream:

> . . . he hopes to find himself a girl, the rarest of rare pieces, and
> live the life of Rudolfo on the balcony, sitting around on the floor
> and experiencing soul-communions. I have my doubts. In the first
> place, he will defeat himself, jump ten miles ahead of himself,
> scare the wits out of some girl with his great choking silences, want
> her so desperately that by his own peculiar logic he can't have her;
> or having her, jump another ten miles beyond both of them and end
> by fleeing to the islands where, propped at the rail of his ship in
> some rancid port, he will ponder his own loneliness.
>   In fact, there is nothing more to say to him. The best one can do
> is deflate the pressure a bit, the terrible romantic pressure, and
> leave him alone. He is a moviegoer, though of course he does not go
> to movies. (M, 216)

The romantic has walked out of the Cave into the Sun! He
has escaped the limits of mere sensation and everydayness, to
concentrate upon the essence of things. Thus Binx's last view of
him: "The romantic is ahead of us, at the window of a lingerie
shop, . . . where black net panties invest legless torsos" (M, 218).
No longer burdened with having to respond to the complexity

that is an ordinary girl, he can regard with awe the (dressing/Platonic) Female Form, Percy's crafty visual pun.

Yet another of Binx's acquaintances, fittingly surnamed Stern, has entered the realm of the Sun. The romantic and the scientist are usually contrasted, the one a soft-headed metaphysical and the other a hard-headed physical type. Thus Binx seems bent upon a futile contradiction when he ponders the two: "Explore connection between romanticism and scientific objectivity. Does a scientifically minded person become a romantic because he is a left-over from his own science?" (M, 88) If this is true, then Binx, by his own admission, had become a romantic after discovering that he was left over from his "vertical search." But Harry Stern has not discovered that he is left over.

The two boys had cooperated on a chemistry experiment one summer, but Binx became obsessed with his experience, not his experiment with the specimens, and so became a distraction to Harry, who

> . . . was absolutely unaffected by the singularities of time and place. His abode was anywhere. It was all the same to him whether he catheterized a pig at four o'clock in the afternoon in New Orleans or at midnight in Transylvania. He was actually like one of those scientists in the movies who don't care about anything but the problem in their heads—now here is a fellow who does have a "flair for research" and will be heard from. Yet . . . he is no more aware of the mystery which surrounds him than a fish is aware of the water it swims in. (M, 52)[24]

Like the romantic, the scientist has escaped time and place, to contemplate the eternal and universal; in Marcel's distinction, he has reduced the mystery of being to a problem. He too is a moviegoer.

Binx's Aunt Emily is yet another type of moviegoer; born to a family dedicated to Southern Stoicism, she represents the type who heeds the call of duty, thus to be a philosopher-king in the Cave. Fundamentally she has the idealizing temperament; hence she imposes her vision upon actuality: "All the stray bits and pieces of the past, all that is feckless and gray about people, she pulls together into an unmistakable visage of the heroic or the craven, the noble or the ignoble. So strong is she that sometimes the person and the past are in fact transfigured by her" (M, 49). Toynbee concludes that the philosopher-king returns to the ordinary world only under compulsion, and that such compulsion ultimately sours his effort: " . . . however admirably he may behave, [he is] handicapped by a fatal lack of zest which checks the impetus of [his] *élan.* This negative, weary, melancholy temper is manifest in the *Meditations* of Marcus Aurelius, the historic philosopher-king who dutifully carried on his shoulders the burden of governing the whole *Orbis Romanus.*"[25] Toynbee's characterization is quite appropriate to Aunt Emily's outlook; further, his choice of an exemplar, Marcus Aurelius, is identical to Aunt Emily's choice (She writes Binx: "These words of the Emperor Marcus Aurelius Antoninus strike me as pretty good advice, for even the orneriest young scamp," M, 78) and to William Alexander Percy's choice.[26]

What of Binx Bolling? Certainly he is not a Walter Wade, knowing nothing but the shadows on the wall and supremely complacent in that knowledge. Neither is he a Harry Stern, knowing nothing but the Sun itself and therefore indifferent to the sun (Binx recalls: "In the course of an afternoon the yellow sunlight moved across old group pictures of the biology faculty. I became bewitched by the presence of the building; for moments at a stretch I sat on the floor and watched the motes rise and fall in the sunlight. I called Harry's attention to the presence but he shrugged and went on with his work," M, 51-52). Nor yet is Binx an Aunt Emily, having known the Sun, but unable, she and her class, to prevent " . . . the going under of the evening land" (M, 54) and therefore convinced that the world must be punished, before it merits another chance. As Binx recalls his aunt's afternoon intellectual teas: " . . . we used to speculate on the new messiah, the scientist-philosopher-mystic who would come striding through the ruins with the *Gita* in one hand and a Geiger counter in the other" (M, 181-182).[27]

Rather Binx is that individual who has been freed from the Cave, has regarded the Sun, has returned to Cave, but is alienated by his knowledge that there is an area of darkness not revealed by either firelight (sensibles) or sunlight (intelligibles). He is genuinely alone, his alienation intensified by his inability to participate in any activity without reflection. In his characteristic irony, he recalls a sociologist's discovery "that a significantly large percentage of solitary moviegoers are Jews" (M, 89); he knows that he is both moviegoer and Jew: "The fact is, . . . I am more Jewish than the Jews I know. They are more at home than I am. I accept my exile" (M, 89). In the novel Sidney Gross if the "at home" Jew (M, 185-186).

In Toynbee's terms, Binx has "Withdrawn," has escaped the Cave to be "turned around"—to the knowledge that his new knowledge does not help.   He lives on Elysian Fields (M, 9)—Plato said that those who have seen the Sun " . . . will not engage in action if they can help it, dreaming that, while still alive, they have been translated to the Islands of the Blest."[28] Yet though he lives "among the happy shades in Elysian Fields" (M, 99), he still lives in the basement of Mrs. Schexnaydre,[29] in the bottom of the bottom, the Cave.   His placement of himself in such a dialectical position, appearing to be one thing when he is another (appearing to read *Standard and Poor* while in fact reading *Arabia Deserta* is another instance[30] is one of those "death house pranks" (M, 193) that Kate discerns in him.

Having read *A Study of History,* "the solution of the problem of time," Binx should be adjusted to his world.   The fact is that Binx did not escape into the timelessness of the Ideal through the "vertical search," instead remains in time, in agony.   He therefore devises rotations," . . . the experiencing of the new beyond the expectation of the experiencing of the new" (M, 144) and aesthetic repetitions, "the reenactment of past experience toward the end of isolating the time segment which has lapsed in order that it, the lapsed time, can be savored of itself and without the usual adulteration of events that clog time like peanuts in brittle" (M, 80).

Both rotations and aesthetic repetitions purport to draw consciousness out of the present into another, better state, the perfect To-Be or the edited Been; both would be timeless.   Both fail. Even after an extraordinarily successful weekend rotation on the Gulf Coast, Binx experiences a dreadful attack of the malaise (M, 166) that signals the resumption of everydayness.   On another occasion, Binx alleges that he has conducted a "successful experiment in repetition" (M, 79) by going to a western movie in the same theater in which he had seen a western movie fourteen years before, there to select only those past-bits that he wants to remember. But then he has to admit:

> As usual it eluded me. There was this: a mockery about the old seats, their plywood split, their bottoms slashed, but enduring nevertheless as if they had waited to see what I had done with my fourteen years. There was this also: a secret sense of wonder about the enduring, about all the nights, the rainy summer nights at twelve and one and two o'clock when the seats endured alone in the empty theater. The enduring is something which must be accounted

for. One cannot simply shrug it off. (M, 80) [As Harry shrugged, (M, 52)]

Binx's emphasis on the phenomenon of endurance is a strong argument that Percy is responding to Bergson's *Creative Evolution* for at least part of his attack upon Toynbee. For in that work, in his distinction between duration and time, Bergson also emphasizes the same phenomenon:

> The universe *endures*. The more we study the nature of time, the more we shall comprehend that duration means invention, the creation of forms, the continual elaboration of the absolutely new. The systems marked off by science *endure* only because they are bound up inseparably with the rest of the universe. It is true that in the universe itself two opposite movements are to be distinguished, . . . "descent" and "ascent." The first only unwinds a roll ready prepared. In principle, it might be accomplished almost instantaneously, like releasing a spring. But the ascending movement, which corresponds to an inner work of ripening or creating, *endures* essentially, and imposes its rhythm on the first, which is inseparable from it.[31]

Wanting to edit his Been, Binx tries to link up only those "moments" that satisfy some requirement of his intellect, but the enduring "old seats, their plywood split, their bottoms slashed," mock his efforts to sanitize the past; as Bergson says, "Real duration is that duration which gnaws on things, and leaves on them the mark of the tooth."[32] Such small changes as the dilapidation of the seats would inform us that duration, in which we have our being, goes on, whether or not we are conscious of it: it is only condensed duration that our intellect can control, can keep frozen in order. Bergson continues:

> If everything is in time, everything changes inwardly, and the same concrete reality never recurs. Repetition is therefore possible only in the abstract: what is repeated is some aspect that our senses, and especially our intellect, have singled out from reality, just because our action, upon which all the effort of our intellect is directed, can move only among repetitions. Thus, concentrated on that which repeats, solely preoccupied in welding the same to the same to the same, intellect turns away from the vision of time. It dislikes what is fluid, and solidifies everything it touches. We do not *think* real time. But we live it, because *life* transcends intellect. The feeling we have of our evolution and of the evolution of all things in pure duration is there, forming around the intellectual concept properly so-called an indistinct fringe that fades off into dark-

ness. Mechanism and finalism agree in taking account only of the bright nucleus shining in the center. They forget that this nucleus has been formed out of the rest by condensation, and that the whole must be used, the fluid as well as and more than the condensed, in order to grasp the inner movement of life.[33]

In his treatment of "Withdrawal-and-Return" Toynbee quotes Bergson's *Two Sources of Morality and Religion,* but not *Creative Evolution.* His neglect of the latter is indicative of his neglect of the central theme of Bergson's argument in the latter, that we live in continually unfolding and therefore mysterious duration, not in the static and known intellectual construct that we call time. Toynbee's "solution of the problem of time," as Binx well knows, is to throw away the sheet that the problem is written on.

If Toynbee will not recognize the presence of duration, it follows that he will not refer to Bergson's brilliant attack on Platonic thinking, Toynbee's own method despite his charge that Platonic thinking leads ultimately to a refusal to leave off contemplating in order to provide leadership for a civilization.[34] In keeping with Toynbee's eclectic liberalism, any visitor is welcome to his church, as long as no beliefs are brought into the sanctuary. Thus he quotes Bergson for his own devices, but not Bergson's model of the thinking process that most people employ most of the time. For this thinking process, "the cinematographical mechanism of thought,"[35] as Bergson calls its, occurs to intellect whenever it initially confronts the fullness of duration.

In a charming illustration Bergson describes the process by which a photographer takes many still shots of a regiment marching past, then attempts to arrange his stills so as to present the illusion of movement. No matter how many stills he may have, he cannot accomplish his intention. He must have a movement, in a projector, an unrolling film upon which he can superimpose his sequence of still shots. But let Bergson say it:

> It is because the film of the cinematograph unrolls, bringing in turn the different photographs of the scene to continue each other, that each actor of the scene recovers his mobility; he strings all his successive attitudes on the invisible movements of the film. The process then consists in extracting from all the movements peculiar to all the figures an impersonal movement abstract and simple, *movement in general,* so to speak: we put this into the apparatus, and we reconstitute the individuality of each particular movement by com-

bining this nameless movement with the personal attitudes. Such
is the contrivance of the cinematograph. And such is also that of
our knowledge. Instead of attaching ourselves to the inner becoming of things, we place ourselves outside them in order to recompose
their becoming artificially. We take snapshots, as it were, of the
passing reality, and, as these are characteristic of reality, we have
only to string them on a becoming, abstract, uniform, and invisible,
situated at the back of the apparatus of knowledge, in order to imitate what there is that is characteristic in this becoming itself.
Whether we would think becoming, or express it, or even perceive
it, we hardly do anything else than set going a kind of cinematograph inside us. We may therefore sum up what we have been saying in the conclusion that the *mechanism of our ordinary knowledge
is of a cinematographical kind.*[36]

It is not merely "the *mechanism of our ordinary knowledge*"
that Bergson intends to describe, though, for he quickly mounts
an attack upon the "philosophers of the Eleatic school," who de-
valued change and exalted permanence, even if the former was
visible and the latter was not. Probably to make his opposition
as radical as possible, Bergson attacks Plato himself, right in the
Divided Line; first he puts words in Plato's mouth, then he
laments the unwisdom that the words reveal:

> . . . reality changes, but . . . it *ought not* to change. Experience con-
> fronts us with becoming: that is *sensible* reality. But the *intelligi-
> ble* reality, that which ought to be, is more real still, and that real-
> ity does not change. Beneath the qualitative becoming, beneath
> the extensive becoming, the mind must seek that which defies
> change, the definable quality, the form or essence, the end. Such
> was the fundamental principle of the philosophy which devel-
> oped throughout the classic age, the philosophy of Forms, or, to use
> a term more akin to the Greek, the philosphy of Ideas.[37]

As processes of thought, then, ordinary knowing and Idealist phi-
losophizing are the same: "That is to say that we end in the philosophy of Ideas when we apply the cinematographical mechanism of the intellect to the analysis of the real."[38]

Nor yet is Bergson finished. What Binx suspects, Bergson
asserts: modern science is not different from, but dependent on
Idealist thinking:

> Modern, like ancient, science proceeds according to the cinemat-
> ographical method. It cannot do otherwise; all science is subject to
> this law. For it is of the essence of science to handle *signs*, which it
> substitutes for the objects themselves. These signs undoubtedly dif-

fer from those of language by their greater precision and their higher efficiency; they are none the less tied down to the general condition of the sign, which is to denote a fixed aspect of the reality under an arrested form. In order to think movement, a constantly renewed effort of the mind is necessary. Signs are made to dispense us with this effort by substituting, for the moving continuity of things, an artificial reconstruction. . . . Science may consider rearrangements that come closer and closer to each other; it may thus increase the number of moments that it isolates, but it always isolates moments. As to what happens in the interval between the moments, science is no more concerned with that than are our common intelligence, our senses and our language: it does not bear on the interval, but only on the extremities. So the cinematographical method forces itself upon our science, as it did already on that of the ancients.[39]

It follows that " . . . for a science that places all the moments of time in the same rank, that admits no essential moment, no culminating point, no apogee, change is no longer a diminution of essence, duration is not a dilution of eternity."[40] Without paradox, then, Binx's "vertical quest" becomes a "horizontal quest."

So Binx remains the moviegoer. Beginning as all human beings do, he viewed only the sensibles; he was a wall-watcher in the Cave, a moviegoer, but leaving the Cave did not mean leaving the cinema. Although Plato and his followers, including Toynbee, may think that a higher reality may be reached, outside the theater of life, their method, ancient or modern, is at the expense of individual existence: for—if we follow Bergson—the higher reality of Idealism or Science is only an exaggerated form of unaided intellection. Is Binx then inevitably to remain in the cinema, eyes fixed on the "intellectual concept," "the bright nucleus," but unable to see any of the "indistinct fringe that fades off into darkness"? Indeed, is he condemned to a life sentence of despair such as he realizes at the climax of the novel? Having tried to separate himself from matter, to come out of the Cave, he has been caught, and his punishment is to be that not only will he be confined in matter, but it will be replaced by feces:

> Now in the thirty-first year of my dark pilgrimage on this earth and knowing less than I ever knew before, having learned only to recognize merde when I see it, having inherited no more from my father than a good nose for merde, for every species of shit that flies—my only talent—smelling merde from every quarter, living in fact in the very century of merde, the great shithouse of scientific humanism where needs are satisfied, everyone becomes an anyone, a warm and creative person, and prospers like a dung beetle, and

one hundred percent of people are humanists and ninety-eight percent believe in God, and men are dead, dead, dead; and the malaise
has settled like a fall-out and what people really fear is not that
the bomb will fall but that the bomb will not fall—on this my thirtieth birthday, I know nothing and there is nothing to do but fall
prey to desire. (M, 228)

Is the only hope the apocalypse that his aunt, even he (M,
231), dreams of? Is his only quest to be the "desire" that a despairing—whether or not he admitted it—Sartre asserts as the ultimate, futile human occupation? Is science—knowledge, the
term once meant—finally fit only to turn our world into dead
waste?

Bergson would have had nothing but amused contempt for
such a series of questions, a series that betrays so little grasp of
the meaning of evolution. The genuine evolution, "rolling
out," is not a film that we project, upon which we superimpose
the few still shots that we are capable of taking, but rather a "rolling out," a generating, a creating, of *more* than we can ever comprehend. Creative evolution is not finally static, but dynamic;
we are not finally to be seen in a still shot, but in continuous
movement. "Yet," Bergson says,

evolutionist philosophy does not hesitate to extend to the things of
life the same methods of explanation which have succeeded in the
case of unorganized matter. It begins by showing us in the intellect
a local effect of evolution, a flame, perhaps accidental, which
lights up the coming and going of living beings in the narrow passage open to their action; and lo! forgetting what is has just told us,
it makes of this lantern glimmering in a tunnel a Sun which can
illuminate the world. Boldly it proceeds, with the powers of conceptual thought alone, to the ideal reconstruction of all things,
even of life. True, it hurtles in its course against such formidable
difficulties, it sees its logic end in such strange contradictions, that
it very speedily renounces its first ambition. "It is no longer reality
itself," it says, "that it will reconstruct, but only an imitation of
the real, or rather a symbolical image; the essence of things escapes us, and will escape us always; we move among relations; the
absolute is not in our province; we are brought to a stand before the
Unknowable."—But for the human intellect, after too much pride,
this is really an excess of humility. If the intellectual form of the
living being has been gradually modeled on the reciprocal actions
and reactions of certain bodies and their material environment,
how should it not reveal to us something of the very essence of
which these bodies are made? Action cannot move in the unreal.
A mind born to speculate or to dream, I admit, might remain outside reality, might deform or transform the real, perhaps even

> create it—as we create the figures of men and animals that our
> imagination cuts out of the passing cloud. But an intellect bent upon
> the act to be performed and the reaction to follow, feeling its object
> so as to get its mobile impression at every instant, is an intellect
> that touches something of the absolute.[41]

No wonder that Binx suffers from a sense of unreality:
"Three o'clock and suddenly awake amid the smell of dreams
and of the years come back and peopled and blown away again
like smoke. A young man am I, twenty nine, but I am as full of
dreams as an ancient" (M, 144). Having ascended the Divided
Line, he has reached the point of contemplation, only to discover, not clarity and precision, but the wavering forms of Ideality.
Induced by his methodology not to act, but to observe the Perfect
Actors, he experiences ever greater alienation. He will continue
to feel himself flying farther and farther from the earth until he
decides to think about the very way that he thinks.

He must, just as Bergson here announces that he does, reject
Plato's myth of the Cave as the model of man's relation to his
world:

> Human intelligence, as we represent it, is not at all what Plato
> taught in the allegory of the cave. Its function is not to look at
> passing shadows nor yet to turn itself round and contemplate the
> glaring sun. It has something else to do. Harnessed, like yoked
> oxen, to a heavy task, we feel the play of our muscles and joints,
> the weight of the plow and the resistance of the soil. To act and to
> know that we are acting, to come into touch with reality and even
> to live it, but only in the measure in which it concerns the work that
> is being accomplished and the furrow that is being plowed, such is
> the function of human intelligence.[42]

But acting is easier said than done. Since the enemy is so
grand, will not the act against it have to be so grand that a mere
human being could not hope to perform it? Bergson's description of the act, presaging Camus's description of Sisyphus' struggle, is designed to convince us of the universal availability of the
act. We plow, we make our mark on matter. Thus to do will we
establish what Heidegger calls "the tool-complex," Sartre, "the
relation of instrumentality."[43] The world is not to see, but to use;
it is not, in Heidegger's terms, "present-at-hand," but "ready-to-
hand." By using the world, we live in Heidegger's "care relationship": first we care for out tools, then we care for others, ultimately we care . . . for Being? Binx has, we discover, begun to

care for his tools (M, 11), "thrown a world," and therefore begun a quest. He wants to care for others: despite his ironic reserve, he dreams of opening a *service* station. At the climax, when he feels that he is suffocating in feces, he is saved by the responsibility of caring for Kate, someone who is worse off than he.

In the Epilogue Binx hints that he cares for Being. He has indeed found "the solution of time"—duration, the scratches on the cinema seat. It is not that he has come out of the Cave; he has discovered that he was never in the Cave, that the Platonic image is simply false. Rather Binx now knows that the true image of man-in-his-world is that of the Prodigal Son, who comes to himself in a strange land and decides to return to his father. His movement is to be a "return," but not in the sense that Plato and Toynbee give the term. Binx has rejected the cinematographical way of looking at things—he is no longer the moviegoer.

It should be clear, too, that the novel asserts Walker Percy's "return." His medical studies and his moviegoing were not, it turns out, dissimilar activities; his comments indicate that he was as much a victim of cinematographical thinking as anyone else. Then came the ordeal of his illness, during which he awakened in a strange country. His reading and ultimately his writing record his struggle to find his way back, his genuine repetition.

Notes

[1] The quotation is taken from Herbert Mitgang, "A Talk with Walker Percy," *New York Times Book Review*, 20 February 1977, pp. 1, 20-21. For other biographical details, I am indebted to Robert Coles, *Walker Percy: An American Search* (Boston, 1978), who offers the fullest account of Percy's life in the Forties and Fifties.

[2] See Karl Löwith, *Meaning in History* (Chicago, 1957). See, also, Mircea Eliade, *The Myth of the Eternal Return* (Princeton, 1971).

[3] Löwith, p. 206

[4] Löwith, p. 14.

[5] Walker Percy, *The Message in the Bottle* (New York, 1975), 140.

[6] *The Message in the Bottle*, p. 59. See also p. 127.

[7] *The Message in the Bottle*, p. 110.

[8] In "From Facts to Fiction," *Book Week*, 25 December 1966, pp. 6, 9, Percy describes his own experience in Toynbeean terms: "What happens is a period of unsuccessful effort during which one works very hard—and fails. There follows a period of discouragement. Then there comes a paradoxical moment of collapse-and-renewal in which one somehow breaks with the past and starts afresh."

[9] See Kenneth W. Thompson's critique of Toynbee's approach to history, in *Toynbee and History*, ed. Ashley Montagu (Boston, 1956), 200-20, especially p. 216.

[10] Martin Luschei, *The Sovereign Wayfarer: Walker Percy's Diagnosis of the Malaise* (Baton Rouge, 1972), very fruitfully applies the terms of this essay to Percy's then-existing canon.

[11] *The Message in the Bottle*, p. 95. It is thus in the nature of Marcel's "recollection," as well.

[12] Zoltán Abádi-Nagy, "A Talk with Walker Percy," *Southern Literary Journal*, 6 (Fall 1973), 16.

[13] *The Message in the Bottle*, p. 96.

[14] Arnold J. Toynbee, *A Study of History*, Volume III, *The Growths of Civilizations* (London, 1934), 249.

[15] The comparison of the spectator in the cave with the spectator in the movie theater is so apt that is has occurred to more than one writer. See the footnote provided by Francis McDonald Cornford, in his well-known translation of the *Republic* (New York, 1945), 228; quite possibly Percy was struck by Cornford's, as well as Toynbee's footnote. For yet other comparisons of moviegoing and wall-watching see Marcel LaPierre, *Les cent visages du cinéma* (Paris, 1948), who entitles Chapter II "Les Ancêtres" and begins by citing the allegory of the Cave, and L. Chauvois, "Le 'cinéma populaire' en Gréce au temps de Platon et sa projection dans l'allégorie de la 'cavern aux idées', *Revue generale des sciences pures et appliquees* (Juillet-Août, 1967), 193-96. The earliest implied comparison that I have found is Bergson's likening of wall-watching and moviegoing, discussed later in the present paper.

[16] In "Moviegoing in *The Moviegoer*," *Southern Quarterly*, 18 (Spring, 1980), 26-42, I discuss Binx's behavior as the alienated spectator by referring to the phenomenology of Marcel, Sartre, and Heidegger. In his interviews Percy has always emphasized the writing of fiction as an exploration of reality.

[17] J. E. Raven, "Sun, Divided Line, and Cave," *Classical Quarterly*, 3 (January-April 1953), 22-32, provides a good review of the literature of the three devices.

[18] Cornford, p. 222. See also John Sallis, *Being and Logos: The Way of Platonic Dialogue* (Pittsburgh, 1975), 414, for a slightly different representation of the Line.

[19] Raven, 24.

[20] See Martin Heidegger, "The Meaning of the Cave," pp. 278-295, in *The Great Thinkers on Plato*, ed. Barry Gross (New York, 1968).

[21] Alfred Edward Taylor, *Plato, the Man and His Work* (New York, 1927), 286.

[22] Walker Percy, *The Moviegoer* (New York, 1967), 69-70. Hereafter, references to (M) are incorporated into the text.

[23] That "leverage point" was sought, as Percy well knows, by René

Descartes. See Norman Kemp Smith, ed. and trans. *Descartes' Philosophical Writings* (London, 1952), 202-3, where, at the beginning of Meditation II, Descartes muses: "Archimedes, that he might displace the whole earth, required only that there might be some one point, fixed and immovable, to serve in leverage; so likewise I shall be entitled to entertain high hopes if I am fortunate to find some one thing that is certain and indubitable." According to Percy, Descartes did succeed in displacing the world, is responsible for much of our alienation.

24 In *Science and the Modern World* (New York, 1948), in the chapter entitled "Abstraction," Alfred North Whitehead discusses what he terms the "abstractive hierarchy," which culminates in a "complex eternal object" called the "vertex" (pp. 168-169). He describes Binx's "vertical search," here illustrated by Harry Stern. Whitehead's distinction between eternal and enduring objects and his analysis of duration, repetition, time, and space, as well as the Fallacy of Misplaced Concreteness, provide very valuable insight into Binx's alienation from the scientific-objective worldview. See *The Message in the Bottle, p. 211.

25 Toynbee, p. 253.

26 I speak to the relationship of Aunt Emily and William Alexander Percy to Marcus Aurelius in "Walker Percy's Southern Stoic," *Southern Literary Journal*, 3 (Fall 1970), 5-31, and *"The Moviegoer* and the Stoic Heritage," in *The Stoic Strain in American Literature*, ed. Duane J. MacMillan (Toronto, 1979), pp. 179-191.

27 I speak to the response to messianic thinking by William Alexander Percy and Walker Percy in "William Alexander Percy, Walker Percy, and the Apocalypse," *Modern Age*, 24 (Fall, 1980), 396-406.

28 Actually a street in New Orleans, Elysian Fields, through Percy's wit, becomes a symbol in his thematic pattern. See Cornford, p. 233, for identification of Elysian Fields as the Islands of the Blest.

29 Brainard Cheney, "To Restore a Fragment Image," *Sewanee Review*, 69 (Autumn 1961), 693, pronounces the name "she's nadir."

30 I speak to Binx's *bad faith*, in which he poses as businessman while hankering after deserts, in "Moviegoing in *The Moviegoer.*"

31 Henri Bergson, *Creative Evolution*, trans. Arthur Mitchell (Westport, Connecticut, 1975), 14.

32 Bergson, p. 52.

33 Bergson, pp. 52-53.

34 Toynbee, p. 251. Paul Friedländer, *Plato*, III, *The Dialogues* (Princeton, 1969), 482, warns: "It is frightening to see how thoroughly Toynbee, world historian of our epoch, misunderstands the 'paradox'—as he rightly recognizes it to be—of the philosopher-king."

35 Bergson, p. 296. Here Bergson says, in a footnote, that he first "compared the mechanism of conceptual thought to that of the cinematograph" in his lectures at the Collège de France, in 1902-1903. Louis Saurel, "La Naissance d'un film," in *Le Cinema: des origines a nos jours*, ed. Henri Fescourt (Paris, 1932), 170, says that there was a demonstration by the Lumiere brothers, on 16 November 1895, of their motion picture invention, for a convocation of the Faculty of Science at the Sorbonne. The program probably contained ten parts, each sixteen meters long, one of which was probably their film, "Le Regiment." Since Bergson's illustration of cinematographical thinking cites the passing of

a regiment, it is possible to speculate that Bergson's philosophical invention resulted from the cinematic invention. If such is the case, when Percy turns philosophy back into cinematic images, one of those intriguing historical circularities
has been achieved. The ultimate historic linkage will be when *The Moviegoer*
is released as a movie.

[36] Bergson, p. 332.

[37] Bergson, p. 341.

[38] Bergson, p. 342.

[39] Bergson, pp. 357-358.

[40] Bergson, p. 374.

[41] Bergson, pp. xx-xxi.

[42] Bergson, pp. 209-210.

[43] I speak to Binx's decision to take action in the world, in "Moviegoing in
The Moviegoer."

Time and Eternity in *The Moviegoer*

"This morning I . . . ,"[1] begins the narrator of Walker Percy's *The Moviegoer* (1961), John Bickerson "Binx" Bolling, a stockbroker and moviegoer of New Orleans. With these three words Binx acknowledges his awareness that time existed before he became aware of it and that the chief and unending problem of his life is how to deal with it. As he begins to describe his response to the events of the week before his thirtieth birthday, it soon becomes apparent that time in some form is always on his mind—which is just another way of saying that consciousness is conscious of time *and* whatever else it may be conscious of. The chief cause of his difficulty with time is that he has in the past relied first on one understanding of it and then on the opposite and that he seems now to be telling time by both of them. If his actions sometimes seem erratic or whimsical, it is because he depends upon two different timepieces, which are not merely set at different points but travel at different speeds. One of these watches is for a stockbroker; it is the time-and-place, of the concrete here and now; time is indeed money. The other is for a moviegoer; it is the time of time-and-space, of the universal and eternal; time freezes into timelessness.

Consciousness for Binx is further complicated by the fact that while he generally lives in controlled time he occasionally suffers from an attack of uncontrolled time. Since there is no significant meaning in Binx's life, he cannot really think that there is much point to the present; if he cannot escape it, he will try to mesmerize himself by rote activity or to distract himself with some form of undemanding interest. As he says: "In the evenings I usually watch television or go to the movies. . . . The fact is I am quite happy in a movie, even a bad movie" (7). In his effort to escape the present, Binx creates controlled excursions to the future and the past. A pre-packaged tour of the future Binx calls a "rotation": "A rotation I define as the experiencing of the new beyond the expectation of the experiencing of the new" (144).[2] In dealing with the past, Binx attempts to cull the best scenes from all the film available and then to convince himself that the best scenes joined chronologically are *all* the scenes; such a selection is a "repetition": "A repetition is the re-enactment of past experience toward the end of isolating the time segment which has lapsed in order that it, the lapsed time, can be savored of itself and without the usual adulteration of events that clog time like peanuts in brittle" (79-80). (Both "rotation" and "repetition" will be discussed later.)   Despite Binx's efforts to control time, though, "wild" time occasionally thrusts its way in, unbidden and unexpected. The possibility that there is an enormous, absolutely unknown and unknowable future causes him both to fear any mention of God and to yearn for "the end of the world" (231). The latter is not a Christian's faithful anticipation, understand, but a Gnostic's revulsion against time and his leaping imagination that the millennium would bring freedom from it. Similarly, the past in all its undoctored fullness keeps returning, like a bill-collector: "One picture I never tire looking at. For ten years I have looked at it on this mantelpiece and tried to understand it" (24).   The picture is of his father and other male relations; it stirs up the kind of memories that cause an experience of guilt, a sure sign that the past is not past. These undigested lumps of the past do not return in chronological order, nor do they occur at a time of day set aside for them, a happy hour, when the slow movement of the present can be switched off. Binx's consciousness is thus a mixture of his controlled endurances and evasions, his complicated dread of, yet yearning for a cosmic future, and his nagging feeling that there is something back there in the past that he needs to know. An analysis of Binx's experience of time, necessarily arranging the various types in sequential combination, is obviously a repetition, a distortion, and Binx's discomfort results precisely from the fact that life cannot be managed the way the cards in solitaire can be stacked. But the distortion must occur if the complexity of time in *The Moviegoer* is to be appreciated.

Binx seems to have become aware of time pretty much the same way everyone else does; suddenly one falls into the river—at a certain moment consciousness becomes aware that it is a part of a flow, yet is different from it, set off, alienated. Such a recognition had become constant by the time Binx had reached college, for he now summarizes those days with the description, "I had spent the four years propped on the front porch of the fraternity house, bemused and dreaming, watching the sun shine through the Spanish moss, lost in the mystery of finding myself alive at such a time and place . . . " (38).

There are, of course, different responses to the mystery of time and place. The two chief Western ways appear to be (1) to become so involved in commerce with time and place, buying and selling them, making a profit from them, that both become commodities and lose their mystery, and (2) to escape them by the sheer mental effort of adding more and more examples of time and place to the generalizations about them until the original time and place lose their primacy, indeed any significance, and become merely local color, small change to the new bills called Time and Space. Eddie Lovell, as Binx describes him, typifies the commercial attitude: "Now he jingles the coins in his pocket. No mystery here!—he is as cogent as a bird dog quartering a field. He understands everything out there and everything out there is something to be understood" (19). In his own dissimulation as a stockbroker, Binx tries to make time and place into money. When Kate Cutrer, his aunt's stepdaughter, asks him, "How do you make your way in the world?" (43), he replies (implying that life is no big-deal mystery): "Is that what you call it? I don't really know. Last month I made three thousand dollars—less capital gains." But Kate is not fooled; she knows that Binx is not content with time and place and is even more frustrated by Time and Space.

Binx had made an attempt to learn to think of Time and Space in college, an attempt entirely to be expected since mastery of the research techniques of one of the physical or biological sciences is for most people the apex of higher education. With a fellow student, Harry Stern, Binx had begun an experiment in biology using pig blood; as it turned out, Binx himself was involved in another research project, which took more and more of his time:

> . . . a peculiar thing happened. I became extraordinarily affected by the summer afternoons in the laboratory. The August sunlight came streaming in the great dusty fanlights and lay in yellow bars across the room. The old building ticked and creaked in the heat. Outside we could hear the cries of summer students playing touch football. In the course of an afternoon the yellow sunlight moved across old group pictures of the biological faculty. I became bewitched by the presence of the building; for moments at a stretch I sat on the floor and watched the motes rise and fall in the sunlight. I called Harry's attention to the presence but he shrugged and went on with his work. He was absolutely unaffected by the

singularities of time and place. His abode was anywhere. . . . . He was actually like one of those scientists in the movies who don't care about anything but the problem in their heads. . . . (51-52)

At that time Binx did not accomplish the transfer of regard that characterizes the scientific attitude. For Binx there was still a "presence" in the here and now, a something that must be Being, for both words come from the same root. Yet Being, according to Platonism (romanticism and scientific objectivity are but its different guises, Binx later discovers [88]), is not found in the specific, the local, the visible, the contemporary, but rather in the general, the universal, the intelligible, the eternal. For Harry, who had learned to look far off (so far off that almost always some instrument must be used), properly had no time for a "presence," which to him was mere Becoming. For Harry the location of Reality was in the idea; it still remained in sensation for Binx. He was aware of the passage of moments, of the human past of other people, of the contemporary impingement of others, of visual, auditory, and other impressions. But these phenomena cannot be organized and directed, for they have autonomy. Binx was a failure as a scientist and so he "moved down to the Quarter where [he] spent the rest of the vacation in quest of the spirit of summer and in the company of an attractive and confused girl from Bennington who fancied herself a poet" (52). If sensation is the test for Reality, then the more pleasant the sensation the more it is sought; since sexual sensation is the most intense, it is "the real thing" (199), as Kate tries to convince herself just as she is coming off an idealistic high. In this frame of mind, that the experience of life is fundamentally the response to sensations (usually short-lived and thankfully so), time becomes a roller coaster of anticipation, participation, depression—one learns to invest as little as possible in the process and to escape, if possible, the end stroke of the cycle.

Binx apparently remained a creature of sensation until his wounding in Korea. That event destroyed his absolute trust in place: Literally he was knocked to the ground, his nose not six inches from a dung beetle (11). Discovering that place could also contain painful sensation, he seems to have thought for the first time of place as something to be avoided. No doubt he must have considered the possibility, by virtue of his wounding, that time only becomes worth consideration when its alternative is realized. No wonder that he can recall that "there awoke in me an immense curiosity" (11), the origin of philosophy, says Plato in the *Theaetetus* (155d). To satisfy that curiosity, Binx vowed a search.

But he soon forgot it, when his place was once again the United States. Or he says he did; it appears that he undertook one, though, even if he does not recall it as such. Having taken up with two young men like himself, he seems to have tried a romantic quest (41). Rather than simply responding to each sensation, he was measuring each sensation against its Perfect Model. The result is to be predicted: "The times we did have fun, like sitting around a fire or having a time with some girls, I had the feeling they were saying to me: 'How about this, Binx? This is really it, isn't it, boy?', that they were practically looking up from their girls to say this. For some reason I sank into a deep melancholy. . . . [Even] the beauty of the smoky blue valleys, instead of giving us joy, became heartbreaking" (41). Binx has his recollection of the failure of his romantic quest on Wednesday; on Sunday, on the train, he returns to the subject, stimulated by Kate, who seems to be entranced by the Beauty of a particular time and place (195). The bitterness of Binx's comments to his audience and his behavior toward Kate reveal just how painful the failure of his quest had been to him: "I try to steer her away from beauty. Beauty is a whore" (196). Rather he tries to get her interested in money. "You don't know what I *mean*,' she cries in the same soft rapture." Then Binx vents his anger and hurt to his audience:

> I know what she means all right. But I know something she doesn't know. Money is a good counterpoise to beauty. Beauty, the quest of beauty alone, is a whoredom. Ten years ago I pursued beauty and gave no thought to money. I listened to the lovely tunes of Mahler and felt a sickness in my soul. Now I pursue money and on the whole feel better.

At some point after he moved to Gentilly Binx took up the search that he had once vowed. He calls it his "vertical search," a good name for it, since it is similar to the ascent to knowledge in the *Republic*.[3] There Plato uses the Description of the Divided Line, the Simile of the Sun, and the Allegory of the Cave to illustrate the two realms of the Apparent and the Ideal (Real), of the Sensible and the Intelligible, Becoming and Being. In his ascent Binx read "only 'fundamental' books, that is, key books on key subjects" (69). The titles he mentions or alludes to are weighted toward physics. He does mention Toynbee's *A Study of History*, terming it "the solution of the problem of time" (69), but he is probably being ironic in that statement. He no doubt seriously sought the answer to the problem of time from Einstein, Schroedinger, and Eddington, who were thought to be restructuring the very questions that could be asked about the nature of time, space, and whatever it is that occurs in them. This time Binx's shift of regard was accomplished.

He informs us that the night he completed his search, he celebrated by going to a movie (70), *It Happened One Night*, a movie that Percy elsewhere cites as a representation of the way that the "alienated I" explores the "It."[4] Binx had become the moviegoer. Binx knows that Arnold Toynbee and F. M. Cornford (and before them, Henri Bergson) liken Plato's wall-watcher to the modern day moviegoer. He knows, too, that just about every modern physicist who has written for the layman—Jeans, Eddington, Heisenberg, von Weisäcker, Frisch—has likened the modern physicist to the wall-watcher. When he calls himself a moviegoer, then, he is creating an elaborate metaphor by which he can illustrate the way he looks at the world, now that he accepts a (Platonist) physics. That way of looking at the world is brilliantly analyzed by Bergson, who devotes the last fourth of *Creative Evolution* to the "Cinematographical Mechanism of Thought and the Mechanistic Illusion": Binx's recital of his life as a moviegoer is a brilliant revelation of the effect that such a way of thinking has upon a particular human experience.

One word more needs to be said about the metaphor of the moviegoer as a modern day Platonist. Binx has read the entire *Republic*, not just the Allegory of the Cave, so that he knows that the action of the Allegory is central to the meaning of the entire work. For in the latter part of Book V Plato returns to the Cave, to stress his belief that the Philosopher who has attained the Sun must return to the Cave, to instruct the wall-watchers. The Allegory thus opens up to degrees of achievement, at every level from pure phenomenalism, which accepts the shadows as the only reality, up to Philosophy, which has escaped the phenomenal to perceive the Forms. Binx thus sees other people according to their way of looking at their world. Some, like Walter Wade, are wall-watchers; others, like the romantic collegian on the bus, are well within the realm of the Sun. His Aunt Emily is the Philosopher-King who has returned to govern and expects to pass on her responsibility to Binx. She has prepared him for his destiny by teaching him the *Meditations* of Marcus Aurelius[5] and the *Crito*. But he simply has not been able to accept her Idealization of Duty (which shields, actually, a contempt for both the "high gods" and her fellowman). Nor can he accept, really, her despair, which is so strong that it secretly worships death. Small wonder that the *Crito* is her Platonic dialogue of choice (226), because it advocates total deference to the laws of the state, even unto death, or because, simply, it is about the death of a lofty philosopher (who is holding fast to his Ideal against mere contingency and also punishing in the worst way the community of wall-watchers who have demanded his death). Thus the relationship between Binx and his aunt has been strained, if formally cordial. She slowly comes to realize that he is, in her eyes, betraying her trust; he, for his part, has never been able to explain to her that her values seem totally inapplicable to his experience of life.

Binx himself had completed the ascent; we have his word for that. But he does not return to the Cave to instruct his fellowman, who does not wish to be instructed and certainly not in the knowledge that Binx gained by mastering the "vertical search," which he describes to Kate: " . . . as you get deeper into the search, you unify. You understand more and more specimens by fewer and fewer formulae" (82). There are, of course, some complications: " . . . it doesn't matter where you are or who you are" (82) "and danger is of becoming no one nowhere" (83). Indeed, Binx discovered that in completing his search he had disposed of the universe, but was himself "left over" (70).[6] Binx therefore conceives of himself as a ghost, drawn to both the world of phenomena and the world of idea, yet alienated from both, continually in between.

That "in between" condition is illustrated by Plato with another of his most vivid images. In the *Timaeus* Plato gives a likely account of the creation of the world.[7] There was first of all God, who confronted chaos. Deciding to give order to chaos, he fashioned a universe after the model provided by the immutable Ideas or Forms. These Forms are, obviously, Eternal, Timeless: they are (they always have been, they always will be—they are Being). Chaos has a condition that can be called duration or lastingness. Now God continued to perfect the universe toward the One, but since it was after all composed of both Being and Not-Being (Becoming, just as easily, though awkwardly, Be-going), it could not be the same as the Forms, which are pure Being. God therefore made an intermediate state, Time, "the moving image of eternity" (37d). Time moves, like Becoming, but is eternal, like Being. Time is not just chaotic duration, for it is ordered by number; Platonic time means, then, what A. E. Taylor describes as " 'Newtonian' time, the 'absolute, true, or mathematical time', which, in the famous words of the *Principia*, 'flows equably'. It is thought of as measured, or rather numbered, by a succession of equal intervals, days or years or what not. . . . The thing meant is thus what is often called depreciatingly 'clock time'. . . . "[8] To apply the metaphor of the moving image of eternity to the Description of the Divided Line would be to stretch it between the lower portion of the Line, the World of Sensibles, and the upper portion, the World of the Intelligible. For Binx, then, the theater itself becomes the world of the Sensibles, of alienated human beings such as these at the Tivoli: "there are only a few solitary moviegoers scattered through the gloom, the afternoon sort and the most ghostly of all, each sunk in his own misery" (74). Such "solitary moviegoers" are often Jews, Binx reports (89), using sociology for his own cosmic purpose; by that assertion he strengthens his description of the moviegoer as a wandering person who yearns to return to "the holy city of Zion" (96), to which Binx alludes in another context. The Reality to be glimpsed in the movie theater is the world of the Intelligible; the Actors are the Forms. The movie film, which places the Forms in specific, limited contexts, i.e., plot, is "the moving image of eternity." Thus when Binx watches a movie, he is in fact revealing his preoccupation with time, his continual awareness that the film illustrates the sheer demarcation between the immanent and the transcendent. Appropriately, when he goes to the movies he generally winds up speculating on the nature of time.

Binx was firmly caught up in Time and Space when he struggled to achieve the "vertical search." He recalls he had lived in his room "as an Anyone living Anywhere" (69). Place thus gave way to Space; the reality of things was transferred to ideas; Whitehead's Fallacy of Misplaced Concreteness occurred. This shift is illustrated in the movie phenomenon that Binx calls "certification":

> Nowadays when a person lives somewhere, in a neighborhood, the place is not certified for him. More than likely he will live there sadly and the emptiness which is inside him will expand until it evacuates the entire neighborhood. But if he sees a movie which

> shows his very neighborhood, it becomes possible for him to live, for a time at least, as a person who is Somewhere and not Anywhere. (63)

Time became Space in that it had to be understood as something measured by eternal references into equal, empty receptacles to be filled up. This action Binx performs with his "rotations" and "repetitions." (It should be noted that there is such an experience as an "existential repetition," by which one really returns to the past to start over at a higher level. But since Binx is caught up in the "aesthetic sphere" he can only conceive of "aesthetic repetitions," nostalgic day-trips to the past, from which one returns unchanged.) Having reached the summit Binx can no longer think of his search as a vertical quest; since he can only cast about forward or backward on the same plane, it is appropriate that he now describe his quest as a "horizontal search" (70), a wandering in the neighborhood.

Such is the state of Binx Bolling's life when he begins to reveal his thoughts to us on Wednesday. By day he is a stockbroker, apparently satisfied with time as the accumulation of tokens of wealth, living in Heidegger's "everydayness," being dictated to by public time, which is in fact nobody's time. This life is possible only by constant dissimulation: He moves among the Walter Wades, the Eddie Lovells, and the Jules Cutrers of the concrete world by adopting a role suitable for each occasion. By night he is a moviegoer, aware of the realm of Perfection available to Romantics and Scientists, but unsatisfactory to himself. This life is bearable only by the constant employment of an ironical detachment, about others and about himself as a role-player. He can appeal to the Actors, such as Rory and Tony and Bill Holden, for Divine Protection and even crow to them, when he achieves Gestural Perfection: "O Tony. O Rory. You never had it so good with direction. Not even you Bill Holden, my noble Will. O ye morning stars together. Farewell forever, malaise" (127). It is ambiguous here whether Binx is alluding to the *Timaeus* (38d), in which the sun and morning stars are said to control time, or to Job (38, 7) in which "the morning stars sang together" in praise of a Perfect Beginning. Either would be appropriate to Binx's conduct with his new secretary at that moment. But the malaise is not permanently vanquished, the malaise which "is the pain of loss. The world is lost to you, the world and the people in it, and there remains only you and the world and you no more able to be in the world than Banquo's ghost"

(120). Fundamentally, then, on the Wednesday of the beginning Binx experiences Time and Space as a void; he is going nowhere in nothing, for all his busy-ness.

Yet as he begins to move through the public space of the City of Man and the Public time of commerce, he does reveal, almost fearfully, that a small event has occurred which has reawakened his interest in a search. On the way home from work, on Thursday afternoon, Binx drops in at the Tivoli, his neighborhood theater. First he must talk to Mrs. de Marco, the ticket seller; he explains: "If I did not talk to the theater owner or ticket seller, I should be lost, cut loose metaphysically speaking. I should be seeing one copy of a film which might be shown anywhere and at anytime. There is a danger of slipping clean out of space and time. It is possible to become a ghost and not know whether one is in downtown Loews in Denver or suburban Bijou in Jacksonville. So it was with me" (75). When he had fully submitted to Platonism, in other words, he had ignored the theater in order to concentrate on the moving images, to see it he could discern the Wayneishness of John Wayne, for example.

But at that very same Tivoli Binx had "first discovered place and time, tasted it like okra. It was during a re-release of *Red River* a couple of years ago that I became aware of the first faint stirrings of curiosity about the particular seat I sat in, the lady in the ticket booth . . . As Montgomery Clift was whipping John Wayne in a fist fight, an absurd scene, I made a mark on my seat arm with my thumbnail. Where, I wondered, will this particular piece of wood be twenty years from now, 543 years from now?" (75). The key word to Binx's recollection is "absurd," "glaringly opposed to manifest truth or reason." Binx *knows* that Montgomery Clift, the actual man, could never beat John Wayne, the actual man, in a fist fight; for once he uses his own immediate experience to reject a supposedly higher level of truth. And if immediate truth is superior in one instance, might it not be in others? Instantly, "curiosity," the beginning of philosophy, floods his consciousness, as he shifts his regard to other particulars of his placement. Especially, if time is not Eternal, then duration, a continuous stream of *more* than we can ever understand by mind, must be acknowledged. That particular piece of wood will exist in some form after he no longer regards it, thus must be a kind of Being, a "presence" that the world of sensation has.

Later that same night, Thursday, Binx (with Kate tagging along) goes to another movie, at the theater on Freret Street, deliberately to conduct an aesthetic repetition. He says that it was "successful" (79), that is, that he was able to splice "fourteen years" together in order to reconstruct time. But then he has to admit:

> There was this: a mockery about the old seats, their plywood split, their bottoms slashed, but enduring nevertheless as if they had waited to see what I had done with my fourteen years. There was this also: a secret sense of wonder about the enduring, about all the nights, the rainy summer nights at twelve and one and two o'clock when the seats endured alone in the empty theater. The enduring is something which must be accounted for. One cannot simply shrug it off. (80)

Harry Stern had shrugged off the "presence," but Binx cannot, for it "endures," manifesting a Bergsonian duration that is immeasurably richer than structured time. Such a strong argument against Platonism would cause Binx to "wonder," to think philosophically, for if there is a "presence," something *is* left after the mind has subjected "the old seats" to analysis, despite Plato's dismissal of an actual couch, in Book Ten of the *Republic*, as a remove from Reality. And if there is something left over in a thing, might he not feel encouraged to think that there was something left over in himself as a "left over" from the "vertical search"?

That "left over" is a clue, but Binx seems unwilling to think about it. After the movie he and Kate walk on the campus behind the laboratory in which he had first tried to achieve scientific detachment. As he talks about the "vertical search," he acknowledges its dangers, that any experience in becoming a "specimen" loses its "presence." But Kate, who has heard all this before, responds: "On the other hand, if you sit back here and take a little carcass out of the garbage can, a specimen which has been used and discarded, there remains something left over, a clue?" (83) Binx agrees, but is disinclined to trace out the connection: that he was left over from the "vertical search," just as something is left over after a lab experiment, just as something is in the theater besides the screen on which an image of Reality is ostensibly being projected. The nature of the cosmos is characterized by duration, which is a continuously evolving mystery, rather than by Eternity and Chaos, the Platonic bifurcation.

Binx's confession of his reawakened sensitivity to place and time explains his comments and actions on Wednesday morning (10-11), when he places himself in the middle of his room to see his world as "ready-to-hand." His things "looked both unfamiliar and at the same time full of clues" (11), so he determines to resume a search for the meaning of the clues: "A man can look at the little pile on his bureau for thirty years and never once see it. It is as invisible as his own hand. Once I saw it, however, the search became possible" (11). Having shifted his gaze back to the Sensibles, he might even find himself, the center of all his things. Since his shift is a direct threat to the value-system of the Philosopher-King, Aunt Emily, it is no surprise that his awakening elicits a summons from her that will re-establish her unquestioned domination.

Seen in this way, the main struggle in the novel is Binx's attempt to nurture the spark of life that he has found in his own soul. Against all threats and blandishments, he must struggle to establish his own time and his own place. From one Wednesday to the next, Binx apparently goes about his quotidian activities, but never far from the surface of his consciousness is the fascination/horror for the Intelligible World represented by his Aunt Emily and his Romantic father, who sought a glorious death because he could not stand a life of Wednesdays.

When Binx stands before Aunt Emily on the second Wednesday (219-27), she brings to bear the massed batteries of the Idealistic School. Her attack is such to destroy Binx with overwhelming ease and he flees to the playground of his easy aesthetic existence. The result is that Binx is once again convinced that no transcendence is possible, that his search for an escape from the either/or is only a useless passion, that only sensation is achievable. And so he wants a female body; in an immanent world the only incarnation available is sexual. At the same time Aunt Emily has put him back in the Cave; he has a vision of the world as feces (228); he is no better than a dung beetle; he has made no progress in the ten years since his nose hit the dirt six inches from that dung beetle. Figuratively in a cave, he imagines that his place is that much closer to Hell: "Elysian Fields glistens like a vat of sulfur" (231). Time, in either form that he knows, either as stockbroker or as moviegoer, is unbearable; the only hope left is the Bomb: "For a long time I have secretly hoped for the end of the world and believed with Kate and my aunt and Sam Yerger and many other people that only after the end could the few

who survive creep out of their holes and discover themselves to
be themselves to be themselves and live as merrily as children
among the viny ruins."[9] Only some such moment as Yeats'
"Second Coming," provided by an Oppenheimer-like "scientist-
philosopher-mystic" (181), will be able to put a stop to the old Platonic bifurcation which keeps men in their "holes," their Cave.

And at that moment Kate comes. Not the Second Coming of
some Gnostic resolution, but just an ordinary human being coming to a particular place at a particular time. Binx can see faith
and love not as dimly perceived Platonic Forms, but as concrete
human actions. Instantly Binx's experience of time changes: "Is
it possible that—it is not too late?" (231). At the same time a
black man—not Cothard, the symbol to Aunt Emily of Western
decline (226), but just an ordinary fellow—emerges from the adja-
cent church, with, in all likelihood, the mark of the ashes on his
forehead, for it is Ash Wednesday. Binx wonders: "It is impossible to say why he is here. Is it part and parcel of the complex business of coming up in the world? Or is it because he believes that
God himself is present here at the corner of Elysian Fields and
Bons Enfants?" (235). Is he here for the City of Man or the City of
God? "Or is he here for both reasons: through some dim dazzling trick of grace, coming for one and receiving the other as
God's own importunate bonus?" (235).

"It is impossible to say," concludes Binx. But it is also impossible to rule it out. The Epilogue makes it clear that Binx, having
suffered by accepting blind rationality, decides to accept the fullness, the duration that is not comprehended by mere intellect.
The Realm of the Sensible is not forever separate from the
Realm of the Intelligible; the City of Man is not forever separate
from the City of God. In the Incarnation each set is joined. Binx
has had to struggle with all his resources to reject the loftiness
and despair that tempts the soul into following Plato, but—with
a mystery of grace that cannot be explained—he has by that moment taken Augustine as his model.[10]

In Book XI of *The Confessions*, Augustine begins Chapter
XXIII by saying, "I have heard from a learned man that the mo-
tions of the sun, moon, and stars constituted time, and I assented
not."[11] With those words Augustine rejects the *Timaeus* of the
philosopher whose follower he had earlier been. But if those easily discerned reference points do not control time, what does? If
nature does not provide universality, how can there be any understanding of time? In Chapter XIV, Augustine freely admits

that in interiorizing time, he has undertaken a most perplexing problem: "For what is time? Who can easily and briefly explain it? Who even in thought can comprehend it, even to the pronouncing of a word concerning it? But what in speaking do we refer to more familiarly and knowingly than time? And certainly we understand when we speak of it; we understand also when we hear it spoken of by another. What, then, is time? If no one asks of me, I know; if I wish to explain to him who asks, I know not." Anyone who has ever attempted to say anything about time, say in an essay about Walker Percy's *The Moviegoer*, will instantly assent to the truth of Augustine's confession and prostrate himself to the brilliance of Augustine's subsequent analysis.

Time, as Augustine describes it, has a very familiar and unassuming character. Time is an individual experience which occurs within the soul, or perhaps a modern might insist upon calling it the consciousness or the psyche. Whatever sentience is called, there is where time is. There are three tenses, but since they must connect in a soul to be real, they are different for each soul. What is universal is not the past, nor the present, nor the future, but the soul which joins them to make time.

Thus Binx must create his own time, given the opportunity that his soul affords him. In the Epilogue Binx has the opportunity to give vivid testimony to his ultimate sense of time. His stepbrother Lonnie is dying, and Binx does not deny that fact when his other siblings ask him. A brother, Donice, attempts to deal with that most mysterious of human concerns, translating death into an experience that he comprehends. Ever practical and unsentimental, Donice asks, "Binx, . . . when Our Lord raises us up on the last day, will Lonnie still be in a wheelchair or will he be like us?" (240). Binx's reply, "He'll be like you," argues an eschatology that extends time into eternity and asserts that a genuine repetition has taken place. He now sees that the wood of Plato's couch was real, just as is the wood of his theater seat, and as is the wood of Lonnie's wheelchair, but that only the soul can be Real. Thus Binx now possesses the faith to believe that though he lives in a concrete time and place he possesses an Eternity that a moviegoer would never see.

Notes

[1] Walker Percy, *The Moviegoer* (New York: Noonday Press, 1967), p. 3. Hereafter, page references are included in the text in parentheses.

[2] In "Walker Percy's Indirect Communications," *Texas Studies in Literature and Language*, 11 (1969), 867-900, I discuss Percy's sources for such terms as "rotation" and "repetition."

[3] I have described Percy's use of the wall-watching/moviegoing image in "Walker Percy's *The Moviegoer*:   the Cinema as Cave," *Southern Studies*, 19 (1980), 331-54.

[4] Percy's discussion occurs in an early essay, "The Man on the Train" (1956); this essay is essential to a reading of *The Moviegoer* or anything else that Percy has written.   It is included in *The Message in the Bottle* (New York: Farrar, Straus and Giroux, 1975), a selection of Percy's essays.

[5] My essays, "Walker Percy's Southern Stoic," *Southern Literary Journal*, 3 (1970), 5-31, and *"The Moviegoer* and the Stoic Heritage," in *The Stoic Strain in American Literature: Essays in Honour of Marston LaFrance*, ed.   Duane J. MacMillan (Toronto: University of Toronto Press, 1979), pp. 179-91, describe the Stoic tradition against which Binx is reacting.

[6] In "Moviegoing in *The Moviegoer*," *Southern Quarterly*, 18 (1980), 26-42, I speak of the use Percy makes of Marcel, Sartre, and Heidegger in creating Binx as a "spectator."

[7] I am indebted to F. M. Cornford, *Plato's Cosmology* (London: Routledge & Kegan Paul, Ltd., 1937), for his very helpful commentary on the *Timaeus*.

[8] I am indebted to A. E. Taylor, *A Commentary on Plato's Timaeus* (Oxford: Clarendon Press, 1928) for his clear explanations to a layman.   The quotation cited is on p. 187.   In "The Concept of Time in the *Timaeus*," pp. 678-91, Taylor takes issue with Bergson's understanding of Plato's concept of time; I am not qualified to judge between Plato and Bergson, but I *choose* Bergson.

[9] In "William Alexander Percy, Walker Percy, and the Apocalypse," *Modern Age*, 24 (1980), 396-406, I treat the sense of the apocalypse held by William Alexander Percy, the model for Aunt Emily and Walker Percy's adoptive father, and Walker Percy's reaction to that sense in his novels.

[10] I have traced the development of *The Moviegoer* from the *Republic* to *The Confessions*, in *"The Moviegoer* and the Allegory of the Cave," *South Carolina Review*, 13 (1981), 13-18.

[11] I am indebted to John F. Callahan, *Four Views of Time in Ancient Philosophy* (New York: Greenwood Press, 1968), for his very helpful treatment of both Plato and Augustine.

English romanticism ... and 1930 science in
The Moviegoer

It is by now pretty generally agreed that the theme of Walker Percy's *The Moviegoer* (1961)[1] is contemporary man's experience of alienation. There has been little attention paid, however, to the source of that alienation for John Bickerson "Binx" Bolling, Percy's representative contemporary man. A reason for this lack of attention may lie in the nature of alienation, itself. There is a hint in that direction in the novel's motto, from Kierkegaard's *The Sickness Unto Death:* "the specific character of despair is precisely this: it is unaware of being despair." The alienated person, like the despairer, may not be aware of or, if aware, able to give voice to his alienation. In that case, what he says about another person's alienation offers a clue to the condition from which he suffers, but cannot name. In *The Moviegoer*, then, very close attention should be paid to Binx's father, whose alienation Binx diagnoses with a heated absoluteness that violates his usual disguise of detached ironist.

His father, Jack ("Binx" is probably a Junior, though he would never acknowledge it), was killed, his son says, by "English romanticism . . . and 1930 science" (88). This statement is, to be ponderous, not literally true; he died in an airplane crash (25). Then "English romanticism . . . and 1930 science" must have been in some way accountable for the state of Jack Bolling's mind, not his health. At first glance, the two concepts seem to be unconnected, but Binx senses, once he spontaneously links them, that the concepts behind the labels must have a relationship, and he vows to discover it (88). The nature of the relationship, it becomes clear, is that "English romanticism," as Binx uses the term, inspired "1930 science." Moreover, it becomes evident, the process of education, of forming a worldview, implied by "English romanticism . . . and 1930 science" is illustrated by moviegoing, the principal image-pattern of the novel. When Binx discusses going to the movies, in other words, he is really talking about the way that he, like his father before him, was educated to look at the world.

To a slight degree, Binx's "English romanticism" is misleading. He does not mean the English Romantic poets; rather he is
alluding to the romantic idealism so pervasive in English higher
education in the latter half of the nineteenth century. Although
he does not mention his name, Binx is really talking about the
tradition inspired by Benjamin Jowett, the legendary Master of
Balliol College, Oxford, whom J. H. Muirhead credits with the
"revival of Platonic study"[2] in England. A very hostile authority
also acknowledges Jowett's remarkable influence:

> Plato's story of the cave has, as everyone knows, been the subject of
> almost infinite controversy: people have tried to make it accord
> with the somewhat thinner details of his account of the Line, and
> with nearly everything said by Plato in the *Republic* and else-
> where, or with everything that others have been inspired to say by
> reading him. This remarkable exegesis was, of course, for many
> years a specifically British preoccupation, ever since Benjamin Jow-
> ett made Plato in general, and the *Republic* in particular, the core
> and centre of Oxford education.[3]

Such popularity continued, refurbished, and spread the image of
"Plato the Gentleman (usually a Christian gentleman)," as T. M.
Robinson describes it.   Jowett was essential to this image,
Robinson continues: "A whole generation of Oxford students . .
. was spellbound by the lectures of Benjamin Jowett, and his
view of Plato as the father of Idealism was bolstered by his best-
known achievement, the first complete translation of Plato since
the Latin version of Marsilio Ficino."[4]
    Jowett's influence survived his death.   A contemporary phil-
osopher remembers, for example, his pre-college holiday, in
1929: "Such works as I did while I was in Santander was mainly
on Plato's *Republic*, which I knew I should have to study when I
came to Oxford."[5] And another student in the Twenties reveals
one of the processes by which "English romanticism" became
"1930 science": "One evening I went to the Jowett Society to hear
Eddington speak, who was all the rage then; his book, *The
Nature of the Physical World*, had immense *reclame*; he was spoken of with veneration as a new Daniel come to judgment.   I
fear I was not properly impressed; the truth was that I didn't
much like this mixture of Quaker quietism with unintelligible
physics."[6] By then, when the physicist was speaking on the philosopher's stage, physics of the Eddington and Jeans kind had become an idealistic philosophy.   Ironically, this mystical physics,

it could be called, was rather quickly attacked by such critics as C. E. M. Joad, in *Philosophical Aspects of Modern Science,* and L. Susan Stebbing, in *Philosophy and the Physicists,* for its naive understanding of philosophy.

In his deceptively casual way Binx Bolling reveals quite a bit about the "English romanticism . . . and 1930 science" intellectual ambience of both his childhood and his adolescence. Ordinarily, perhaps, the two states are not so easily separated, but in Binx's case a radical severance occurred. He first became aware of his life in the home of "Dr. Wills" Bolling, his grandfather, the patriarch of an old family of Feliciana Parish, Louisiana; there he lived with his father (a physician like his father, Dr. Wills), and his mother, a nurse, born Anna Castagne, and his brother Scott, who died when Binx was eight years old. After his father died when Binx was eleven years old, his mother had returned to work, and Binx was taken into the New Orleans home of Emily Bolling Cutrer, his great-aunt, where he spent his adolescence.

Although Binx relates only a few scattered memories of his father, he reveals enough to give an impression of the kind of father that he was. Jack Bolling had wanted each experience to be a Perfect Moment, a rare event whose Possibility to stir emotion was attained. Binx describes one such pursuit of the Ideal, when he was eight:

> . . . we came my father and I to the Field Museum, a long dismal peristyle dwindling away into the howling distance, and inside stood before a tableau of Stone Age Man, father mother and child crouched around an artificial ember in postures of minatory quiet—until, feeling my father's eye on me, I turned and saw what he required of me—very special father and son we were that summer, he staking his everything this time on a perfect comradeship—and I, seeing in his eyes the terrible request, requiring from me his very life; I, through a child's cool perversity or some atavistic recoil from an intimacy too intimate, turned him down, turned away, refused him what I knew I could not give. (p. 204)

That obligatory reverential moment before the "tableau" brilliantly conveys the quaint, tragic optimism of the scientific humanism of the 1930's. In those pre-war days it was still possible to believe that mankind was engaged in an orderly progression from the Cave Man to the Century of Progress. One had but to believe in the progressive moment in history such as Arnold Toynbee, a Balliol fellow and tutor, discerned and to keep abreast of the breathtaking developments in science.

Jack Bolling seems to have tried to convince himself that
sooner or later one of the discoveries would provide the key understanding for his immanent universe. Binx remembers that
one night his father called his young sons out to look through a
telescope at "the horsehead nebula in Orion" (p. 91). Perhaps
Jack had just read Sir Arthur Eddington's *New Pathways in
Science (1935)*, which contains a magnificient plate of that "dark
nebulosity."[7] It was a time when the discovery of the expanding
universe was accepted as the ultimate scientific explanation.
But, Binx remembers, "that was the end of the telescope," "a fas-
cinating scientific hobby" (p. 91) that soon ceased to fascinate.
For, having accepted the assertion that the universe is infinitely
expanding, Jack could only realize that he had just gotten lost in
a "desert of emptiness," as Sir Arthur calls the universe.[8] Then
"he began to read Browning and saw himself in need of a world
of men" (p. 91), Binx remembers. Jack had been reading "the
works of Fabre," the great authority on the social organization of
insects, so perhaps he was consoling himself with the belief that
in an indifferent universe the only hope was man's capacity for
joint endeavors. There would have to be organization, for
science seemed to be telling him that individual man was the
victim of various kinds of determinism. Binx admits that he
early read Freud (p. 138), probably in emulation of his father. In
those days there was much talk on the Bolling porch of "psychological make-ups and the effect of glands on our dismal dark behavior" (p. 154, p. 86).

What happened was that even as Jack Bolling tried harder
and harder to perceive and rely upon a universal reality that
could be exhaustively explained by science, he was experiencing
his own life with less and less satisfaction. It came to the point,
Binx learns from his mother, that nothing personal, even eating,
was *"important* enough" (p. 153). So alienated from his own life
did he become that he took to his bed in depression, suffering his
wife to read *The Greene Murder Case* to him as she fed him (p.
152).[9]

So deep was Jack's personal gloom that only the outbreak of
World War II could rouse him. The war would obviously be
apocalyptic, become a cosmic conflict between mighty antagon-
ists, whose opposed philosophies transcended the mere national
ambitions of each country composing a bloc. Jack would have
seen the war in allegorical terms, the Children of Light versus
the Power of Darkness. For him the Children of Light were led

by England, the culmination of that Western tradition which originated in the land bounded by Homer's "wine dark sea" (p. 157). He immediately volunteered for and was accepted by the RCAF as a flight surgeon. Ordered to Greece, he no doubt exulted in the opportunity to act, for once, like a Byron; he was killed during the Battle of Crete, in 1941, with a copy of *A Shropshire Lad* in his pocket (p. 25). As a Platonist he would have accepted the image of the *Republic:* one must leave the cave of appearance, perceive the truth in the Sun, the Ideal, then return to lead those still captive in the cave. Only, Binx might well think, his father, like Icarus, came too near the sun over Crete and perished in that "wine dark sea" (p. 25).

Jack's fall is also Binx's fall, a fall into a sense of loss and time. Fittingly, Binx had been "off at school" (p. 156), when his father made his discovery that he could escape everydayness by becoming part of a great effort to turn back the barbarians. Jack's success in escaping alienation by a socially-approved gesture ensures that his son will suffer the same kind of distancing from the world. Whereas his father had lain in Dr. Will's house fixedly watching the ceiling fan (p. 156), Binx grows up "staring straight up at the plaster medallion" (p. 6) in his bedroom at his aunt's house.

Aunt Emily might at first seem to be a different sort from Binx's father. "Aunt Emily no longer talks of psychological makeups" (p. 154), Binx notes. She may have lost her infatuation with "1930 science," indeed, but this is not to say that she has not behaved as a Bolling. It may be deduced that she too had been so alienated that she had longed for a cause that would give her life a meaning, for she had jumped at the chance to become a nurse during the Spanish Civil War. The only trouble was that she survived it, returning to marry Jules Cutrer, a widower with a child, in six months (p. 27), then to settle down with a vengeance. But though Jules is a wealthy and successful broker and he and Emily fully participate in the social life of New Orleans, she has by no means escaped the alienation so ingrained in the Bolling personality.

Rather than emphasize the expansion of the universe as the determining factor of her outlook, Emily chooses entropy as her fundamental truth. "I don't quite know what we're doing on this insignificant cinder spinning away in a dark corner of the universe" (p. 54), she admits to Binx, grimly intending humor, but unaware of just how smug that "quite" makes her sound. For while she appears to be acknowledging her limits, she creates a cumulative impression of one who knows very well everything that one needs to know. She pays lip service to the "high gods" (p. 54, p. 224), but she really accepts her formulation of the world as the ultimate reality. Binx realizes: "For her too the fabric is dissolving, but for her even the dissolving makes sense. She understands the chaos to come" (p. 54). She is far more pessimistic than her nephew Jack had been.

There is no hope. She is certain that "the age of the Catos is gone" (p. 49). Only memory remains, as her mantel and "glassed-in cases of medals" (p. 175) attest: tellingly, the cabinet of the past was sealed in 1938, the year that she returned to New Orleans. As far as she can tell, "the barbarians [are] at the inner gate and who defends the West?" (p. 33) She might well think of herself as a Marcus Aurelius at the frozen Danube, trying nobly to shield a southern people, who grow ever more decadent and unworthy of continuation. As that Stoic took some small comfort in committing his *Meditations* to himself, so Aunt Emily relies upon his words and even advises Binx to hark to them:

> Every moment think steadily as a Roman and a man, to do what thou hast in hand with perfect and simple dignity, and a feeling of affection and freedom and justice. These words of the Emperor Marcus Aurelius Antoninus strike me as pretty good advice, for even the orniest young scamp. (p. 78)

It is indeed a wintry kingdom, in which life is but a duty and death a relief.

Thus, although Binx is never explicit about his feelings, it can be inferred that he must finally conceive of his father as one who abandoned, even rejected, him. Granted Jack Bolling had his problems, and the adult Binx can intellectually accept that fact: but in the adult Binx there still must be the son who was cast adrift too soon. There must lurk in his being, too, a depression associated with his Aunt Emily, who, although she took him in as a duty, has always erected an emblem for him (p. 49), rather than accepting him as (he knows) he is. She can only find him wanting, since he can never live up to her expectations. Binx can only have grown up with an overwhelming sense of doubt about himself and an equally strong need to hide his hurt behind an early-developed mask.

His Aunt Emily had told him that he must "act like a soldier" (p. 4), and so he had: his war—Korean—had come along, and Binx had gone, apparently with great willingness, for he had filled "long, sensitive and articulate letters" to his Aunt with such sentiments as:

> Japan is lovely this time of year. How strange to think of going into combat! Not so much fear—since my chances are very good—as wonder, wonder that everything should be so full of expectancy, every tick of the watch, every rhododendron blossom. Tolstoy and St Exupery were right about war, etc. (p. 87)

The only trouble was, he survived.

There was a moment in Korea when, by virtue of being wounded, Binx realized that he was immersed in the mud, in the *en-soi*, as the dung beetle six inches from his nose (p. 10-11). So when he returned from the war he eventually began a quest for some sort of deliverance from it. The course he had taken would have earned Aunt Emily's approval; she believes in the Great Books (p. 51) and could only have commended his effort. In effect, she is the Philosopher-King who returned to the Cave, to prepare Binx to follow the same upward path, out of the cave of becoming into the sunlight of Being.[10] The titles which he cites to represent his "vertical" search—Tolstoy's *War and Peace*, Toynbee's *A Study of History*, Schroedinger's *What is Life?*, Einstein's *The Universe as I See It*, Eddington's *The Expanding Universe*, and *The Chemistry of Life* (pp. 69-70)—effectively combine the slightly different slants on Platonism taken by his father and his aunt.

No doubt he began with Plato in his education (the etymology is revealing) in the Great Books, for Aunt Emily had thus taught him (p. 226)—she must have introduced him to all the other dialogues before they read the *Crito*. Since the *Republic* occupies so central a position in Plato's thought and canon, and since Aunt Emily was so evidently modeling herself after the Philosopher-King, Binx must have been supersensitive to the reliance on the Allegory of the Cave that recurs in the Great Books of the Western tradition and must have realized that reading the Great Books was an act of climbing out of the cave. At the same time, Binx was also reading "1930 science," especially physics. There he must have noticed how often the physicist-writer-for-the-layman likens the physicist-investigator to the Platonic inhabitant of the Cave, who must devise a method for penetrating the shadows on the wall in order to "see" or at least "prove" the presence of invisible ultimate reality.   Such likenings abound: Pierre Duhem, *La Théorie Physique: Son Objet, Sa Structure (1908)*, Henri Bergson, *Creative Evolution (1911)*, Sir Arthur Eddington, *The Nature of the Physical World (1927)*, Sir James Jeans, *The Mysterious Universe (1930)*, Werner Heisen-berg, "On the History of the Physical Interpretation of Nature" (1932), Sir James Jeans, *Physics and Philosophy (1942)*, Sir Charles Sher-rington, *Man on His Nature (1951)*, and Erwin Schroedinger, *Mind and Matter (1958)*.[11] It is likely that Binx would have known these books, for the physics texts to which he specifically refers are of the same kind or by the same authors.

Binx must also have noted a second likening, that of the Platonic wall-watcher to the modern-day moviegoer. Since he appears to have been a devotee of movies ever since he saw *All Quiet on the Western Front*, one of his first, in August of 1941 (p. 79), he would have been supersensitive to any references in his reading to cinematography. He would have discovered that Bergson in *Creative Evolution*, Toynbee in *A Study of History*, and Francis Cornford in his translation of the *Republic* make either an allusion (Bergson) or a direct reference (Toynbee and Cornford) to moviegoing as a contemporary equivalent for the wall-watching image.[12]

Binx declares that he completed his "vertical search" in Birmingham one night, when he read *The Chemistry of Life* (p. 70).[13] Then he went out to see *It Happened One Night*. He had, in adopting the wall-watching behavior of both Platonist and physicist, become a moviegoer. There is one hitch: "The only difficulty was that though the universe had been disposed of, I myself was left over."[14] He becomes, therefore, a moviegoer who cannot lose his awareness of himself in the dark theater or of the technical processes necessary to present the images on the screen. The two awarenesses are not of course really separate.

If "1930 science" has rejected the "billiard ball picture" of the universe and, modernizing Plato, adopted the "moviegoer picture" of Cartesian man monitoring the universe, then it is understandable that Binx would be obsessed with the actual cinematographic process. For he would make a continuous attempt to see if the new "picture" adequately represented the lofty truths of physical science to the layman.[15] To put it another way, what does the cinematographic *process*—quite apart from the sequence of images projected on the film—"say" to the layman? And is what the cinematographic process says an accurate illustration of a general set of modern scientific theories?

Most physicists who have used the wall-watching image would most likely agree with Sir James Jeans, when he extracts certain meanings from the Allegory of the Cave (as he *almost* links wall-watching with moviegoing!):

> Our phenomenal world consists of the activities of matter and photons; the theatre of this activity is space and time. Thus the walls of the cave in which we are imprisoned are space and time; the shadows of reality which we see projected on the walls by the sunshine outside are the material particles which we see moving against a background of space and time, while the reality outside the cave which produces these shadows is outside space and time.[16]

Binx is certainly aware of those material particles of which Sir James speaks: "As the train rocks along on its unique voyage through space-time, thousands of tiny thing-events bombard us like cosmic particles" (p. 190), he says. So sensitive to his alienation is he that he often feels that he is being assaulted by undifferentiated cosmic dust.[17] At the same time, he could imagine the particles to be the stinging sand whipped up by the winds of Arabia Deserta.[18] But when he is in a movie theater, Binx is affected by the same less immediate considerations as Sir James, space and time. Arbitrarily, in the present essay, space will be almost ignored; suffice it to say that whether the experience is one of space or place depends upon the particular conception that one has of time, as either eternity or duration; while space and time cannot therefore in any full discussion be separated, here the emphasis will be on time, since it is the quality that has been "pictured" by the image of the cinematographic process.

In appearance, *cinematic* can hardly be distinguished from *kinematic*. And there is more kinship in meaning than might be expected. But customarily the words appear in such vastly different contexts that the reflection that one concept could provide the other is lost. This relationship was closer in the 1930's, when the concept of time as a linearity began to be replaced by the concept of time as a circularity (or, to put it another way, when the Platonic concept of time-as-circularity began once again to be asserted, after the long domination of the Christian concept of time-as-linearity). Thus when physicists used the image of cinematography as process, rather than their more commonly used image of the representation projected on the screen *by* the process, they used it to illustrate the foremost consideration of modern kinematics, what Eddington described as "time's arrow," the irreversibility of time as a condition of entropy.[19] Schroedinger uses the image as clearly as anyone:

> With very few exceptions (that really are exceptions) the course of events in nature is irreversible. If we try to imagine a time-sequence of phenomena exactly opposite to one that is actually observed—as in a cinema-film projected in reverse order—such a reverse sequence, though it can be easily imagined, would nearly always be in gross contradiction to well-established laws of physical science.[20]

Eddington's use is somewhat more involved, but consistent with Schroedinger's:

> The view is sometimes held that the dynamic quality of time does not exist in the physical universe and is a wholly subjective impression. Experience presents the physical world as a cinematograph film which is being unrolled in a certain direction; but is suggested that that is a property of the way the film is inserted into the cinematograph lantern of consciousness, and that there is in the film itself nothing to decide which way it should be unrolled. If this view were right the 'going on of time' ought not to appear in our picture of the external world.[21]

When Binx goes to the movies, in other words, he is betraying a strong tendency to follow his father and his aunt, to see the world as interpreted by "English romanticism . . . and 1930 science." The temptation to see larger-than-life actions on the screen is a metaphor for his father's devaluation of ordinary life (becoming) in favor of the Perfect Gesture (being). The temptation to see the unrolling of the films as a metaphor for the deterioration of the universe is an attitude that Binx was taught by his aunt. Both father and aunt are therefore moviegoers.

Yet Binx the moviegoer is aware that moviegoing is his greatest deception. He may act the soldier or the businessman—Kate Cutrer perceives that for his aunt he can be "a proper Bolling" and at the same time for her father he can be "a go-getter" (43). But these roles are limited in comparison to his role as a moviegoer/wall-watcher, which subsumes all his other roles. He does not accept the image of the movie screen as a valid "picture" of ultimate reality, even though he may talk of "certification" (p. 63)—the conferral of reality upon the phenomenal by reproducing it in a movie—and allude to movie stars as

Platonic Forms. Nor does he accept the "picture" of time as the unrolling-consciousness-rerolling process of cinematographic projection. He is aware, by virtue of his "vertical" education, that the unwinding film is like "the moving picture of reality," as time is defined in the *Timaeus*.[22] But he *is* aware, not engrossed; each instance of himself as an unengrossed viewer in a movie is therefore his continued effort to suggest that he, like Sartre's officious waiter, is *more* than the role that he betrays by overacting. That *more* is of course his sense of transcendence. With such a "left over" characteristic, he cannot truly be either a classical Platonist or a modern physicist. Binx never really watches the movie; his rare comment about screen actions usually imply their phoniness, and his interest is more often directed to such unremarkable things as fellow moviegoers, seats, and ticket-sellers.

He has, though, no belief which will get him out of the movies, out of the cave. The changes in his life will not occur because of some physical act by which he makes some radical achievement in the social world. The various involvements of the narrative, thus, while they characterize the success of his posturing, do not point to any conclusion for the novel. The novel has therefore been misleading to socially-minded critics, who wish to impose the very same Platonic sociological Forms that it warns against.

Binx once awoke to a condition not recognized by sociology: he came to himself in the *hylē*, the viscous, the mud, the shit. *He* is the "dung beetle" (p. 11) of his Korea reminiscence. The essential movement of the novel traces his despairing observation that "English romanticism . . . and 1930 science" do not provide an escape from the *hylē*. At the same time he feels himself sinking deeper with each struggle. The bottom is reached when his aunt, as representative of those two value-systems, disowns him (p. 227). It is then that Binx realizes the true nature of his life: he is smothering in shit (p. 228).[23] He lives in a "great shithouse of scientific humanism," in which everyone else is prospering "like a dung beetle" (p. 228). He realizes, now, what his true inheritance from his father is: "a good nose for merde, for every species of shit that flies" (p. 228). And, like his father, he seems to be sliding down into the *en soi*, the great *"Antivalue,"* as Sartre calls sliminess.[24] On his thirtieth birthday, when he should be establishing his independence from his father's example, he is finally accepting Jack's utter despair. His father eventually found his apocalypse, and Binx now clarifies his occasional welcoming reference to an atomic war: either he would die or he and other survivors would "creep out of their holes and discover themselves to be themselves and live as merrily as children among the viny ruins" (p. 231). Until that time, he can only practice seduction, turn to desire, by which physical incarnation permits consciousness to be embodied, if only for a few minutes.

There he stands, in an "evil-smelling" (p. 228) telephone booth, making a desperate and unsuccessful call to his latest secretary. He must be aware that the graffiti at which he idly glances speak of the kind of "love" that he now proposes. At that moment he is pulled back by a loving hand. It is no doubt thought to be a "romantic," even "sentimental" scene and has been, in these "realistic" times, often passed over in embarrassed silence. Perhaps, though, Kate's arrival is a motion of love, a miraculous action, and that is really what is offensive these days. Binx seems to see it as a divine presence, for he immediately links it with the mysterious occurrences in the nearby church. Both Kate's action and the church's presence argue that the Spirit can be incarnated; on the intersubjective level Kate reveals that love can still make a heaven of this world, and on the historical level, for the believer, Christ's entry into time ended forever the dualism that Plato had described. With a knowledge of Christ, all things, as Paul says, may be counted as dung (Philippians iii 8).

Binx is, it turns out, not so despairing as his audience. He yields, confesses a readiness to believe: "Is it possible that—it is not too late?" The Epilogue merely confirms that Binx has summoned the faith to accept both Kate and Christ, to accept each as a "dazzling trick of grace" (p. 235). With such faith, Binx need not expect miracles from either life or science; he can therefore enter medical school, pick up his father's life where his father discarded it. Having transcended "English romanticism . . . and 1930 science," Binx has found a new Father and can forgive the one he lost.

Notes

[1] The edition cited is (New York: Noonday Press, 1967). Page references to the novel will be incorporated into the text.

[2] John H. Muirhead, *The Platonic Tradition in Anglo-Saxon Philosophy* (London: George Allen & Unwin, 1931), p. 413.

[3] J. N. Findlay, *The Discipline of the Cave* (London: George Allen & Unwin, 1966), p. 22.

[4] Thomas More Robinson, "Plato Oxoniensis," *University of Toronto Quarterly*, 37 (October, 1967), 90, 91. Robinson discerns four Platos: "Plato the Gentleman (usually a Christian gentleman), Plato the Repressed Homosexual, Plato the Totalitarian, Plato the Analyst."

[5] A. J. Ayer, *Part of My Life: The Memoirs of a Philosopher* (New York: Harcourt Brace Jovanovich, 1977), p. 71.

[6] A. L. Rowse, *A Cornishman at Oxford* (London: Jonathan Cape, 1965), p. 245.

[7] Sir Arthur Eddington, *New Pathways in Science* (Cambridge: The University Press, 1935), facing p. 202.

[8] Eddington, p. 184, introduces the chapter "Cosmic Clouds and Nebulae" with this image: "First let me remind you of the vastness of this space and the extreme isolation of the stars from one another. The stars are small oases of matter in a desert of emptiness. For a traveller in this desert we may take a ray of light. His journey from one oasis to the next, say, from the nearest star to our sun, takes four years; he takes only eleven hours to cross the whole extent of the solar system; and then the journey is through empty desert again for six years or so. That is if the light ray were to zigzag from star to star; if it goes unheedingly on a straight course through the universe it will probably miss the oases altogether as a traveller in a desert would do." Such desert imagery recalls *Arabia Deserta*, Binx's "single book" (p. 78).

[9] In "The Man on the Train" Percy writes: "An Erle Stanley Gardner novel is a true experience in alienation. A man who finishes his twentieth Perry Mason is that much nearer total despair than when he started." See *The Message in the Bottle* (New York: Farrar, Straus and Giroux, 1975), p. 83.

[10] I have traced the indebtedness of *The Moviegoer* to the *Republic*, in "Walker Percy's *The Moviegoer*: the Cinema as Cave," *Southern Studies*, 19 (Winter 1980), 331-354.

[11] The likening continues after Binx makes his confession in 1960. Otto Frische uses the image in *Atomic Physics Today* (1961) and Carl Friedrich von Weizsäcker has used it in several of his works, including *The Unity of Nature* (1971).

[12] The French, who take their cinematography seriously, have continually discovered the likeness. See: Jean Przyluski, "Le theatre d'ambres et la caverne de Platon," *Byzantion*, 13 (1938), 595-603, which mentions A. Dies' article in *Bulletin de l'Association Guillame Bude* (Janvier 1927), not seen by the present writer; Marcel LaPierre, *Les cent visages du cinema* (Paris: Editions Bernard Grasset, 1948), Chapter II; L. Chauvois, "Lè cinéma populaire' en Grèce au tems de Platon et sa projection dans l'allégorie de la 'cavern aux idées'," *Revue generale des sciences pures et appliquees*, 84 (Juillet-Aout 1967), 193-196. Percy might have come across the likeness in some book or magazine devoted to

the movies, for he early became not only a moviegoer, but a student of movies. See his college article, "The Movie Magazine: A Low 'slick'," *Carolina Magazine* [University of North Carolina], 64 (March 1935), 4-9.

[13] I can only guess at the identity of this book: *The Physics and Chemistry of Life*, "a SCIENTIFIC AMERICAN book" (New York: Simon and Schuster, 1955), which consists of a collection of essays on the state of scientific knowledge to date. That date would make it a likely attraction for Binx in his scientific enthusiasm. The book, so the editors announce, is intended for the likes of him (p. vii):

> This book is concerned with life as a physical process. The questions raised here are the kind that can be answered wholly within the discipline that explain the behavior of nonliving atoms and molecules. The first chapter advances an explanation of how life was originally ignited in the elements of the earth. The last chapter describes the beginning of our understanding of the electrical basis of thought. The speculations of these two authors are sustained by the work in a dozen different fields of investigation reported by the other contributors to the book. There are gaps and unknowns in the picture. But it is a connected one, and it is increasingly worthy of the attention of priests, philosophers and poets.

To conclude their analogy to scientific picturing, the editors put the picture into its proper context (p. x): "The theater for all this immense variety of biochemical activity is the microsopic living cell." The last essay, incidentally, in which W. Grey Walter discusses "The Electrical Activity of the Brain," might be an origin of Percy's third novel, *Love in the Ruins*. Walter's description of his brain scanner, the Toposcope, could well have stimulated Percy to begin thinking about a "lapsometer."

[14] I have spoken of the theme of "left over," Sartre's *de trop*, in "Moviegoing in *The Moviegoer*," *Southern Quarterly*, 19 (Spring 1980), 26-42.

[15] Marshall McLuhan, *Understanding Media* (New York: Signet Books, 1964), in a chapter entitled "The Reel World," offers a very helpful discussion of the movie as the appropriate medium for a mechanistic culture.

[16] Although the excerpt comes from *Physics and Philosophy* (1942), it is quoted here from *The Mystery of Matter*, ed. Louise B. Young (New York: Oxford University Press, 1965), pp. 127-129, to illustrate the popularity with scientists of the picture of the investigator as Platonic wall-watcher.

[17] Owen Barfield, whom Percy had read (*Message in the Bottle*, p. 292), speaks of "the particles" as "the unrepresented," that which is conceived by the modern world to have an existence that is independent of consciousness.

[18] Binx would feel drawn to the desert imagery of *Arabia Deserta*, his one-book library, because of its lunar aspect. But he also might feel a sympathy for the author, Charles M. Doughty, a Christian among infidels who quests for a holy city.

[19] Thus Sir Arthur puts it, in *The Nature of the Physical World* (New York: MacMillan Company, 1933), p. 89:

> But the association of 'becoming' with entropy-change is not to be understood in the same way. It is clearly not sufficient that the

change in the random element of the world should deliver an impulse at the end of a nerve, leaving the mind to create in response to this stimulus the fancy that it is turning the reel of a cinematograph. Unless we have been altogether misreading the significance of the world outside us—by interpreting it in terms of evolution and progress, instead of a static extension—we must regard the feeling of 'becoming' as (in some respects at least) a true mental insight into the physical condition which determines it.

[20] Erwin Schroedinger, *Mind and Matter* (Cambridge: The University Press, 1958), p. 83.

[21] *New Pathways in Science*, p. 53.   Bernhard Bavink, *The Anatomy of Modern Science* (London: G. Bell & Sons, Ltd., 1932; translation of fourth German edition), reveals that the movie image occurred in the German scientific community (p. 49).:

> It is easy to see that, if matter really consists of completely separated particles, all processes taking place in it, which apparently continuous, such as sound waves, heat conduction, or the like, are in fact, in sub-microscopic dimensions, by no means so continuous as they appear. . . . It would thus be, to use a modern analogy, a cinematograph, in which a discontinuous succession of pictures produced the false impressions of continuous succession of change.

[22] See my "Time and Eternity in *The Moviegoer*, " *Southern Humanities Review*, 16 (Spring 1982), 129-141.

[23] Norman O. Brown, *Life Against Death* (New York: Vintage Books, 1961), enables us to understand Binx's excremental vision: "Our much prized 'objectivity' toward our own bodies, other persons, and the universe, all our calculating 'rationality,' is, from the psychoanalytical point of view, an ambivalent mixture of love and hate, an attitude appropriate only toward excrement, and appropriate to excrement only in an animal that has lost his own body and life" (p. 295). Further, Brown writes: " . . . the philosophical and scientific concept of 'matter' is, from the psychoanalytical point of view, radically infected by the excremental imagination" (p. 295).   Finally, Brown concludes: "Nor can psychoanalysis abstain from wondering whether the contradictions in the scientific concept of 'matter,' so searchingly probed by Emile Meyerson, do not reflect the unconscious projection—palpable in Plato or in Berkeley's tar-water philosophy—of man's anal disturbance into his picture of the world" (p. 296).

[24] Jean-Paul Sartre, *Being and Nothingness*, trans. Hazel E. Barnes (New York: Philosophical Library, 1956), p. 611.   But the whole treatment of the slimy should be read.

Walker Percy as Martian Visitor:
The Message in the Bottle

During a relatively short period, Walker Percy has had a remarkable career as a novelist. Winner of the National Book
Award for his first published novel, *The Moviegoer* (1961), he
has subsequently written *The Last Gentleman* (1966) and *Love in
the Ruins* (1971). With the three novels he has gained the appreciation, respect, and trust of a large number of us for his ability to
communicate what it is like to flourish in the contemporary objective-empirical world and yet desperately yearn to transcend
that mode of existence.

Before the novels, though, Percy had begun to publish articles
in scholarly journals. His targets ranged widely here, from the re-
views, *Sewanee* and *Partisan*, to *Thought*, *Modern Schoolman*,
and *New Scholasticism*, to *Personalist*, *Journal of Philosophy*,
Philosophy and Phenomenological Research, and *Psychiatry*—an accomplishment probably as rare as a triple play. The
variety of journals able to tolerate Percy's ideas is all the more
remarkable when it is revealed, as *The Message in the Bot-tle* so
discloses, that all of the essays are basically about the same set of
ideas and that these ideas would not be completely congen-ial
with any of the journals. That set of ideas explores the significance of the distinctively human ability to receive and convey
symbols through language—the only phenomenon on which to
base an anthropology, maintains Percy—although, strange to say,
Percy has never published in a journal specializing in either linguistics or anthropology.

In the essays that comprise *The Message in the Bottle*, in
other essays, and in his responses to interviewers Percy's willingness to discuss personal history has provided us with a body of
information sufficient to suggest a context for his prevailing
ideas. This is not to say, of course, that a knowledge of the data
of his life adequately explicates his writing, any more than a
knowledge of the ingredients for a recipe conveys the taste of the
dish. Rather, it is simply to say that such knowledge should

point us in the direction of his work. Which is not at all too modest an accomplishment, for it has been my experience that many a reader (this one included) has missed a Percy novel or essay because he came at it from the wrong direction.

Orphaned by the age of fourteen, Percy was adopted by his father's cousin, William Alexander Percy, the gentleman who wrote *Lanterns on the Levee*. Percy grew to manhood, then, in the presence of a figure who exemplified the patrician code of traditional Southern culture—"the stern inner summons to man's full estate, to duty, to honor, to generosity toward his fellowmen and above all to his inferiors," as Percy describes the value-system in "Stoicism in the South." In time Percy chose his profession, medicine, as a means by which he could please Uncle Will, so he told Martin Luschei, and one can imagine what his life might have become: a lovable, if cranky Lionel Barrymore of Greenville, Mississippi, excused for his outrageous opinions and conduct because of his function as latest incarnation of Percy *noblesse.*

Whether or not Percy would have found the practice of medicine a gesture which satisfied the stern inner summons, only he can say. It would have served his bent toward science quite well, he has admitted in "From Facts to Fiction," a bent unaffected by his later reservations about most contemporary practitioners of the scientific method. "It struck me then, as now, as an idea of the most revolutionary simplicity and beauty: namely, that even the *dis*-order of *dis*-ease, which one generally takes to be the disruption of order, could be approached and understood and treated according to scientific principles governing the response of the patient to the causative agents of disease. This response *was* the disease as the physician sees it!"

However the active profession of medicine might have met his social or individual inclinations, it was denied him, when he contracted tuberculosis in the laboratory, after graduating from College of Physicians and Surgeons, Columbia University, in 1941. Despite the lengthy bed-rest that was the standard treatment of the disease at the time, Percy suffered a relapse and decided to abandon his career as a physician. In the next few years he married, moved to Covington, La. (an action not nearly so insignificant as it might seem: Covington is neither Cambridge, Mass., where people are at home in theories, nor Greenville, Miss., where people are at home in themselves), converted to Catholicism, and read widely among a group of writers foreign to his previous interests: "I began to read, no longer McLeod's *Physiology* or Gay's *Bacteriology*, but the great Russian novelists, especially Dostoevsky; the modern French novelists, especially Camus; the existentialist philosophers, Jaspers (also a physician), Marcel, and Heidegger."

Martin Luschei, in his study of Percy, *The Sovereign Wayfarer*, very profitably employs one of Percy's ideas to characterize the crisis which was brought to a head by the tuberculosis. He speaks of the "ordeal," and by so doing he addresses the psychological, rather than the physical, effects of the illness. Percy had become a rather solid abstractionist, practicing science, perhaps not yet aware of the "secret about the scientific method" which he reveals in *The Message in the Bottle:* "The secret is this: Science cannot utter a single word about an individual molecule, thing, or creature in so far as it is an individual but only in so far as it is like other individuals. The layman thinks that only science can utter the true word about anything, individuals included. But the layman is an individual. So science cannot say a single word to him or about him except as he resembles others" (p. 22). So committed to the method was he that he had submitted himself to Freudian therapy for three years.

Time and again Percy writes that, as a result of an ordeal, a person looks at his life from a new perspective: "the young man recovers consciousness" (60); the businessman "regains consciousness" (109); "When the novelist writes of a man 'coming to himself' through some such catalyst as catastrophe or ordeal, he may be offering obscure testimony to a gross disorder of consciousness and to the need of recovering oneself as neither angel nor organism but as a wayfaring creature somewhere between" (113). The onset of a new perspective through disaster is acknowledged by Binx Bolling, in Percy's *The Moviegoer.* So frequently has Percy discussed the phenomenon, indeed, that it seems a virtual certainty that he underwent just such an experience during his illness.

Two sets of terms in the passage just cited are significant in understanding the recovery that Percy made through his ordeal. First, it is of primary importance to sense the complexity he discovers in "consciousness"; not merely the state of awareness or sensibility, consciousness for Percy is "an exercise in intersubjectivity": "I am not only conscious *of* something; I am conscious of it as being what it is for you and me. If there is a wisdom in etymologies, the word *consciousness* is surely a case in point; for consciousness, one suddenly realizes, means a knowing-with!" (274). Second, to be neither angel nor organism is to rule out the forms of human behavior proposed by German idealism and American empiricism, respectively. Man does not grasp his placement in the world by constructing a set of universal modes that anticipate all possible individual behaviors and thus cancel them; neither does man stand any possibility of knowing himself if he investigates himself as an organism governed by the laws of stimulus and response.

Man was rather in the middle, an embodied mind, in Percy's new anthropology, and he was inevitably drawn to consider language as the only route to experience transcendent solidarity (and establish reality), now that identity with angels and animals had been rejected:

> Where does one start with a theory of man if the theory of man as an organism in an environment doesn't work and all the attributes of man which were accepted in the old modern age are now called into question: his soul, mind, freedom, will, God-likeness?
> There is only one place to start: the place where man's singularity is there for all to see and cannot be called into question, even in a new age in which everything else is in dispute.
> That singularity is language. (7)

Lest the reconstruction of his itinerary imply a deliberation, as if Percy immediately knew his destination, let it be said that he had to begin where everybody else has had to begin, between Bishop Berkeley and Samuel Johnson. There has always been the question: what is the connection between the thing and the sound (which can be transcribed) by which I can distinguish it? Percy began to grapple with the question not as a problem in linguistics, but as problem in the study of the only creature which uses language, a study which has now occupied twenty-five years, which has by his own admission maintained the intensity of a mild obsession.

Early in the struggle he made some fundamental discoveries about his methodology. In our specializing world there are some two hundred disciplines that study the different aspects of man, but none that seems to deal with man as talker and listener. But it seemed to Percy that the vast amount of information developed about man by the various disciplines blinded their professors to what it was that was not known, i.e., what happens when language is employed. So he realized that he would have to approach man not as a scientist, but as a Martian, looking not at the questions formulated by the answers already developed, but rather at the activity that most immediately distinguished a man for some visitor who had never before met one, his noisiness.

The second realization was that the investigation would be doubly strenuous: he would have not merely to develop his own theories, but would have to be constantly on guard, lest he lapse into accepting without question some of the theories provided by those who saw nothing curious about language, regarding it either as a rather droll and picturesque communications device, like the Pony Express, that would be phased out as man reached his telepathic potential or as a quirky category of standard stimulus-response behavior, a type of activity that no self-respecting rat would ever perform.

A consequence of both realizations was Percy's decision to turn to fiction whenever he became stymied in his study; thus he describes how he cultivated *The Message in the Bottle:* "It is the meager fruit of twenty years' off-and-on thinking about the subject, of coming at it from one direction, followed by failure and depression and giving up, followed by making up novels to raise my spirits, followed by a new try from a different direction or from an old direction but at a different level, followed by failure, followed by making up another novel, and so on" (10). This alternation is not a disjoint sequence analogous to Lincoln's shifting from a consideration of Burnside's ineptitude and Union casualty reports to the retailing of a homespun joke, a diversion from the weighty to the humorous for sanity's sake.

Rather, Percy's action is the masterful decision of a thinker who knows how he must approach his particular problem.   In the first place, leaving quite aside the truth that change *per se* is usually restful, Percy learned that the vocation of the novelist demanded from him an independence from an unquestioning acceptance of conventional wisdom: " . . . only a Martian can see man as he is, because man is too close to himself and his vision too fragmented.   An a nonpsychologist, a nonanthropologist, a nontheologian, a nontechnologist—as in fact nothing more than a novelist—I qualify through my ignorance as a terrestial Martian.   Since I am only a novelist, a somewhat estranged and detached person whose business it is to see things and people as if he had never seen them before, it is possible for me not only to observe people as data but to observe scientists observing people as data—in short to take a Martian view" (11). Second, Percy must have seen that his ideas had a way of leading to conclusions that had not been or could not be tested in laboratory situations; hence he must have hit upon the writing of novels as a means of testing out and verifying his theories according to their truthfulness to a human situation. These patently pragmatic reasons for writing a novel may explain why Percy's description of his fictional technique seems to sound so much like the scientific method: "My writing involves many false starts, many blind detours, many blind passages, many goings ahead and backing up where something has been tried and doesn't work. Sometimes, the first half will be all right and the second half doesn't work at all. You don't know why it doesn't work, it doesn't swing, it doesn't cook, it doesn't go; so, you just back up. It's mysterious, this thing of not knowing why it doesn't work. All you know is that when it *does* work, you know it." His characterization of the process, also in "From Facts to Fiction," amplifies his attitude toward the process: "What comes to my mind when I think of a writer sitting down to create something new, however modest the creation, is not the picture of a man setting out to entertain or instruct or edify a reader. It is the picture rather of a scientist who has come to the deadend of a traditional hypothesis which no longer accounts for the data at hand."

As a product of a scientific, empirical education, Percy spent a great deal of time in the early Fifties attempting to accept the behaviorists' model of a language transaction, in which every talking (writing) is a stimulus and every hearing (reading) is a response that activates. But no matter how many refinements he imposed upon the basic model, it still did not seem to account for all language transactions. In time all his questions about the language event congregated in one place, as when the eye, attempting to respond to the various, competing appeals of a painting, finally in desperation seizes upon one, often minor but immensely human, detail, with the intuition that if the one part could be understood, all the other parts would subordinate themselves to that understanding.

This reduction to the microcosm was Helen Keller's account, in her autobiography, of how she, as a girl of eight, came to perceive that while sometimes a word commands a response, more often it is an answer to a question. Helen's thought process suddenly arced, so that she knew that "the wonderful cool something" flowing over one hand was named by the word "w-a-t-e-r" that Miss Sullivan was tracing in her other hand. In that instant curiosity burst forth, and Helen was almost frenetic to learn the names of everything else in her world.

Percy's intuition from Helen's experience was that it transcended a stimulus-response model, that it did not involve a causal relation. On the contrary, both the word *water*, provided by the Namer, and the presence of the object, provided by the senses, arrive simultaneously in the consciousness of the Hearer (77) and are linked by the structure of grammar, hence the evolution of the sentence. Percy's account of his discovery betrays the delight inherent in naming (283):

> My breakthrough was the sudden inkling that the triangle was absolutely irreducible. Here indeed was nothing less, I suspected, than the ultimate and elemental unit not only of language but of the very condition of the awakening of human intelligence and consciousness.
>
> What to call it? "Triad"? "Triangle"? "Thirdness"? Perhaps "Delta phenomenon," the Greek letter signifying irreducibility.
>
> Alpha was the beginning, omega will be the end, but somewhere in between, some five billion years after alpha, and x years before omega, there first occurred delta, Δ.
>
> The Delta phenomenon lies at the heart of every event that has ever occurred in which a sentence is uttered or understood, a name is given or received, a painting painted and viewed.
>
> What Helen had discovered, broken through to, was the Delta phenomenon (40).

Percy later expands upon the significance of the Delta phenomenon: " . . . the standard syntactical sentence of language, the coupling of subject and predicate, is a special case of the more fundamental human capacity to couple any two things at all and through the mirror of the one see the other. Thus, the child's sudden inkling that the thing ball 'is' the sound *ball* is the progenitor not only of all future sentences about balls but also of his grasp of metaphor, art, and music" (308).

Percy speculated that eight-year-old Helen's sudden experience, delayed because of her special circumstances, was the same experience that most two-year-olds gradually participate in. Further, he felt that, if ontogeny really does recapitulate phylogeny, Helen's breakthrough would be the best reconstruction of what happened in the dawn of consciousness, perhaps during the era of *Homo neanderthalensis,* when brain size "suddenly" increased fifty-four percent (42): "What took place when the first man uttered a mouthy little sound and the second man understood it, not as a sign to be responded to, but as 'meaning' something they beheld in common? The first creature who did this is almost by minimal empirical definition the first man" (154).

It is totally appropriate that the conception of the language event as the essence/mystery which marks the beginning of man should become the beginning of all of Percy's investigations. In the years that followed, he amplified his theory of man-as-symbol monger in essays that were satisfying as integral units. Perhaps the best known is "The Man on the Train," which offers descriptions of some of his most useful techniques, "alienation," the "objective-empirical," "rotation," "repetition," "zone crossing," and "certification." Or "The Loss of the Creature," which identifies "the sovereign wayfarer" and "the consumer of experience," may be preferred. And "The Message in the Bottle," with its discussion of the "castaway" and its distinction between "news" and "knowledge," has its adherents.

Percy's amplification of the theory of the Delta phenomenon is indebted in part to a diverse assemblage of thinkers. First to be mentioned must be Thomas Aquinas, whose thought provided no single impetus to the development of the theory, but rather the bedrock for Percy's thinking about transempirical reality. Then Charles S. Pierce should be acknowledged, not because he contributed so much to Percy's thought, but because, as Percy discovered, even though a scientist he had anticipated Percy's basic disagreement with a stimulus-response, which he called a "dyadic relation" (161), model of language. Percy must have felt doubly rewarded when, after discovering Pierce's writing which supported his theory, he found Pierce's argument (322) that the scientific mind somehow riffles through nearly countless hypotheses to select the correct one in short order. If both he and Pierce, obviously independent of each other, had sorted through the pack and pulled out the identical card, not just the same suit or even value, then the card must be the right one. Beyond those two sources are the writers whose ideas rushed in to fill the void during Percy's ordeal, when he discovered "that the more science progressed and even as it benefitted man, the less it said about what it is like to be a man living in the world" ("From Facts to Fiction"): Sören Kierkegaard, Gabriel Marcel, Martin Buber, among others previously mentioned. Then, too, there are the specialists in linguistics, Chomsky foremost, for Percy cannot be accused of leapfrogging the research in the field to proclaim his revelation—he is much too dedicated to science for that maneuver.

On the basis of the Delta phenomenon, with the indispensable help of the Namer (who must, however, possess authority and intention [76], the Hearer develops "autonomous object interest" (255), in other words, asks a question about a symbol, rather than responds to a signal: "Once it dawns upon one, whether deaf-mute or not, that *this is water*, then the first question is *What is that*, and so on, toward the end that *everything is something* . There has come into existence an all-construing mode of cognition in which everything must be formulated symbolically and known intentionally *as* something" (281). Then the Hearer is able to couple names and things and can, by this act, assert, classify, and use the "discovering power of analogy" (77). At the same time "a community" (172) has been formed; this community is not an "environment," which has gaps, but is, rather, a "world," which is global (173): "The greatest difference between the environment (*Umwelt*) of a sign-using organism and the world (*Welt*) of the speaking organism is that there are gaps in the former but none in the latter. The nonspeaking organism only notices what is relevant biologically; the speaking organism disposes of the entire horizon symbolically. Gaps that cannot be closed by perception and reason are closed by magic and myth" (203). But in establishing a "world" man seems necessarily to recognize his distance (196) from that world, hence his sense of alienation and/or his attempt to separate himself from it even further by regarding it as purely material, open to exhaustive study and ultimate scrutiny (a separation which is, paradoxically, a submersion of the non-material, the self, in the material). At that point Percy concludes by reminding his reader that, while the significance of the coupling of name and thing may now be asserted, nothing is known about the coupler: "The apex of the triangle, the coupler, is a complete mystery. What it is, an 'I,' a 'self,' or some neurophysiological correlate thereof, I could not begin to say" (327). "The one thing in the world which by its nature is not susceptible of a stable symbolic transformation is *myself*! I, who symbolize the world in order to know it, am destined to remain forever unknown to myself" (283). The only thing that man can know about himself by symbolization has been implied, that if he is not content with the objective-empirical he can only be alienated, a castaway (119-149). With the identification of man as the castaway may lie the reason for the title of the collection of essays, *The Message in the Bottle*, rather than *The Delta Phenomenon*. For the latter title would name the whole work as a scientific triumph (which it may be), whereas the former title reminds the reader that at a certain point science will not suffice. The message in the bottle that the castaway picks up will not contain knowledge, but news from across the seas.

And finally a word about Percy's future novels. There has always been that close relationship between the ideas of Percy's essays and the content of his novels. His two first-person protagonists, Binx Bolling and Tom More, use—to good effect—many of Percy's own terms to comment upon their experience. As well, they and Will Barrett, the limited third-person protagonist of *The Last Gentleman*, are endowed by their creator with attitudes and habits of behavior discussed in the essays.

Such weaving of expository material into the narrative fabric of his novels does not argue, though, that Percy has been a stylistic innovator. On the contrary he has adhered to a fairly conventional form for his novels, depending upon his mastery of the distancing factor of humor—especially irony, satire, burlesque—for his main impact. Now, however, he has available, through right of discovery, a model for advancing point of view beyond interior monologue, where Joyce and Faulkner left it forty years ago. Perhaps, then, in a future novel, acting upon his contention that consciousness is a collaboration, that thinking is symbolization resulting from intersubjectivity, that the self cannot know itself through symbolization, Percy will create a new first-person narration that will offer a radical complexity—and truthfulness—to the rendering of consciousness in fiction.

. . .

Note (1987). Such narration is employed in *Lancelot* and *The Second Coming*. *Lancelot* employs a "Deprived Consciousness," a hearer who will not listen to a namer. *The Second Coming* employs a hearer and a namer, who gain an "enhanced consciousness" through their union in love.

Tom More: Cartesian Physician

I - Archimedes

In *Love in the Ruins* (1971) a voice abruptly announces the place, time, and date. Then, with an ominous "Now in these latter days" (LR, 3), the speaker begins to recite a memorandum into a tape recorder, intended for any "survivors poking around the ruins of Howard Johnson's a hundred years from now" (LR, 28). From this account, they would be able to learn the cause of the catastrophe that the speaker, to judge from his eschatological reference, obviously expects. The concept of last days or last things originated in Christ's teaching, and since the speaker refers to Christ in the same sentence, it is tempting to think that he is a Christian. But this may not be the case; as Eric Voegelin points out, in *The New Science of Politics* (1952), gradually a secular concept arose to oppose the Christian vision of apocalypse. According to Voegelin, the secular apocalypse is envisioned as the last great world struggle, from which will emerge the leader who is to create the millennial state. This apocalyptic vision is the foundation of modern gnosticism, the antithesis of Christianity and the most pervasive, dominant system of thought since the seventeenth century. In Percy's novel, it soon becomes evident that the speaker is a thoroughgoing gnostic, who conceives of the apocalypse as a secular event and believes that he can either preclude its occurrence or, if it occurs, use it to further that progressive movement in history that all gnostics detect.

As he continues to dictate, the speaker provides himself with a background. His name is Tom More, though he does not think to give it for the record. He is a citizen of Louisiana, a descendant of a Roman Catholic family whose ancestry includes Sir Thomas More, the English martyr. He professes himself a Roman Catholic, "albeit a bad one" (LR, 6); the facility with which he recites his creed suggests that he may not even be a bad one, but rather only a nominal one. A wealthy, middle-aged widower, Tom is, he declares, "a physician, a not very successful psychiatrist . . . but a genius nevertheless . . . " (LR, 11). Perhaps he would be somewhat more modest if he considered his genius merely a personal adornment, but something that he says early in his rambling talk indicates that he believes himself to have an impersonal destiny.   Speaking of his early success in research, Tom admits, "There followed twenty years of silence and decline" (LR, 24). The last three words sound like a Toynbee buzz phrase, and, sure enough, Tom expands on them: "Toynbee, I believe, speaks of the Return, of the man who fails and goes away, is exiled, takes counsel with himself, hits on something, sees daylight—and returns to triumph" (LR, 25). Fascinated by History as he is, Tom would know Arnold Toynbee's *As Study of History*, a "universal" history that detects great patterns in the past events and tempts the reader to think that these patterns prefigure the future.   Tom seems especially familiar with the third volume, *The Growths of Civilizations* (1934), which elaborates the pattern of "Withdraval-and-Return." Since Tom believes that his past fits the Toynbeean pattern, he is secretly confident that he will emerge as a great leader.

Tom is, in other words, one of Eric Voegelin's modern gnostics.[1] Everytime he discovers a three-part sequence in history, a gnostic predilection, he gives himself away.   Take, for example, the day of the year, July 4, the significance of which he does not mention, but probably notes well. As a history-minded American, he would know certain momentous events: on July 4, 1776, the colonies declared their independence from Great Britain and thus created the union; on July 4, 1863, the United States forced both the Confederate surrender at Vicksburg and the retreat at Gettysburg and thus maintained the union.   On July 4, 1983, Tom More feels, he will join Washington and Lincoln, when he uses his machine to preserve the union. At other times Tom thinks of sequences that are personified by great men. Very early, he imagines what will happen when he wins the Nobel Prize (for he does not really believe that the world will end): the director of the institute at which he works will cry out, "A toast to our local Pasteur!   No, rather the new Copernicus! The latter-day Archimedes . . . " (LR, 7). Or, just a little later, he recalls, "When I was a young man, the question at the time was: where are the Catholic Einsteins, Salks, Oppenheimers?" (LR, 23) in both cases, *he* is to be the individual to transcend the triad. Still later, he recalls explaining how his achievement will com-

plete the greatest triad: it "will undoubtedly be recognized as one
of the three great breakthroughs of the Christian era, the others
being Newton hitting on his principles and Einstein on his field
theory, perhaps even the greatest of all because my discovery
alone gives promise of bridging the dread chasm between body
and mind that has sundered the soul of Western man for five
hundred years" (LR, 90).

With such high regard for his own achievement, Tom is not
afraid to invite individual comparison with some of the most
highly regarded personages of History. His fine choice of words
in his introductory statement ("I came to myself in a grove of
young pines") hints that he will pit himself against Dante. but
whereas Dante began in a dark wood and had to struggle to
locate that transcendent meaning which resides in God alone,
Tom soon intimates that he will demonstrate that man's
consciousness, alone, is sufficient to discern the ultimate meaning, which is immanent. Rather than slog through the Inferno
and Purgatory in order to reach Paradise—the Garden of Eden
and finally Heaven itself—Tom has already reached Paradise
(Estates).

Positioning himself at the cloverleaf is also a telling behavior. A short while before switching on his tape recorder, Tom
had left the abandoned motel in which he has hidden the three
women with whom, in one way or another, he is connected. To
protect them, he implies, he had to take the high ground, from
which he can observe any approaching enemy. Reasonable
enough—but he repeats his location so often that it must have
some private significance for him. He must be following as pre-
cedents "the man in the cloverleaf" and "the technopolitan man
. . . on the go" that Harvey Cox celebrates in *The Secular City*
(1965). Although Cox labors in a divinity school, he offers a
gnostic, tripartite plan of History: mankind has progressed from
a *tribal* phase through a *town* phase into a *technopolitan* phase.
"Contemporary man has become the cosmopolitan. The world
has become his city and his city has reached out to include the
world. The name for the process by which this has come about is
secularization."[2] Implicit in such a notion is the belief that it is
the city of man, rather than the city of God which occupies (and
ought to occupy) man. He must resolve his own problems by
personifying two other Cox images: the "man at the switch-
board," who unites a diverse community by technology, and the
"driver in the cloverleaf," who interacts with others not through

outmoded institutions, but through personal, anonymous mobility. By his identification with the cloverleaf, then, Tom indicates that he has abandoned the two cities concept of Saint Augustine. He sees the geometric form before him simply as a highway intersection, not as a cross.

Tom now "knows" that, by his genius, Paradise (Estates) can be regained. There is no need, therefore, to develop pictures of better worlds that could be accomplished through basic individual or institutional change. Tom has thus transcended his ancestor, Sir Thomas More, something of an authority or father figure. Sir Thomas had only been able to sketch a possible community, in *Utopia* (1516); ultimately he refused to resolve differences between the two cities by deferring to the city of man and so he suffered martyrdom. Tom implies that no such divided loyalties need plague man's estate. Good American that he is, he will give the old world a wave of his glorious gadget and thus restore it to its prelapsarian perfection. His Eve, Doris, "a lusty Shenandoah Valley girl, Apple Queen of the Apple Blossom Festival" (LR, 13), may be dead, but this Adam will not be bothered by the past: "Fletcher Christian began a new life with three wives on faraway Pitcairn, green as green and unhaunted by old Western ghosts. I shall be happy with my three girls" (LR, 46). Tom is positive that he can be as sovereign as Robinson Crusoe *and* as scientific as Faust *and* as free as Don Juan.

The possibility of his future, indeed the future of humanity, depends upon whether or not his machine (the ultimate in technology) will have the opportunity to cure the race of its maladjustments before mankind destroys itself. Refusing to accept alienation as a condition inherent in human consciousness, Tom believes that it has developed only as a result of the triumph of Descartes' philosophy. Thus, far beyond any of the other Personages of History, Descartes is the one with whom Tom wishes to contend, for only by besting him can he fulfill his Toynbeean destiny, to advance Civilization. Very early in his dictation, Tom reveals that great expectation for himself. Fantasizing the scene in which his colleagues react to the announcement that he has won the Nobel Prize, Tom has the director allude to Descartes when he crowns his series of tributes with "the latter-day Archimedes" (LR, 7).

Tom is sufficiently well read to know that Descartes had craved that accolade for himself. In the second of his *Meditations Concerning First Philosophy* (1641) he expands" on the na-

ture of the human mind: that it is better known than the body."
Beginning by admitting the profoundly unsettling effect of the
First Meditation upon his own mind, Descartes nevertheless
vows to continue his line of reasoning, that is, to strip his mind
of every idea that can be doubted. If he finds that nothing is certain, then that idea at least is certain. Descartes believes that he
cannot offer a new philosophy unless he can base it on a certainty: "To move the earth from its place, Archimedes asked for
nothing but one small spot that should be firm and stable; similarly great things are to be hoped for if I shall find at least one
thing that is certain and unshaken."[3]

By the end of the Second Meditation Descartes had found his
Archimedean lever, the *cogito* : "it must finally be concluded
that this axion, *I am, I exist*, everytime it is pronounced by me, or
mentally conceived, necessarily is true." Thus the bedrock of the
Cartesian system has been reached: I think; I think of God, therefore He exists; I credit Him with my existence and go on about
my business, which is to know the world. The preceding summary is simplistic, but sufficient here. The point is, that everything in the Cartesian system rests on the subject/object relationship, the observer and the observed, *res cogitans* and *res extensa*.
By such a magnificiently simple process, Descartes removed man
(and God) from the world, so that man could study it objectively:
thus was born the scientific method. But in removing man
from his world, Descartes contributed mightily to man's sense of
loneliness for that world.

Tom More speaks vividly of the alienation caused by Cartesian intellectualism as a "dread chasm . . . " (LR, 90). He is convinced that he offers " . . . the first hope of bridging the dread
chasm that has rent the soul of Western man ever since the famous philosopher Descartes ripped body loose from mind and
turned the very soul into a ghost that haunts its own house"
(LR, 191) (He has apparently read Gilbert Ryle's *The Concept of
Mind* [1949], which scornfully rejects Cartesian thought as "the
dogma of the Ghost in the Machine."). But it should be understood that Tom does not share such rejection of the basic validity
of Cartesianism; he believes the premise of the Second Meditation, that the mind can be so well known that it is as body. In
describing some of his early tinkering with his lapsometer, Tom
speaks of "pineal activity" (LR, 36) and identifies the pineal as
"the site of inner selfhood" (LR, 38). He thus accepts Descartes'
teaching that the pineal is the home of the soul. That idea was

long ago rejected by science; but Tom's willingness to base his methodology upon a universally discredited Cartesian doctrine indicates just how deeply committed to Cartesianism he really is.

Having accepted the ultimate implication of Cartesian psychology, that mind (including his own) is matter, Tom had developed his machine, "More's Qualitative Quantitative Ontological Lapsometer" (LR, 30). He had been at first content to measure the matter, but now, through an adaptation (resulting from assistance not credited), his machine can modify the behavior of the matter. This much of a thread of organization has emerged from Tom's dictation. He then proceeds with the scientific format that his introduction had promised; he offers a series of case studies that demonstrate the effectiveness of his machine merely as a diagnostic tool. Imagine the results, runs his implication, now that he can both diagnose *and* treat: he will be the universal doctor, more worthy of the title "Angelic Doctor" than even Thomas Aquinas. Small wonder that he can all but ignore a small, contrary voice that occasionally surfaces in his dictation, like a demon in one of the possessed: "Physician, heal thyself . . . " (LR, 4).

II — Don Juan and Faust

It is certainly appropriate that Tom More lapse into a dream just at the time when he is daydreaming of using his lapsometer to undo the Cartesian split. For Descartes had credited the inspiration of his entire system to a dream which he had had on November 10, 1619. That dream has been the subject of frequent analysis. Such an analytical activity has rarely been disinterested, though: Descartes' proponents have always been somewhat embarrassed, his opponents more than a little amused, by the fact that modern rationalism had an irrational birth.

One of the recent foes of Cartesian thought, Jacques Maritain, was so struck by the irony of the matter that he gleefully entitled his attack *The Dream of Descartes* (1944).[4] Maritain is a mischievous opponent: first he deals with the actual dream in apparent sincerity, then he reveals his thesis, that the entire body of Cartesian thought is a dream, a pipe dream, a "Mid-Autumnal Night's Dream conjured up by a mischievous genius in a philosopher's brain . . ." (DD, 29). What Maritain has to say about

Descartes' Dream is most applicable to an investigation of Tom
More.   Indeed, Tom More may have read *The Dream of
Descartes*, so often does he refer to the same ideas, even use the
same terms, to make his attack upon Cartesian intellectualism.
If he did read the book, he apparently failed to see that some of
Maritain's points touch him as deeply as Descartes.   "Physician,
heal thyself . . ."
    Maritain is very much aware of a contrast that many his-
torians have used to draw the tension that developed in seven-
teenth-century France: "The misfortune of our classical age is to
have been as though caught fast in the conflict between two gen-
iuses, one of which was making of man an angel full of clear
ideas—the other a monster of darkness" (DD, 184).   He is obviously alluding to Pascal's often quoted observation that "man is
neither angel nor beast, and the mischief is that he who would
play the angel plays the beast"[5]—in order to place Descartes and
Pascal himself in counterpoint.   No doubt Maritain is aware that
the contrast could be deepened by including certain similarities
in the lives of the two men.   Pascal also had a profound experience on a November night, in 1654—during which he abandoned Cartesianism as he accepted Christianity.   Pascal, too, it
may be inferred, seems to have regarded Archimedes as a model;
his biographer, the Abbé Jean Steinmann, subtitles the first section of Pascal's life, up until his conversion, "the Young Archimedes."   Later, though, in the *Pensées*, Pascal cites Archimedes,
not to underscore the loftiness of his own scientific ambitions,
but to describe the world-moving power of Jesus Christ.[6]
    Maritain does not develop the full contrast that could be
made, though, acknowledging only: "If we had to choose between Descartes and Pascal, it is obviously Pascal's part that we
would take."   The truth is, that Maritain the Thomist must re-
gretfully reject Pascal's philosophy, even though Pascal is the enemy of his enemy: "The fact remains that Pascal, knocking his
saintly and generous heart against the narrow precincts of the
Jansenist system, also failed (as did Descartes in a contrary sense)
to understand nature and reason" (DD, 184).   Maritain thus neg-
lects Pascal's beast, to concentrate upon Descartes' angel.
    Indeed, *angelism* is the recurrent concept that links Mari-
tain's five essays.   Thus it is introduced, to conclude the first,
title essay: "Science as Descartes conceives it is a human science
which would be at the same time divine by revelation, or better
still, would be the very science of God and of the Angels.   If this

is so, it is no doubt by virtue of the idealism and, if I may use the word, of *the angelism* which in general characterizes Cartesian philosophy . . ." (DD, 28). The concluding essay, "The Cartesian Heritage," carefully catches up all the themes that have been introduced. Maritain does not deny the magnificent improvement of the material conditions of life that the Cartesian revolution has brought about. He emphasizes that he is speaking of what he considers the *abuses* of the system—but he is remorseless in their denunciation. There is, first of all, his charge that "every modern philosopher is a Cartesian in the sense that he looks upon himself as starting off in the absolute, and as having the mission of bringing men a new conception of the world" (DD, 167). Such a state of affairs has undoubtedly led to the enormous popularity of gnostic programs, but also to the equally widespread sense of severance, isolation, and relativity, as each gnostic promise contends with every other. Since each gnostic prophet offers man a view of reality in which ideas have more substance than things themselves, man comes more and more to distrust his own senses, to disown his body; he has become ". . . an angel inhabiting a machine . . ." (DD, 179). He puts an absolute value on his ability to know, yet because of the way in which he conceives of thoughts as objects, as idea-pictures, he has given his mind over to determinism. Hence his body (including his mind) has been subjected to ". . . Cartesian physicians, iatromechanists or iatrochemists, [who] treat it as an automaton or retort" (DD, 181). Thus he can be treated only by technique, " that is, by means extraneous to himself" (DD, 182), not by respectful attention to his sovereign wisdom, which he has forfeited. He has lost his sense of having a place in the world, is told that his only choice is to adjust himself to its terms. "What remains of man? A consumer crowned by science" (DD, 182).

When Maritain sketches the Cartesian philosopher-physician, he catches a palpable likeness of Tom More. Just before he dozes off, Tom conveys his conviction of having a mission to save the world through iatrotechnology: "I can save you, America! I know something! I know what is wrong! I hit on something, made a breakthrough, came on a discovery! I can save the terrible God-blessed Americans from themselves! With my machine! Listen to me. Don't give up. It is not too late. You are still the last hope. There is no one else. Bad as we are, there is no one else" (LR, 58). "With my machine!"—thus always the promise of scientific humanism.

Tom's actual dream (LR, 61-352), then, comprising the body of the novel, is Voegelin's gnostic dream (NSP, 167-173), Maritain's Cartesian dream, that man can, through sheer thought, become an angel. As dreamwork, the dream presents a reality which does not respect such human conventions as cause and effect, chronology, and mutual exclusiveness. It seems to contain both free, unconscious, highly symbolic content and some semiconscious imposition of structure: Tom seems sufficiently aware of being in a dream, for example, to impose a July 1-2-3-4, morning-to-night order to it, the former suggesting his obsession to be a political messiah. It also is both historical and prophetic, both individual and archetypal: Tom reveals not only his own complex, confused, specific motivations, but also the singular and intensified strivings that have been traditionally associated with the figures of Don Juan and Faust.

In an excellent essay, "Two Gnostic Precursors of Scientific Humanism: Faust and Don Juan," Jean Brun has warned the contemporary world against dismissing Faust as a "simple magician" involved with the Devil and Don Juan as merely "a cruel, fickle, and exeptionally cynical tormenter of hearts." It is true that since their origin in the sixteenth century both have been so popular as to become trivialized in some versions of their respective myths. But the core of each myth is the story of a man who believes that salvation can be gained through knowledge. That story will never become trivial or dated. Incorporating the aspiration of Faust and Don Juan in his actions, Tom More illustrates two specific observations by Maritain: as a Don Juan, Tom has become nothing but a "consumer crowned by science"; as a Faust, he has "recourse to strange collusions with magic and occultism" (DD, 102).

III—Robinson Crusoe

Perhaps the chief reason that Tom More has taken up his position at the cloverleaf is that such a move fits into his fantasy of the hero of civilization who withdraws-and-returns. Since that hero frequently goes to the mountain to experience his vision, Tom has gone to the only available elevation. He is not therefore averse to nap, for he must come into contact with the ultimate before he can come off the (man-made) mountain with the message; the dream that he has, then, will be affected by the preoccupations of his waking state. Early in his dream, his friend Max Gottlieb (does Tom see him as a Sinclair Lewis character?) speaks of him: "The prodigal has returned" (LR, 108); whether or not Max really said that does not matter—the point is that Tom, having either remembered or imagined the reference, fancies its application to himself: he has been away, now he is back, victorious.

There is another movement in the dream content, but below Tom's semiconscious awareness. That theme moves from Tom's discovery of the domination of the body, to his belief that he has discovered a means of making man an angel and thus free of the body, to the revelation—of which he is ignorant—that his discovery has only made the mind into body and therefore exaggerated the domination of body. Broken out in hives, bodily orifices swelling shut, he dreams of curing the world: "Physician, heal thyself..."

In the beginning Tom had existed in an Adamic state with his wife and daughter. In those days he would come home from Communion in such happiness for the health and wellbeing of his family that he would dance, in worship of the transcendent in the immanent, like King David before the Ark (LR, 13, 138). It was an Old-Testament world, one in which God was physically present—in an ark or a burning bush (or a ruby-glowing TV tower?)—and accessible. Then daughter Samantha developed a brain tumor. The disease presaged for Tom a fall from Old Testament security into contemporary alienation; twice he attaches a "modern" image to it: "... the neuroblastoma had pushed one eye out and around the nosebridge so that Samantha looked like a two-eye Picasso profile..." (LR, 72, 373).

Walker Percy's friend and fellow Catholic, Flannery O'Connor, herself suffering from a fatal cancer, meditated upon such a mocking cell-blob. In her introduction to *A Memoir of Mary Ann* (1961), she writes of a little girl soon to die: "Her small face was straight and bright on one side. The other side was protuberant, the eye was bandaged, the nose and mouth crowded slightly out of place." Never one to mince words, Flannery O'Connor was frank enough to admit that the defect was "... plainly grotesque." She knew what many of her contemporaries would make of such a metastasis:

> One of the tendencies of our age is to use the suffering of children to
> discredit the goodness of God, and once you have discredited His
> goodness, you are done with Him . . . Ivan Karamazov cannot be-
> lieve, as long as one child is in torment; Camus' hero cannot accept
> the divinity of Christ, because of the massacre of the innocents. In
> this popular pity, we mark our gain in sensibility and our loss in vi-
> sion. If other ages felt less, they saw more, even though they saw
> with the blind, prophetical, unsentimental eyes of acceptance,
> which is to say, of faith. In the absence of faith now, we govern by
> tenderness. It is a tenderness which, long since cut off from the per-
> son of Christ, is wrapped in theory.[9]

When Samantha dies, Tom and Doris cannot rise to Flannery
O'Connor's vision. Doris dismisses God, to follow strange gods
in Mexico. Tom loses his faith, to become wrapped up in theory.

Already a specialist in encephalography, Tom redoubles his
efforts to develop a more sophisticated instrument for brain scan-
ning. Slowly, though, his interest begins to shift, as had Freud's,
from the neurological to the psychological. He pays great attention to the various Brodmann areas, especially those in the pre-
frontal lobe, that make the brain unique to humanity. As he
"proves" in the case studies he cites while awake, he discovers
that many patients are helped just by having their private conditions named.

As Tom becomes involved in theoretical research, in angelism, so he becomes involved with Moira, a secretary in the Love
Clinic. Moira has the presence of a spirit, so typical and vague
are her good looks: she reminds Tom of "the Draw Me girl in
magazine contests" (LR, 134, 259). Neither is she situated in
place or time: she likes motels and interstates, has no notion of
chronology. She regards Tom as a father-figure, even as he sees
her as a child. A believer in rotation, that is, the unexpected encounter that redeems the ordinary, she is a thoroughgoing romantic. She represents that kind of idealizing romanticism that
is so similar to universalizing science. It should be clear that
Tom does not really love her; he loves the tiny aspect of Woman
that she as woman reflects. He is, as Jean Brun labels Don Juan,
"the courtier of the Multiple," "the gnostic of the *pleroma*, or the
ultimate fulfillment."

Although he is embarrassed by the activities at Love, at the
emphasis upon coition as a technique that is separable from any
consciousness, Tom is more like the Love scientists than he will
admit. They want to abstract information about x couplings in
order to construct THE COPULATION, while Tom wishes to ob-

serve x copies of another private part, the consciousness, in order to construct THE COGITO. Moira is equally reluctant to admit the carnality of coition. While she sleeps with Tom and works at Love, she is all the same very idealistic about the act itself and understands it not as an attempt at secular incarnation, but as a third entity: he, she, their love (LR, 136-137). Her use of a scented douche, *Cupid's Quiver*, suggests her intentions to gain the Good Housekeeping Seal of Approval for her vagina—conceiving of it as a container for little love darts is hardly giving flesh its due.

Recently Tom has become involved with a second woman, one who represents his fall into bestialism. Formerly content to study his object at a distance, he now dreams of invading it. As it happens, he finishes his prototype machine and an article for *Brain* on Christmas Eve, so he goes to the Paradise Country Club to celebrate. He thinks that he has developed the technique by which man can once again be incarnated, put into his body, put into his world: he has bridged the dread chasm of Descartes. In effect, too, he has made Christ superfluous, so rather than celebrating the Incarnation, he drinks to his own breakthrough.

Back in Paradise, as it were, Tom meets Lola Rhoades. In contradistinction to Moira, Lola is an abstraction (Woman) experienced concretely (LR, 213), as a five foot nine inch redhead. Her inner being is expressed by her dedication to the 'cello and her habit of hissing pieces from Dvorak (in whose *New World Symphony*, many Americans imagine they hear "Goin' Home"). Since she manipulates her world as much as she wants, indeed imagines it as her instrument to play, she is not in anxiety, is fit as a fiddle and ready for love. Projecting a firm sense of self, she is, to Tom, "a lovely inorganic girl" (LR, 92), "a marble Venus with a warm horned hand" (LR, 95). Phenomenologically Tom reacts to her as sheer matter, pure *en soi*. He frequently senses her viscous properties: the calluses on her fingertips, as they pad-dle his palm (LR, 93, 94, 280) or "strew stars along his flank" (LR, 95, 338) in a Sartrean caress; the strength of her thighs as she grasps him like her 'cello (LR, 95) or as she locks her legs around his waist in loveplay (LR, 340); the way in which she hems him in as they stand talking (LR, 89, 93) and cradles him in her lap (LR, 239) and hugs him (LR, 277).

Lola is the comfort of the maternal/material, of a Southern concreteness that tempts Tom to engage in aesthetic repetition or nostalgia: "Music ransoms us from the past, declares an amnes-

ty, brackets and sets aside the old puzzles" (LR, 339). Emerging
from a conservative background (her father, "Dusty," is, what
else, a right wing proctologist) and inhabiting a phony Tara, Lola
represents a spurious wholeness, a reality utterly devoid of reflection. Tom takes great pleasure in responding to her as just lovely, healthy, red meat; indeed, she refers to herself in the third person, as an object. Lola as an *Erdgeist* tempts Tom as Faust to seek
the *Urgrund*; what Jean Brun says of Faust applies to Tom, now
that he has lost faith in the Trinity, but found divine technique:
"Now Faust is precisely this pilgrim of the continuous, the gnostic who wants to see the God-Nature face to face by crossing over
the abyss that separates man and God." Tom no longer relies
solely upon the Multiple but will penetrate to the Absolute
through the apparent, even if he has to take up with the Devil,
Art Immelman, to do it.

On Christmas Eve Lola plies Tom with Ramos gin fizzes, a
drink combining gin and egg whites. Since he is allergic to albu-
men, Tom suffers an anaphylaxis, as his body becomes lumpy
with wheals that swell his apertures shut. Just as his philosophy
has become too "bodily," so his body is reacting against too much
body, the protein of the egg white. He is barely saved, between
Lola's legs. So, suffering from post-coital depression (all too often the climax of secular incarnation), sick, medicated, stitched
up and hung over, he ends Christmas a failed suicide. Thought
to be unstable, he is placed in the hospital, in which he prays to
Saint Thomas More and God and pleads for Ellen Oglethorp, the
ward nurse, to comfort him.

His mortification does not last, though. Soon he is working
feverishly to outshine the Establishment doctors, those Cartesian
practitioners who have not the imagination to see that he has
demolished Descartes. At the Pit, he seduces the Love scientists,
to prove that they are wrong, that sex is all in the head (even Dr.
Helga Heine is concerned: "*Alles ist Geist*," [LR, 236]), and to
show the Behaviorists that their behavior is not simply a predictable response. But, rather than unifying people, as he is always
promising, Tom, with his busy helper, Art Immelmann, causes
chaos.

Having demonstrated the efficacy (?) of his technique in the
Pit, having confounded his elders in their temple, on July 3, he
undergoes an experience on July 4 that must be highly symbolic
to him. Captured, he is placed in the abandoned church; but by
wit and instrumentation he escapes. So he has escaped from the

old world of the thought-confinements of the Church. He can go forth to the motel, the new Eden in which he, like Fletcher Christian, will enjoy his three women. But once again he is acting too secularly, reacting too strongly to the body; he gets drunk on gin fizzes, egg-addles his mind with thoughts of immanency, before withdrawing to the cloverleaf.

Then, after two stuporous hours, occurs More's Dream—in less than fifteen minutes! Awaking, he realizes that the End did not come—and should realize that he is not going to Return. Down the slope he falls, to find life going on pretty much as usual. He is still drunk (LR, 356), in anaphylaxis, dozing, perhaps hallucinating. He is, in other words, no more capable of inviolable thinking than if he were dreaming. That fact is made evident to him when his busy helper, Art Immelmann, prepares to take Ellen with him to Copenhagen. Tom's unchecked desire to be a Cartesian physician has, so to speak, gotten control of his ability to recognize a single human being and his need for that person. His only hope is to pray, to Saint Thomas More, whom he had thought to supplant. Tom has returned, not as a Toynbeean genius, but as a prodigal who must seek atonement, happily a term coined by the saint himself. Ellen is saved, but so is Tom, as the Devil departs.

The Epilogue, five years later, occurs on Christmas Eve, but this time Tom is celebrating the Incarnation, even making confession. He is also celebrating marriage and family, having renounced Kierkegaard's aesthetic sphere of Don Juan and Faust. As he hoes his collards, he thinks of those men who sowed ideas in him, Maritain, Descartes, Pascal, Kierkegaard. He thinks, too, of Gilbert Ryle, for he speaks of the "poor lonesome ghost locked in its own machinery" (LR, 383); the Cartesian myth, argues Ryle, leads to this conception of consciousness: "The mind is its own place and in his inner life each of us lives the life of a ghostly Robinson Crusoe. People can see, hear and jolt one another's bodies, but they are irremediably blind and deaf to the workings of one another's minds and inoperative upon them."

Tom More now accepts Ryle's contention that the split does not need to exist. The individual can have a world: "Poor as I am, I feel like God's spoiled child. I am Robinson Crusoe set down on the best possible island with a library, a laboratory, a lusty Presbyterian wife, a cozy tree house, an idea, and all the time in the world" (LR, 383). More the *Swiss Family Robinson* than *Robinson Crusoe*. Surely, then, Tom must be thinking of Kierkegaard's definition of "divine father-love, the one unshakable thing in life, the true Archimedian point."[10]

Notes

[1] Cleanth Brooks, in "Walker Percy and Modern Gnosticism," *Southern Review*, n.s. 13 (Autumn 1977), 677-678, was the first critic to discern the resemblance between Eric Voegelin and Walker Percy.

[2] Harvey Cox, *The Secular City* (New York: Macmillan, 1965). Percy reveals his awareness of *The Secular City* in his essay, "Notes for a Novel about the End of the World," a 1967-68 anticipation of *Love in the Ruins*, reprinted in his *The Message in the Bottle* (New York: Farrar, Straus and Giroux, 1975), pp. 101-118.

[3] René Descartes, *The Essential Writings*, trans. John J. Blom (New York: Harper and Row, 1977), p. 196. In "The Sundered Self and the Riven World: *Love in the Ruins*," in *The Art of Walker Percy: Stratagems for Being*, ed. Panthea Reid Broughton (Baton Rouge: Louisiana State University Press, 1979), pp. 115-136, J. Gerald Kennedy provides an excellent discussion of the theme of the "Cartesian split" in *Love in the Ruins*. The present essay intends to join Mr Brooks' identification of Tom More as a gnostic with Mr Kennedy's analysis of him as a Cartesian and thus to reveal more fully Walker Percy's understanding of the gnostic nature of modern scientific humanism.

[4] Jacques Maritain, *The Dream of Descartes* (New York: Philosophical Library, 1944). Hereafter page references are contained in the text as (DD). In his earliest published essay, "Symbol as Need" (1954), reprinted in *The Message in the Bottle*, pp. 288-297, Percy reveals his familiarity with both Maritain's work and Descartes' concept of the *cogito*.

[5] H. F. Stewart, ed. and trans., Pascal's *Pensées* (New York: Pantheon Books, 1950), p. 91.

[6] Jean Steinmann, *Pascal*, trans, Martin Turnell (New York: Harcourt, Brace and World, 1966), p. 282.

[7] Allen Tate also contributed to Percy's development of the theme of angelism. See "Naming and Being," *Personalist*, 41 (Spring 1960), 152. Percy also credits Arthur Koestler's *The Ghost in the Machine* as an influence upon his novel; see Marcus Smith, "Talking about Talking: An Interview with Walker Percy," *New Orleans Review*, 5 (One, 1976), 17.

[8] Jean Brun, "Two Gnostic Precursors of Scientific Humanism: Faust and Don Juan," *International Philosophical Quarterly*, 3 (May 1963), 227-235. Brun acknowledges (232) that "Kierkegaard is the author who has made the most profound comparison between Don Juan and Faust." Percy reveals just how closely he has read *Either/Or* in his interviews; see, for example, Charles T. Bunting, "An Afternoon With Walker Percy," *Notes on Mississippi Writers*, 4 (Fall 1971), 52; and Bradley R. Dewey, "Walker Percy talks about Kierkegaard,"

Journal of Religion, 54 (July 1974), 284.

⁹ Dominican Nuns of Our Lady of Perpetual Help Home, *A Memoir of Mary Ann* (New York: Farrar, Straus and Cudahy, 1961), p. iii.

¹⁰ Paul Sponheim, *Kierkegaard on Christ and Christian Coherence* (New York: Harper and Row, 1968), p. 212, so translates Kierkegaard's journal entry III A 73.

Both Sinclair Lewis' Arrowsmith *(1925) and Walker Percy's* Love in the Ruins *(1971) offer valuable treatments of American medical history for students of medical education.* Arrowsmith, *relying upon the newly-won techniques of realism, offers a satiric view of the physician who is corrupted by the middle-class values of America in the Twenties, but a very positive view of the newly-emerging discipline of medical research.* Love in the Ruins, *relying upon such anti-realistic techniques as burlesque and the absurd, offers a satiric view of the physician who becomes obsessed with a philosophy of medical research that denies the basic humanity of its subject matter.*

Love in the Ruins:
Sequel to *Arrowsmith*

In a recent issue of this journal, Gert H. Brieger has written of Sinclair Lewis' "*Arrowsmith* and the History of Medicine in America."[1] His purpose, he informs us, is " . . . to call attention to the richness of its themes for the teaching of a course on the development of medicine and public health in 20th century America."[2]

Brieger offers a clear and convincing exposition of his purpose. He locates the source of Lewis' interest in the medical profession in the fact that Lewis' father and brother were both physicians. He describes Lewis' reliance upon Dr. Paul de Kruif, the bacteriologist, for the technical information necessary to establish a credible background of research attitudes and activities for *Arrowsmith*. He indicates that Dr. de Kruif was particularly helpful in portraying two scientists whom Lewis deeply admired,

Drs. Frederick G. Novy and Jacques Loeb, whose traits fused into the character of Max Gottlieb, the admirable scientist who so inspires the protagonist, Martin Arrowsmith. These various elements, Brieger implies, provided Lewis with sufficient technical knowledge to trace the development of Arrowsmith from a physician, susceptible to a bombardment of demand for his time and energy, to a researcher, immune by his isolation in the laboratory to any threats against his dedication to the furtherance of knowledge. Arrowsmith's personal quest, then, from Middle West to Chicago to New York and finally to New England, through a variety of medical practices and research institutions, represents, in Brieger's words, " . . . a main reading source for teaching much about the history of 20th century medicine in America."[3]

A particular facet of that history is emphasized in an article which Brieger cites, Charles E. Rosenberg's "Martin Arrowsmith: the Scientist as Hero."[4] Treating the literary properties of the novel somewhat more than Brieger does, Rosenberg examines the significance of the novel as a development in Lewis' career. Famed as a satirist of the anti-intellectual middle class because of such novels as *Main Street* (1920) and *Babbit* (1922), Lewis sought for his next novel a subject that would allow him to provide a more positive theme, to portray a heroic subject, rather than humorous objects. He projected, in Rosenberg's words, " . . . a novel of the American labor movement, its hero to be a Christlike leader modeled after Eugene Debs."[5] But when he met de Kruif, he seems at once to have sensed that science provided a better background than labor for the kind of novel that he had in mind. Successful leadership in labor, as in any mass movement, to be convincingly presented, would inevitably involve his protagonist in historical complexities that would hamper his capacity to initiate bold, novel, unilateral action and in pragmatic compromises that would diminish his ideal proportions. Thus Lewis wisely shifted his background to one in which his protagonist could reasonably be expected to advance toward physical and social solitude and ascend to ever more uncompromising intellectual judgments. To personify the alternative routes that Martin Arrowsmith could take, Lewis depicted, on the one hand, the various physicians and institutional scientists and administrators, who are, in one way or another, corrupted by involvement with the values of the middle class, and, on the other hand, Max Gottlieb, the superbly aloof researcher, whose values, actually just emerging in the United States, Lewis imagined to be antithetical   to   those   of   his   despised   bourgeoisie.

While the sociable physicians and institutional researchers of the 1925 novel have merely merged into the type, *boobus Americanus*, that Mencken named and Lewis is remembered as having satirized, Max Gottlieb has become one of those fictional characters who, because he represents an idea with such purity, vividness, or poignance, transcends the work in which he originated, such as have Faust and Don Juan.   Rosenberg is particularly acute in identifying the quality which has kept Max Gottlieb alive: "Gottlieb is a symbol not only of the transfer of European knowledge and technique to the New World, but an expression of the particular mystique of German academic life.   His worship of research *qua* research and his reverent attitude toward this pursuit of knowledge are very much the product of the German university."[6] Rosenberg specifies the knowledge of which he speaks: "It is knowledge obtained in rigidly controlled experiments,   knowledge   analyzed   and   expressed   in   quantitative terms."[7] Such knowledge depends upon technique: "When Gottlieb feels that Arrowsmith has learned the elementary principles of his trade, he warns that true scientific competence requires a knowledge of higher mathematics and physical chemistry.   'All living things are physico-chemical,' he points out to his desciple; 'how can you expect to make progress if you do not know physical chemistry and how can you know physical chemistry without much mathematics?' "[8] As Rosenberg very clearly demonstrates, Gottlieb derives from Jacques Loeb, whose *Mechanistic Conception of Life* (1912) and other works did so much to popularize in America the idea of every aspect of life—from single cell to psychology—being determined by a force, call it drive, tropism, or whatever.   In Gottlieb, then, we recognize, whether to our horror or to our awe, a prototype of the influential multitude among our contemporary scientists who posit a world without will.

In a sense, Walker Percy's 1971 novel *Love in the Ruins*[9] is a sequel to *Arrowsmith*, for it also has a character named Max Gottlieb.   But since the time of this novel is 1983, he cannot be the same man.   Rather, is he perhaps the grandson of the Gottlieb born in Saxony in 1850, who had a son, Robert Koch, who was born in the United States in 1893?   More American than German, Robert, after serving as an army lieutenant in World War I, graduated from C.C.N.Y. and went into business.   If he is

the father of Percy's Max Gottlieb, he must have moved to Pittsburgh and prospered, for Percy's Max the doctor comes from that
city. At the present, Dr. Gottlieb, certainly no more than forty-
five, is chief resident of a hospital in a Louisiana federal complex
that includes a medical school, a NASA facility, a Behavioral
Institute, a Geriatrics Center, and a Love Clinic. He has not inherited his grandfather's physique; unlike the elder, tall Max,
this Max, " . . . when he rises, like Toulouse-Lautrec, he doesn't
rise much" (p. 108). He has, though, been indoctrinated with his
grandfather's reliance upon knowledge and technique; as he tells
Dr. Thomas More, in evaluating his grand project: "You've got
a gift for correlation, but there's too much subjectivity here and
your series is too short" (p. 114).

It cannot be chance or even unconscious artistry that named
Percy's character Max Gottlieb. Rather it was a very deliberate
strategy by a brilliant middle-aged novelist, who, as an adolescent, read widely in fiction and worshipped science in those
years when, as our first Nobel Laureate in literature, Sinclair
Lewis dominated American reading; who majored in chemistry
at the University of North Carolina; who received his M.D. from
Columbia University; and who became a writer only after an attack by tuberculosis forced him to think seriously, for the first
time, about the value of life, which is another way of saying, *his*
life's values.[10] By establishing an undeniable link to *Arrowsmith*, the novel of the state of science in the Twenties, Percy
was, in other words, brazenly risking comparison with Lewis
and drawing attention to *his* novel of the state of science in the
Eighties, when knowledge and technology make available ever
greater improvements in the physical well-being of
mankind—but also make it increasingly likely that mankind
will destroy itself.[11]

Like the character that Lewis was first contemplating, Percy's
protagonist, Dr. Thomas More, is a Christlike figure. But I has-
ten to add that he has those likenesses not because Percy endowed him with them and thus wishes us to view him as such
an exalted figure, but because he deludes himself into thinking
that he is like Christ. The entire novel is presented from the
point of view of More, the narrator, who alludes to himself as a
Christ. But his repeated hint that he is like Christ is really not accurate, for he is not content to act an imitation of Christ. Rather,
he really thinks of himself as the *new* Christ—as so many mes-
siahs have thought—who will accomplish by a secular means

what he thinks Christ failed to do. Tom is thus that visionary, so common in the last several centuries, who preaches that a transcendent idea, forged out of intellect and implemented by technology, will be sufficient to achieve the millenium.

As the novel opens, the time is 5:00 p.m., July 4, and Tom More, holed up in the southwestern cusp of an interstate intersection, awaits the Apocalypse. Figuratively, he is between states, as well, between the old human present of ramshackled, barely functioning institutions, which is just going out, and the future, which, whatever it will be, cannot be like the present. More thinks that he is the only human being capable of enabling the race to achieve a perfect future, in which the state will wither away because every individual will be totally adjusted and thus have no need of collective security—or regulation. The only other futures that he can envision are either total collectivity imposed by totalitarianism (he has obviously read *1984*) or total destruction, either of which will happen because the Bomb has exploded, after his idea has been spurned, and, indeed, he awakens from a nap to wonder if It has happened. After talking for over two hours, he falls asleep again, to dream. The next three hundred pages represent his dreamwork during a ten-minute nap.

Accustomed as we are to the fictional convention that first-person narrators are reliable, even though in reality we rarely completely trust subjective experience, we may not realize that this man is drunk and probably experiencing distorted senses because of a shot of epinephrine. Caught up in More's vivid description of his surroundings—he is dictating what amounts to a "black box" tape, so that any survivor of the Apocalypse who might happen upon it a hundred years from now might learn how the old world ended—we shudder at the sight. Across the way is a scene of destruction sure to strike terror in any American: A deserted shopping mall, with derelict cars dead on the parking lot; a Catholic church, abandoned after a three-way schism; a HoJo, with cracked orange tiles and not a Rotarian in sight; and a drive-in movie, whose speaker posts have been overwhelmed by poison ivy. This desolation resulted from the riots five years past, when the old system of compromise and sympathy failed to hold and extremism and selfishness became the norm in almost every aspect of American life. Tom thus feels justified in calling this period " . . . these dread latter days . . . " (p. 3), a phrase of which the Old Testament prophets were so fond, when they denounced a fallen-away Israel.

Tom's view is colored, therefore, by the terror of our times, just as Martin Arrowsmith's view was tinged by a rosy hue of faith in an unending science-led progress.   Tom's view is also shadowed by his personal past. He grew up pretty much without thinking about it—as a person will—and he became a physician. He married Doris, a Shenandoah Apple Queen with no blemishes. They moved to Paradise Estates, a guarded subdivision, and, then, on schedule, they produced one child, Samantha. He and Samantha went to the Catholic Church, while Doris, an ex-Episcopalian, believed in every cult and movement she read or heard of and in nothing, really. All in all, both Tom and Doris managed to keep belief and behavior completely separated. They lived, in short, an Edenic life in Paradise Estates, under the ruby glow of the tower of a television station, which transmitted its picture of a national life roughly approximate to their own.

Then their daughter became ill with a neuroblastoma that, before it killed her, " . . . pushed one eye out and around the nose-bridge so that Samantha looked like a two-eyed Picasso profile" (p. 72). Tom's description of his daughter exposes his modern repugnance for any sort of human body that does not conform to our very strict norms for appearance. And, too, surely his physician's consciousness is offended by the sight of runaway cells. Samantha's death is the occasion of her parents' fall from Paradise (Estates); Samantha's death represents that modern proof of the absence of a loving God: the death of an innocent. There is no real bond between Doris and Tom, no incarnation, so that their daughter's death causes their marriage to crumble. Doris, having never believed in the spirit, follows a mystical way to Mexico, but since her brand of mysticism is without any humanity, she soon dematerializes (leaves, it must be said, only a puff of smoke, for Tom inherits her fortune of R. J. Reynolds stock). Tom, having too easily believed in the spirit, becomes entirely occupied with the flesh: he becomes an alcoholic and a lecher, albeit less of the latter when more of the former.

In his work, Tom does something that many a surviving parent does: he devotes himself to attacking the cause of his child's death. Since his specialty is already encephalography, he redoubles his efforts to invent technology for and obtain knowledge from the electro-encephalograph, " . . . with which instrument, as you know, one tapes electrodes to the skull and records brain waves, which in turn may reveal such abnormalities as tumors, strokes, fits, and so on" (p. 28). But feverish work and indul-

gence of his body do not tranquilize his mind; rather, it fractionates, for " . . . seizures of alternating terror and delight with intervening periods of intense longing" (p. 28) force him to commit
himself to the psychiatric wing of his hospital. There he conceives of his great idea: " . . . if the encephalograph works, why
not devise a gadget without wires that will measure the electrical
activity of the separate centers of the brain? Hardly a radical
idea. But here was the problem: given such a machine, given
such readings, could the readings then be correlated with the
manifold woes of the Western world, its terrors and rages and
murderous impulses? And if so, could the latter be treated by
treating the former?" (pp. 28-29). In a way, Tom More is following the path of Freud, who was a neurologist, tracing measurable
nerve impulses, before he became a psychologist, exploring the
invisible world of thought. It should be noted that Tom is unaware that his research is no longer devoted to the condition
that caused Samantha's death, but to the condition caused *by* her
death. That condition, his profound alienation, he then projects
upon the entire world. No wonder that a small voice occasionally intrudes on his narration: "Physician, heal thyself." And
there is, to labor the obvious, something suspect about a great
idea that is hatched by a hatcher " . . . surrounded by thirty-nine
other madmen moaning and whimpering like souls in the inner circle of hell" (p. 28).

More becomes rather professorial when he describes the prototype that he and a colleague, Colley, developed:

> My invention unites two principles familiar to any sophomore
> in high school physics. One is the principle of electrical induction.
> Any electrical activity creates a magnetic field, which in turn will
> induce a current in a wire passed through the field. The other is
> the principle of location by triangulation. Using microcircuitry
> techniques, Colley and I rigged up two tiny electronic 'listeners,'
> something like the parabolic reflectors with which one can hear a
> whisper at two hundred feet. Using our double receiver, we could
> 'hear' the electrical activity of a pinhead-sized area anywhere in
> the brain: in the cortex, the pineal body, the midbrain—anywhere.
> (p. 29)

By Christmas Eve, 1982, Tom has perfected his machine,
which he calls "More's Qualitative Quantitative Ontological
Lapsometer." It will, in other words, precisely record the activity
of the various Brodmann areas of the brain, each the seat of a
specific intellectual/emotional/motor activity, according to local-

ization theorists, and a combined reading of all areas would give
an indication of the ontological whole and the degree of lapse or
aberration from absolute equanimity or "zero" pointer reading
on the screen. At last, a "scientific," absolutely empirical method
of calibrating the mental mechanism! With that precision in
diagnosis, it should be a relatively simple task of trial and error
to develop the proper dosage of electrical/chemical response to
"true up" the old noggin. With understandable pride, Tom has
completed his article for *Brain* that very afternoon.

Then, having worked (and presumably solved the problem of
mind by transforming it into matter), Tom is off to the Country
Club to play (and attempt to solve the problem of his own mind
by alcohol and genital neural impulse). There he picks up Lola
Rhoades, daughter of a prominent right-wing proctologist, to im-
press her with his day's successes: " . . . that this very day I perfected my invention and finished my article, which will undoubtedly be recognized as one of the three great scientific breakthroughs of the Christian era, the others being Newton hitting
on his principles and Einstein on his field theory, perhaps even
the greatest of all because my discovery gives promise of bridging
the dread chasm between body and mind that has sundered the
soul of Western man for five hundred years" (p. 90). Well read
as he is, Tom knows the implication of his bragging. If Newton
was the basis of the worldpicture of classical physics and Einstein
the basis of the worldpicture of modern physics, he will be the
basis of the future worldpicture, which will reflect a physical and
metaphysical reconciliation. No longer will science be distracted
by controversy over duality, for he will reincarnate the observer
into the observed. Thus he will heal the Cartesian split, that
"dread chasm" between observing subject and observed object.
In fact, depending upon the gnostic fondness for "threeness," he
sees himself as the new Christ, returning mankind to lost Eden
and thus obviating the need for the original Christ, who was ineffectual, anyway. No wonder that on this Christmas Eve, Tom
does not commemorate the birth of the One who promised incarnation by His sacrifice—not when he can celebrate his instrument, which assures salvation by technology.

Although he fancies himself a materialist—like so many of
his intellectual contemporaries—the fact is that he is—like so
many of his intellectual contemporaries—haunted by
abstraction. Guilty of Whitehead's "fallacy of misplaced concreteness," he sorts each datum into its type before he ever re-

sponds to it, then responds to it as if it had all the characteristics of its type. Thus, for example, he conceives of the type Woman and then fractionates it into subtypes. Then, when he meets a woman, rather than respond to the mystery of her individuality, he subsumes her under one of his subtypes. Lola is thus "/a/lovely inorganic girl" (p. 92), the personification of his newly materialized world: "A big lovely girl, big and white and cool-warm, a marble Venus with a warm horned hand" (p. 95). Like the *en soi*, of which he imagines she is a part, she begins to envelop him, and he wants to be absorbed. Even so, he cannot get enough flesh fast enough, so, before they fornicate, he tosses off Ramos gin fizzes, as much for their egg whites as for their gin, in order to get those raw proteins. As a result, he suffers anaphylaxis, just as she wraps her legs around him, and he nearly suffocates from engorgement. Saved by epinephrine, he falls into depression and, apparently on Christmas morning, attempts suicide. His post-coital melancholia plainly results from his failure to achieve a lasting incarnation by sexual (secular) means.

While he has consorted with his goddess of the material for only six months, he has kept company with his goddess of the immaterial, Moira Schaffner, for some indefinite period. It is exactly appropriate that Tom does not state exactly how long he has known her, for she is essentially imprecise—everywhere, but nowhere; always, but never now. She is Woman experienced as the Abstract, with an appearance as perfect, vague, and indistinguishable as " . . . the Draw Me girl in magazines contests" (p. 134). She loves HoJo's in exotic places, so that she can experience the universal unaffected by any familiar context. She is a romantic who loves Love, not an individual—when she and Tom fornicate, they do not engage in an action, but rather share a possession. She works as a secretary at the Love Clinic, where countless orgasms, almost all by autostimulation, are observed for technique, so that the Perfect Technique can be published and televised. She is, in fact, a personification of the philosophy that pervades all of the Fedville complex. All the scientists have dissociated themselves from the concept of the whole person, to isolate functions in series, devise norms, and create techniques. His recurrent fascination with Moira suggests Tom's continuing hankering for abstraction.

The only trouble is . . . that once he has perfected his lapsometer as a diagnostic tool for measuring an individual's ontological discomfort, he begins to dream of its adaptation into a means of universal cure. He would like to create Utopia and thus transcend his ancestor, who merely wrote *Utopia*. At this point, there enters his office one Art Immelmann (false heavenman, i.e., false angel, get it?), looking for all the world like a drug salesman. It turns out, though, that he *is* an angel—he says that he represents the great foundations, or did he say, government funding agencies? In no time, Art whips out a contract, which would support Tom's research and development of a therapeutic component. Percy is, as you have guessed, unabashedly using a parody of the Faust legend. But his insight that legend can be applied here is marvelous: the Faust legend originated just at the time when the techniques of the modern scientist were being formulated. The man who wished to penetrate the veil of a nature under the sovereignty of God would indeed be selling his soul to the Devil. The modern era has been called the Faustian age because the seeker after knowledge has continually dared to investigate hitherto tabooed areas of experience. Immelmann, Mephistopheles, realizes that if Tom can eliminate man's alienation (which is inseparable from his consciousness of himself as an imperfection), man would no longer seek God—or strive for anything. It is, after all, dissatisfaction that pushes us forward.

Confident, though, that he will receive support from his own Fedville complex, Tom spurns the Immelman offer. When Tom gets his interview with the director, " . . . a tough old party, a lean leathery emeritus behaviorist . . . " (p. 202) (read B. F. Skinner?), Tom explains that the lapsometer measures the fall, the distance between what man is and what he knows that he could be. The director is traditional enough to recognize that Tom's secular explanation sounds pretty much like the Christian Fall. Since, to the director, all such "religious" talk is "unscientific," therefore nonsense, he thinks that Tom is still mad. Thus he rightly rejects Tom's appeal for support, but for the wrong reasons.

Tom is scheduled to pit his diagnostic skill against a star behaviorist colleague that very afternoon before his assembled colleagues and the medical students. Having thought of himself as the new Christ, he has suffered a ferocious blow to his pride. Thus, when he runs into Immelmann in the bathroom, he is very susceptible to blandishment. In a scene reminiscent of the Devil's offer of the power and the glory to Christ (Luke IV), Immelmann promises Tom the highest human achievement, transcendence as imagined by both romantic and scientist, to ex-

perience the abstract concretely and the concrete abstractly—like
the artist, to intuit Woman (Type) in ultimate sensuousness
(knowledge by quality); and, like the scientist, to extract Woman
(Type) particle from each woman in a series, without commitment (knowledge by quantity); to know by going deep (Faust)
and to know by going wide (Don Juan). Tom signs the contract,
and the Devil screws his universal therapeutic attachment on
Tom's lapsometer.

Now Tom will show those who have scorned him! But
what should have been his triumph is instead a debacle. Immelmann scatters a hundred adapted lapsometers, each with its " . . .
snout-like attachment" (p. 245), among the audience, and each is
promptly used, like a water pistol at an American Legion convention. Since no one knows how to read the level of alienation or
how to make the setting necessary merely to counter it, all sorts
of random and exaggerated alternations take place in the pit,
which collapses into absolute chaos. The attempt to achieve consciousness unaffected by mood, that modern dream, creates the
exact opposite. Tom is led away by his good friend, Max Gottlieb,
who gives him a shot, to alter *his* behavior.

The next day, July 4, is the ultimate in the book—and, Tom
fears, the ultimate in the world. The President is supposed to
speak nearby, and Tom fears that, with his lapsometer confirm-
ing the already extremist position that everyone has already
taken, all hell will break loose. Although he is briefly captured
in an abandoned church, he escapes through an air-conditioning
duct, thus symbolizing for himself his escape from religion into
the secular, creating for himself his own ritual of rebirth.

In his brave new world, he conceives himself to be the only
possible savior. The date is significant: July 4, 1776, marked our
beginning; July 4, 1863, marked our continuation by human sacrifice; and July 4, 1983, will mark our salvation by technology. But
only if Tom leads the entire effort. Rather, his day is one of mis-
adventure; he does seclude his two girl friends and his nurse in
a well-stocked survival position in the abandoned HoJo, but beyond that, he is never in the crucial places; all he succeeds at is
getting good and drunk. And that is when he retreats to the hill-
side cusp of the interstate, like many another millennial visionary before him, to await the End of the World—and goes to
sleep.

When he awakens at 7:15 p.m., the world has not ended; instead, when he drunkenly stumbles down the hill, a golf tourna-

ment is in full swing! Things are pretty much as usual, only more so. The kids have apparently torn up the lapsometers, for people are no saner or meaner than they usually are. But Art Immelmann is still about (it is funny that Immelmann seems to be about only when Tom is drunk and that most other people appear not to notice him), and he threatens to take Tom's dedicated nurse, Ellen Oglethorpe, off to Copenhagen, if not the ultimate secular city, certainly the most charming one. What would a doctor novel be without a dedicated nurse? Tom cannot stop him—until he prays to Saint Thomas More to intervene. In other words, Tom (the scientific view) still needs Saint Thomas More (certainly intellectual, but faithful) for help in protecting Ellen Oglethorpe (post-religious sense of decency) from destruction. With that prayer, Tom collapses, as Art disappears in a puff of smoke. Then Ellen takes over the care of Tom and leads him home.

There is an epilogue, set on Christmas Eve, 1988. Tom is now married to Ellen, and they have two children. They live in some restored slave quarters, not in Paradise Estates. For although the Apocalypse had not occurred, a social revolution did, so that the blacks are now dominant in Louisiana. They took over the medical society and the golf course (which, as everyone knows, have a symbiotic relationship). Then they inherited the white man's alienation, so that Tom has a poor, but growing black practice. He still uses his lapsometer, but without any sort of mood-adapter. He no longer seeks to know absolutes: it is enough at present, to diagnose the vague sense of malaise and give it a name, so that a person may strive for the alleviation of his own, unique condition. The date is enormously significant—not July 4, but December 24. No longer keyed to secular events and delusions of messiahship, Tom goes to Mass and, for the first time in eleven years, Confession. Then he goes home, to barbeque supper, as in olden days; after a few drinks, he is " . . . cutting the fool like David before the ark . . . " (p. 402). And well he should , for the Holy, as in David's case, has been brought home. It is enough to work and wait, take delight in the world around him, help his neighbors, cherish his family, and love his wife, which he promptly proceeds to do, in their new $603.95 Sears Best, king-size.

What is there, then, in *Love in the Ruins* that connects it to the history of medicine in America? If Lewis caught the spirit of American medicine just at the time when research was developing a necessary intellectual rigor, Percy has caught it at a time when it could become weakened by an unnecessary intellectual rigidity. Differences in style must be noted in the two writers. Lewis was famed for daring to use a realism faithful to common-sense experience, thus rebelling against the sentimentality that had dominated his predecessors. Percy goes beyond common-sense realism, to use burlesque, pastiche, the absurd, thus rebelling against the merely visible and therefore stretching the range of vision. If it was in Lewis' time a triumph of the artist to show things as they are, it is in Percy's time even more a triumph to show things as they could become, if left unchecked.

What is the value of *Love in the Ruins* to a course in medical education? I hesitate to say anything here, for a novel is a notoriously bad teacher. But, at the risk of pontificating, I offer four themes that might be drawn from the novel by a group reading and discussion:

(1) That if we lose the faith that enables us to accept a future that is unknowable until we actually meet it, we begin to think of an impending Apocalypse, in which case we either despair or act with abandon, excusing our indulgence by the nearness of the end, or repose our trust in some secular messiah.

(2) That the alienation that an individual experiences may be nothing more than his sense of possibility unfulfilled, not a disease for which drugs are routinely prescribed.

(3) That while the scientific method must be lauded for its success in typing nature, it inevitably abuses the human, who does not conform to type.

(4) That while we must specialize in our technique, we must always understand that technique must be humanized by an overarching generalist philosophy. This goes, as my final word, for an English professor, as for any other specialist in the world.

Notes

[1] Brieger GL. Arrowsmith and the history of medicine in America. Möbius 1982; 3 (July):32-38.

[2] Ibid., 36.

[3] Ibid., 34.

[4] Rosenberg CE. Martin Arrowsmith: The scientist as hero. American Quarterly 1963; 15:447-58.

[5] Ibid., 449.

[6] Ibid., 452.

[7] Ibid., 454.

[8] Ibid., 456.

[9] Percy W. Love in the ruins. New York: Farrar, Straus and Giroux, 1971. (Hereafter, page references are incorporated into the text.)

[10] Coles R. Walker Percy: An American search. Boston: Little, Brown, 1978.

[11] In Notes for a Novel about the End of the World, first published in 1967, Percy refers specifically to Dodsworth, Main Street, and Babbit and extensively to Lewis himself. See: Percy W. The message in the bottle. New York: Farrar, Straus and Giroux, 1975, 101-18.

Walker Percy's Silent Character

In the short time since its publication, *Lancelot* (1977), [1]
Walker Percy's fourth novel, has received wide critical attention.
Virtually all of the response to the novel has concentrated on
the person of Lancelot Andrewes Lamar, the narrator and protagonist of a lurid tale of sex, drugs, and murder. Lance controls the
flow and content of the material, is never checked or refuted, as
is, for example, Quentin Compson, in Faulkner's *Absalom,
Absalom!*. The narration is divided into nine chapters, which
end on moments of mystery or of tableau, action impending or
action completed, the former promoting Lance as the teller, the
latter, as actor. Lance thus seems to dominate the world experienced and the world observed, the subjective and the objective
spheres of the novel. Although there is another character present throughout Lance's entire narration, that person's voice is
not actually heard until the last two pages of the novel, then
only in the responses "yes" and "no."[2]

But the novel does contain another structure besides the chapter, the sequences of daily meetings between Lance and his visitor. In form the two structures may be contrasted:

PAGES COVERED

Chapter
(Explicit 3-6, 9-37, 41-67, 71-102, 105-131, 135-160, 163-182, 185-246,
Structure) 249-257

Meeting
(Implicit 3-6, 9—84, 84—160, 163—246, 249-257
Structure)

The temporal structure draws attention to the beginning and
ending of each encounter, the length of which is presumably determined by the amount of time or patience that the visitor has
to spare. At those times Lance, with exaggerated hospitality, pays
attention to his visitor's appearance and behavior; at those times
the reader, through a medium trustworthy for the recording—

but not the interpretation—of detail, can observe both the visitor's immediate response to Lance's narration and interpolation and the visitor's delayed response, manifested after a night's interval for reflection. Either way, the reader is reminded that Lance is not speaking in a vacuum, that the ideas he expresses and the order which he gives them and the imagery which he uses to embody them are at least in part determined by his awareness of the specific person who is visiting him.

Thus Lance loses the apparent monopoly on world-creating provided by his incessant talking, for his reference to a second person explodes his world; the reader is, by that reference, reminded of the ordinary world of shared responses to physical phenomena (and the human institutions that arise from such intersubjectivity).[3] So the reader is provided with a contrast to Lance's stream of rhetoric, seductive because lulling; so, too, the reader develops an appreciation for the gaps in the narration —the nights when the visitor contemplates Lance's story—as the reader realizes that they are significant parts of the total fable, in that they are essential to thematic development. The reader therefore contributes to the character growth of the unheard auditor by imagining what his life is like, apart from his time in the cell with Lance. The reader will no doubt err in his efforts to imagine the traits of the visitor as Lance responds to them, but no more so than he might misjudge the character of anyone else with whom he has a relationship. However much he may fail to establish as facts the individual data of the visitor's unrevealed existence, yet he will establish its basic outline. In so doing he raises the shadowy visitor to his full prominence as the one who stands waiting to say the one word that will make any difference in Lance Lamar's life.

November 1, All Saints Day

The first meeting opens with the arrival of one man in the "cell" (p. 3) of another, a very talkative man who soon reveals his name, Lancelot Andrewes Lamar. The visitor is offered the only chair, but indicates that he prefers to stand; in that posture he can look out the window at a cemetery and an ordinary city street. Professing confusion about his circumstances, Lance learns from his visitor, whom he thinks he has known, that he is confined in a "Center for Aberrant Behavior."

Talking on, Lance notes that the two had passed in the hall the previous day; he feels that each had recognized the other and that his visitor had started to speak, but then decided against it (p. 4). The most reasonable conclusion that can be drawn is that the visitor must have thought himself unworthy to speak. Now the visitor is unclear about the reason for his being in the cell; did Lance, through the staff, invite him? The reader can only guess at the visitor's questions or very brief comments by back-forming from Lance's repeating of or response to them. Lance offers his reasons for his invitation—he had noted a "certain kin-ship of spirit" between his visitor and himself, but more impor-tantly he had been impressed with his visitor's desicion not to talk, even though he is apparently a "psychiatrist or a priest or a priest-psychiatrist" (p. 4), despite not wearing a garb that would signify either psychiatrist or priest, but rather "phony casuals" (p. 5). Lance has refused to see all the other staff mem-bers—"psychiatrists, ministers, priests, group therapy, and what-not" (p. 5)—presumably because each, trained to speak in the tru-isms of his profession of hear only that part of a patient's re-sponse which could be subsumed under them, would not permit him to speak about his unique condition. But his visitor, merely by his attentive silence and by his personal past serving as a stim-ulant, will enable Lance, he feels, to recover and order his own past.

Attentive to the facial expressions of his visitor, Lance jumps to a conclusion: "I perceive that you're not a patient but that something is wrong with you. You're more abstracted than usu-al. Are you in love?" (p. 6). Lance may be as guilty of pre-conception as the staff members he has just mentioned; thinking of himself as an occupant of a "nuthouse" (p. 3), he makes the unwarranted assumption that everyone else is a member of another category, *them*: it is entirely possible that his visitor is also a patient. Lance also speculates that his visitor's preoccu-pied air results from his being frustrated or distracted by love. The visitor smiles at Lance's speculation, as if to suggest that there might be truth in the works, though not in the sense that Lance is attaching to them. At that point, the visitor indicates that he must leave.

November 2, All Souls Day

The visitor returns to Lance's cell, again to stand by the window, indicating by his habitual posture an openness to the mixture of the sacred and the profane which is ordinary reality. Presumably the visitor has only recently arrived at the Center for Aberrant Behavior, in New Orleans, else Lance who thinks he has been an occupant for a year, would have seen him much earlier. Lance does confess that he had seen his visitor pass the cemetery the day before yesterday (p. 9). Then this morning, Lance had observed the other man shake his head and move on, when a woman approached him in the cemetery. Lance concludes that the only interpretation of his visitor's action is that his visitor had refused a request to pray for the dead (p. 11). If Lance's conclusion is correct, then his visitor has clearly revealed his spiritual condition: he has lost that love of his fellowman that is manifested by the willingness to pray for another. He seems unworthy to be a representative of the Church Militant, those Christians yet alive, if he will not pray for the Church Expectant, those Christians dead but not yet received into the presence of God. His refusal is especially glaring on All Souls Day, that one day besides Christman Day when a priest is permitted to celebrate as many as three Masses. Yet his refusal to pray for his fellowmen does not suggest a turning away from God; the *Dies Irae* sequence in the Mass for All Souls Day must hover in his mind as he listens to Lance, reminding him of the falsity of his position, if he professes to love God but not his fellowmen.

Lance bases his interpretation of his visitor's action in the graveyard on his new knowledge that his visitor is a priest-physician (p. 10). This new information explains his greeting to his visitor: "I have a confession to make" (p. 9): it is the first of several times during his narration that he mockingly refers to the Catholic practice of confession. He continues to suspect that his visitor has fallen in love (p. 11); now that he knows that his visitor is a priest, he perhaps thinks that the man has taken a lay job in order to support himself if he should leave the priesthood.

Seeming to be in no hurry to get to the point of his invitation, Lance indulges himself in memories of his visitor, whose identity he now admits he remembers. The two of them had been born into similar backgrounds, Lance Lamar at Belle Isle, Harry Percy at Northumberland, estates on the River Road up

from New Orleans. Both families were of English stock, members of the gentry, had looked down on the French Catholics and
the American Snopeses. The two boys had gone to school and
college together, joined the same fraternity, had shared the experience of drunkedness and fornication.

The two boys had indicated their perceptions of one another
by their nicknames. Harry had called Lance "Sir Lancelot," apparently in anticipation of the lofty and admirable behavior he expected Lance to display as he matured. Lance had called Harry by
various familiar names.   "Harry Hotspur" and "Northumberland" reflected allusions to Harry's family name and a pugnacity,
charming because ineffectual.   In allusion to the same popular
source of information about Henry Hotspur, Shakespeare's
Henry IV,   Lance had also called him "Prince Hal," in view of
the fact that he seemed happy only in whorehouses.   Such nicknames suggest that Lance expected Harry to mature into the
same kind of life of extroverted superiority that he envisioned
for himself.   Still deriving references from the family name,
Lance had called him "Percival" and "Parsifal" (p. 10): no doubt
the Arthurian connotation was to suggest that Harry, like Lance,
was also a native of Camelot.   There is no reason to thind that
Lance had attached to his friend any of the religious doubt associated with the character in some renditions of the Pervical legend.   The boys were separated during high school, but rejoined
in college.

By that tie each boy had declared his individual personality.
Lance remembers himself as a social and athletic success, a satisfactory, but by no means intellectual student.   He remembers
Harry as an introverted intellectual, melancholy and abstracted:
"I remember [. . .] the first time I had seen you since childhood.
You were sitting in the fratercity house alone, drinking and reading Verlaine" (p. 13).   Though impressed with someone who
read Verlaine, Lance is still not sure that Harry's behavior had
not been an "act" (p. 15) then.   He had not sensed that Verlaine,
the sensual man who had become a celebrated convert to Catholicism, might be just the poet who would appeal to Harry.

Lance grants the fact that Harry was moody and implies a reason: "The men in your family tended toward depression and early suicide" (p. 15).   Then, thinking of himself, he adds: "Yet look
who's depressed now."   To which Harry responds in such a way
that Lance observes: "You cock the same sardonic eye at me you
cocked when you looked up from Verlaine."   As well his visitor

should express skepticism at Lance's statement. For Lance gives no evidence that he is suffering from depression, while at the same time he is, characteristically, so without empathy that he cannot see that his visitor might be the one suffering from melancholy. Indeed, given his family history, Harry is there, it is not beyond conjecture, because he attempted or threatened to attempt suicide.

The idea of Harry behaving in such extreme fashion becomes more tenable when Lance recalls another "act" Harry had performed in college. On an excursion boat for a fraternity-sorority party, Harry had jumped overboard, to swim to a desert island (p. 16). It is a desperate act, the attempt to escape alienation by rotation, to escape the ordinary by a radical plunge into the new. It is also, literally, a "leap," the kind of action, as Lance now sees (p. 61), that prefigured Harry's conversion to Catholicism and decision to take holy orders. Anyone so deperately alone that he would "go from unbeliever to priest, leapfrogging on the way some eight hundred million ordinary Catholics" (p. 16) would understandably focus on the sustaining power of love in his preparation for the priesthood. It would be entirely appropriate for him to adopt the religious name of John. Lance, the unbeliever who knows quite a bit about Christian doctrine and patristic tradition, questions whether Harry meant to imitate John the Baptist, "a loner out in the wilderness," or John the Evangelist, "who loved so much" (p. 10), but the development of Harry's character strongly argues that he meant to pattern himself by the example of the Evangelist. Lance knows as much, for he begins to play on the words "good news," the literal meaning of *evangelion*.

In time Lance begins to allude to the reasons for his present condition. It is impossible to determine just how much is known about his previous behavior by Harry, who should now be thought of as John, the name that he chose to indicate his new life, the life that he is not now living up to. Early on the second day Lance cites headlines that purport to explain his confinement: "BELLE ISLE BURNS. BODIES OF FILM STARS CHARRED BEYOND RECOGNITION. SCION OF OLD FAMILY CRAZED BY GRIEF AND RAGE. SUFFERS BURNS TRYING TO SAVE WIFE" (p. 13). At the same time he makes an assumption: "Then you know my story?" But there is no behavior by Father John that reveals that he has any more knowledge of Lance's recent history than does the reader.

That second day, then, Father John learns of Lance's charge
that his wife Margot had committed adultery in 1968, the proof
of which is a daughter who possesses a blood type not determined by his own. Lance baits Father John in his role as doctor
by saying that since fornication is only "cells touching cells" (p.
17), he shoud have had no great concern about his wife's behavior. Father John could, of course, respond by citing either Mosaic
law or Christ's action in the garden. But he refrains, merely continuing to look out the window.

Lance then assesses the state of mind aroused by his discovery.   This subject Father John seem to recognize as being of
enormous consequence, for he encourages Lance to explore it (p.
44). Lance recalls that he was bored (in fact suffering from everydayness), that his "discovery" enabled him to be "interested" and
"curious," to enjoy that passionless thirst for knowledge that has
been identified as so characteristic of our age.[4] Father John apparently recognizes the deadliness of such symptoms, for he admits
a shock at their presence. Lance, evidently pleased with his success at affecting his visitor, starts to inject copious commentary
into his narration. He was interested, he says, in discovering the
truth of Margot's infidelity, to see if it would lead to the revelation of "a *sin*" (p. 52), that unexplainable act which would
prove the existence of God.   For if there is an absolute evil, he
wants to argue, then there must be an absolute good.   Such spec-
ulative attempts deny sin as a human act of disobedience to God
and raise it into a Contending Principle.   Father John ignores
such dualistic notions, so Lance attempts to cover his tracks by
saying that he had only been joking (p. 52).

Lance also begins to derive schemes of universal history from
his own experiences.   These schemes will prophesy the future;
he, as a knower, perceiving the essential movements of the past,
will announce the inevitable unfolding of the time to come. He
argues from his own experience, of course, implicitly justifying
his own past behavior, indeed elevating it to bold prominence by
demonstrating that it was not only inevitable but the prototype
by which the future may be understood. He introduces his "sexual theory of history" (p. 35) to a smiling priest, but the priest's
reaction does not inhibit him from continuing.

Father John therefore actively calls him back to his analysis of
his feelings at the time when he discovered Margot's infidelity
(p. 41). Then he occasionally nods (pp. 42, 55), as a means of encouragement. But apparently concluding that Lance is incapable

of thinking that he might also have been a cause of his wife's behavior, the priest begins to assert the theme of love (p. 55).
Lance bitterly rejects the existence of the kind of love that the
priest intends; rather, he launches again into the many ways that
the drive to carnal satisfaction may be observed; old men molest-
ing children (p. 55), wives, even his own mother, betraying hus-
bands. Perhaps women are so evil by nature, he seems to imply,
that they are fated to tempt men into sexual frenzy. Some such
thought prefaces his description of his seduction by Margot, at
which time he became so infatuated with her sexuality that he
made a religious shrine of her genitalia (p. 81). It does not occur
to him that he ignored the totality of her humanness, in order to
view her simply as an object. Only such "love" is possible now,
he asserts, and to prove it, he tells of the death of Lucy, his first
wife, his spiritual love. On that dying note, the day's narration
ends.

November 3

When Father John arrives in the cell for his third visit, Lance
immediately notes his appearance: "You look awful. You look
like the patient this morning, not me. Why so pale and sad? After all, you're supposed to have the good news, not me" (p. 84).
It may be assumed that the priest has had difficulty sleeping. Possibly he might have changed his mind about prayer and spent
the night in prayer for his friend. Or it could be that his sleeplessness was caused by some source of perturbation unconnected
with his visits to the cell; this source of his discomfort is unlikely, granted, but we cannot ignore it just because we are reading a
novel (for everyone knows that novelists, practicing economy,
never introduce unusable material). Most likely his troubled
night was in response to Lance's story. But Lance had really told
nothing on the previous day that would seem to elicit a severe
reaction. If, therefore, the priest suffered his sleeplessness because of Lance's story, it must be because of what he anticipates
hearing before the story is all told.

If that is the case, why return to the cell? It could be that he returns merely for old times' sake, out of a sense of duty to an old
friend. Or it could be a Christian act. Lance's story has been of
the most trivial nature, a man's suspicion of his wife's unfaith-

fulness, hardly a rare phenomenon in the world's history. Common, all too common, indeed the subject of comedy at times —yet it might have been just such common, paltry behavior that had depressed the priest in Africa. Rather than fighting the great isolated evil deed, he may have been confronted by a mass of low, base activities that seemed simply to be unworthy of a dedicated person's time. Rather than Africa being the locus of a great rotation, then, the possibility of a continuous intense struggle, it had presented only the same profane commonness that had caused his alienation in Louisiana. Thus he had become depressed, perhaps even sick unto death. He had not, perhaps, committed some great active sin himself—he had merely lost faith in the significance of his own role, lost faith in God's purpose in placing him in such an ordinary place, forgetting that he had authority. He would, then, have had an unfortunate experience in "love," as Lance continues to assert, in that he could not love God if he could not love the most trivial of His flock.

Returning to Lance's cell thus would represent a demanding act of will. The priest would have to acknowledge the same paltriness in his childhood friend that he had fled in Africa. The priest must have wrestled the previous night to accept the truth that some of the basic stuff of human existence is—inescapably—everydayness. When, therefore, he returns to the cell, he must be determined to resume his role as comforter.

Lance very slyly points out that if the priest believes, then he should bear the "good news" (p. 84), the gospel of which Christ spoke. But Father John continues to refrain from speaking, merely to ask questions that encourage Lance to work his way through his own experience. Failing to entice Father John out of his strategy, Lance employs the term for his own devices, saying that he has "good news": he is making headway with the girl in the next cell.

Now Lance begins to make the connection between Margot's long-past infidelity and the possibility that she was still unfaithful (p. 89). Again he wants to bait the priest-as-doctor with the proposition that fornication "amounts to no more than molecules encountering molecules and little bursts of electrons along tiny nerves," but his visitor returns to his own single theme, did Lance love his wife? For, if he did, forgiveness, not detection, should have been his sole purpose. Lance, stubbornly, refuses to conceive of "love" except as a physical act, but at least he is provoked to go on with his story.

Throughout that very long day the priest has to recall Lance from his theorizing to his narration, which is a confession, whether or not it is admitted. When Lance digresses into his allegations about his mother's behavior, the priest is particularly saddened and prompts Lance to resume his story (pp. 96-97). Then Father John seems to want to precipitate the crisis, for he soon induces a response from Lance: "Jacoby? I haven't told you about him? The headlines? BELLE ISLE BURNS: DIRECTOR MURDERED AND MUTILATED! EX-GRID STAR HELD FOR QUESTIONING!" (p. 105). The abruptness of the introduction of Jacoby's name into Lance's narration suggests that the priest is either uncommonly astute, better still prescient, for Lance has barely mentioned Jacoby's name, or that the priest does possess some other source of information than Lance himself. If the latter, then the strain of the previous night is all the more understandable, for who would want to visit an old friend who had insanely committed an arson that caused deaths and committed a murder and a mutilation of the corpse? It is, undoubtedly, the mutilation of the corpse, an act which Lance never discusses, which most clearly suggests his insanity.

Lance continues his story of spying on his wife and her associates in the making of a motion picture. But along the way he also attributes the worst possible behavior to anyone whom he happens to mention, especially it that person is female: Margot's seven-year-old daughter Siobhan, whose paternity he has just disclaimed, shows her "little biscuit" (p. 117) as an enticement; his mother had betrayed his father (p. 130). Such allegations cause his auditor to change the expression on his face, so that Lance is provoked to speak directly to him. Arguing that the modern world is so shameful that no distinctions can be made, Lance asserts that nothing makes any difference, certainly not the Christian response of loving everything (p. 131), which—by tolerating everything, Lance would charge—hastens the decline of quality and the predominance of mediocrity. The priest is at the point of arguing with Lance, but then refrains. Lance continues then to search for "bad news," having rejected the "good news" to which he had earlier alluded.

The quest for "bad news" leads him to tell of his efforts to discover an "infinite evil" (p. 140). Having ruled out God, Lance settles upon sex as the supreme immanent good. But if sexual pleasure is the infinite good, then sexual transgression would be the infinite evil (pp. 140-141), so he intends to discover the truth

about Margot's practices behind closed doors. That intention is
fulfilled, as he tells the priest, by his use of hidden television
cameras. The recounting of what he had learned so enrages him
that he disgresses into a fulmination about the paltriness of
these modern times. He could accept the restraints of Christianity, if it were true, he says (p. 154), or he could live with the broadsword traditions of his ancestors (p. 155), violent though they
may have been. But he cannot live with things as they are.

Thus he begins to lay out for his childhood friend his vision
of a "new order" (p. 156), which is his version of a trinitarian sequence of historical periods originated by Joachim of Fiori. The
totality of Joachim's thought is referred to as the "Eternal Evangel," hence Lance's frequent allusion to "good news." Secure in
his "intellectual" *euangelion*, he mocks Father John's faith-
demanding gospel. Father John recognizes all the symptoms of
an insane man caught up in a Gnostic dream,[5] one who is clever-
ly using the Christological concept of "authority" for a most un-
Christian purpose of creating a fascist party. No wonder that
Father John appears shaken by Lance's story and asks in wonderment what has happened to his old friend. He may have known
the results of Lance's behavior earlier, when he had asked about
Jacoby, but it is clear that he had known nothing of the state of
mind that produced them.

November 4

When the priest arrives in the cell, Lance immediately notes
his change of dress: "How come you're wearing your priest uniform today? Are you girding for battle or dressed up like Lee for
the surrender?" (p. 163). Father John simply continues his silence. But his mere continued presence is a clear indication that
he now accepts his duty in the world, however paltry that world
may be. And his dress argues that he will henceforth present
himself as the visible church, as a clear alternative to the profan-
ity in which he finds himself.

Lance resumes his story. What he has told so far has revealed the way in which, having denied the Incarnation, he had
attached sacred significance to the material world. He makes his
psychology quite vivid by his repetition of the performance of
cunnilingus on Margot (p. 217); he was, he indicates, creating an

"ark," locating the divine, taking "communion" (p. 171). Having elevated his worship of sexuality to such a loftiness, having made the sexual a transcendent immanence, in Sartre's terms, he is preparing the priest to understand the ferocity with which he reacted when he discovered that he had been separated from the medium of his transcendence.[6] Thus he explains in great detail how he had entrapped his wife and her guests. Along the way, as before, the priest responds, but refrains to preach; he questions with muted voice (pp. 179, 214), conveys meaning by facial expression (pp. 180, 182), or merely nods (pp. 200, 235): in these ways he attempts to get Lance to question his conviction that only his version of an event which he describes could be the valid one. Similarly the priest continues to call Lance back to the story whenever he lapses into the theorizing that would justify his behavior (p. 224).

On one occasion Father John offers a refutation to Lance's entire "philosophy" of sin, when he quietly asserts that Christ as the fact of redemption saved mankind from its Old Testament past and now saves each man from his own past (p. 224). The priest's motivation for his continued presence is thus clearly spelled out. If Lance is to be saved from his past, he must first confess it. The motto from Dante which introduces the novel strongly supports the interpretation of Lance and Father John that is being offered at this point.

As Lance gets himself more deeply involved in those events which had aroused his fury the previous year, he seems to become increasingly antagonistic toward the priest as representative of the God who allowed such sinfulness to exist. He implies that his old friend had chosen God out of weakness: "From the beginning you and I were different. You were obsessed with God. I was obsessed with—what?" (p. 216). What, he cannot say, or does not realize, is that he, too, has been just as obsessed with God. But, lacking the faith to accept Him, he has instead tried to "prove" Him by discovering the Absolute Evil that makes His existence a logical necessity. He has, in fact, therefore worshipped evil, found hate (p. 235) as the ruling principle of the universe. And since sex is the medium and hatred is the message, then rape is the primary act of life: "The meaning and goal and omega point of evolution is at last clear" (p. 223). Lance seems to be deliberately using phrases that the priest would recognize. In referring to the omega point, Lance mocks not only the Book of Revelation, which is organized around the theme of

Christ as the Alpha-Omega, but also the thinking of Teilhard de
Chardin, the noble Jesuit scientist, who saw a love-energy moti-
vating the processes of evolution toward the Omega point of
Christ as the Center or Pole of Convergence of the universe.

Lance's "meaning," that hatred rules the universe, inspires
his sodomizing of Raine Robinette (p. 236)[7]: he defines his act as
an attempt to gain knowledge of the Devil, but the consummation brings him no closer to absolute reality, the Infinite Evil
which would "prove" the Infinite Good. At the end of his story,
then, he can only exhibit a numbness as he murders Jacoby. The
explosion which follows is a grand comment upon the fragmen-
tation of his sanity. He thinks of himself as Lucifer (p. 246), since
he must literally have been blown out of his house. But his
image is exactly inappropriate, for he describes Lucifer as being
"blown out of Hell" (perhaps he is thinking of the Sartrean hell
of other people)—the priest would certainly note his error: Lucifer was cast from Heaven for vaunting.[8]

November 5

When he arrives in the cell, Father John exhibits a state of
concentration and repressed energy. An ebullient Lance chaffs
him: "Stop pacing up and down. I'm the prisoner, not you.
Why the long face, the frowning preoccupation?" (p. 249). From
theother evidences of the priest's resurgent faith, his donning of
his true apparel and his praying in the cemetery (p. 254), it can be
argued that he is increasingly restive under his self-imposed silence: he wants to speak.

Lance mockingly tells of his "good news" (p. 249): he is to be
released that day. The priest betrays a reaction to Lance's revelation, a reaction which Lance interprets as disapproval. But there
is not reason to think that Father John's reaction is based on a belief that Lance should receive further punishment. Rather the
priest must wonder if his old friend is competent to function by
himself and must lament the fact that he has been unable to
prompt Lance into any sort of reflection, the necessary precondi-
tion for a change of heart.

As Lance begins to dwell upon his plans for going to the Shenandoah Valley to create the new Eden and start his revolutionary movement, the priest continues to ask an occasional ques-

tion to prompt Lance to talk through his experience. Lance confesses nothing, though, except a feeling of numbness and coldness (p. 253); he knows that his old friend is encouraging him to accept the responsibility for his actions, but he specifically refuses: "No, no confession forthcoming, Father, as you well know." What Lance is implying is his knowledge of the act of confession; he has expressed no contrition, and he therefore is not prepared for confession.

Father John tries again by reminding Lance that he had said at the beginning that he wanted to ask a question. Lance says that he has no question because there can be no answer to it, but, still, he will ask: "Why did I discover nothing at the heart of evil?" (p. 253). He has his answer, of course, the nothing in his own heart of evil. But he will not admit to that possibility. The priest knows that there is only one cure for Lance's condition, so once again, with sadness on his face, he asks if Lance will ever love again (p. 254). As always, Lance rejects love in favor of knowledge. The priest must still be pacing, for Lance tells him to come to the window to look down at the world. Amused to think of himself as Satan tempting Christ, Lance betrays the narrowness of his vision by the narrowness of his field of vision. He can see part of a sign: "*Free &*" (p. 250). He can see the existence of free will in man's behavior, but he rejects the other condition accepted by Christians, responsibility, for it requires the acknowledgement of someone to whom one is responsible.

As he gazes out, Lance proudly implies that he has a sharp vision. He notes, for example: "You know, something has changed in you. I have the feeling that while I was talking and changing, you were listening and changing" (p. 254). He is, of course, both wrong and right: he has not changed, but the priest has. Lance has heard that Father John plans "to take a little church in Alabama" (p. 256). Perhaps this is the decision with which Father John had wrestled earlier in the week—if not on that particular night. It represents Father John's willingness once again to go into the mundane world, to watch and wait.

Having just laid out his own grandios plans in apocalyptic style, Lance mocks the apparently inferior eschatological life of a country priest. His scorn seems to be sufficient finally to provoke Father John to speak, for the priest looks directly at his tempter. Lance fancies an openness of communication between them, so he asks questions. And for the first time Father John answers—clear, unequivocal "Yesses" and "Noes." His response underlines the decision that he has made. He agrees with Lance that the modern world is contaminated by hyprocrisy and baseness. He agrees that there must be a change. But he rejects Lance's immanent solution and redidicates himself to his faith, which is rejected by Lance as "just more of the same" (p. 257). Lance says that "all we can agree on is that it will not be their way. Out there," and Father John agrees. Then Lance ways that the change will be toward his way of Father John's way. And Father John agrees. But it should not be understood that by accepting the construction of an either/or, Father John is giving any sort of assent to Lance's "or."

Lance's way is the way of insane fury, a fury of unreflective violence inspired by a perverted vision of the past, a fury that will destroy the future if love does not prevail. For Lance is still mad, as far as Father John is concerned, so that his agreement that Anna (Lance must be taken with the suggestiveness of her name: the Biblical Anna awaited the new time) will go to the Shenandoah Valley to be the Bride of Lance's New Jerusalem has to be an answer given to humor Lance's absurd parody of the last chapter of Revelations. The last "yes," that Father John would like to tell Lance something, is also ironic. The priest has tried to tell Lance something by his silence throughout their five days together and is telling him once again by his decision to minister in Alabama. But he could say no more than that one word—"Come"—that is repeated so frequently in the Apocalypse that Lance is so fond of. He will not reason with Lance, for it is reason misused that keeps Lance from hearing. Father John knows, as Percy himself has said, that " . . . in these times everyone is an apostle of sorts, ringing doorbells and bidding his neighbor to believe this and do that. In such times, when radio and television say nothing else but 'Come!' it may be that the best way to say 'Come!' is to remain silent. Sometimes silence itself is a 'Come!' "[9] Father John has stood there those five days then as a silent invitation, as a character who could be no more eloquent, and Lance, knowing what the silence says, has fought to protect himself by his noise. The next step is up to Lance.

Notes

[1] Walker Percy, *Lancelot* (New York, 1977). Hereafter, page references to the novel will be incorporated into the text in parentheses.

[2] Percy has acknowledged that the conception of a silent character was not easily developed:

> I wrote the book in several versions, and none of them worked. I had two complete characters, long conversations between them. But as soon as the priest opened his mouth it was no damn good. Maybe it's because religious language is shot, just *defunct*, you know.
>
> The trick was to make the priest real without him saying anything, to make his silence operable.

William Delaney, "A Southern Novelist Whose CB Crackles with Kierkegaard," Washington *Star*, March 20, 1977, C4.

While Percy independently devised his strategy of a silent character, it is interesting to note that two of his early influences, "Sören Kierkegaard and Martin Heidegger, each anticipated him in considering silence as a mode of discourse. Kresten Nordentoft, in *Kierkegaard's Psychology*, trans. Bruce H. Kirmmse (Pittsburgh, 1972), p. 248, quotes Kierkegaard's distinction, in *A Literary Review*, between talkativeness and silence: "what is it to *chatter*? It is the abolition of the passionate disjunction between talking and remaining silent. Only the person who is essentially capable of remaining silent is essentially capable of speaking." Heidegger, in *Being and Time*, trans. John Macquarrie and Edward Robinson (New York, 1962), p. 208, is even more detailed about the significance of silence:

> *Keeping silent* is another essential possibility of discourse, and it has the same existential foundation. In talking with on another, the person who keeps silent can "make one understand" (that is, he can develop an understanding), and he can do so more authentically than the person who is never short of words. Speaking at length [Viel- sprechen] about something does not offer the slightest guarantee that thereby understanding is advanced. On the contrary, talking extensively about something, covers it up and brings what is understood to a sham clarity—the unintelligibility of the trivial. But to keep silent does not mean to be dumb. On the contrary, if a man is dumb, he still has a tendency to "speak." Such a person has not proved that he can keep silence; indeed, he entirely lacks the possibility of proving anything of the sort. And the person who is accustomed by Nature to speak little is no better able to show that he is keeping silent or that he is the sort of person who can do so. He who never says anything cannot keep silent at any given mo-

ment. Keeping silent authentically is possible only in genuine discoursing. To be able to deep silent, Dasein must have something to say—that is, it must have at its disposal an authentic and rich disclosedness of itself. In that case one's reticence [Verschwiegenheit] makes something manifest, and does away with "idle talk" ["Gerede"]. As a mode of discoursing, reticence Articulates the intelligibility of Dasein in so primordial a manner that it gives rise to a potentiality-for-hearing which is genuine, and to a Being-with-one-another which is transparent.

3 Percy has been much interested in actions of intersubjectivity. On this subject he follows Buber and Marcel and rejects Sartre. See his "Symbol, Consciousness, and Intersubjectivity," in *The Message in the Bottle* (New York, 1975), pp. 265-276. See, indeed, this entire study of language. Percy is obsessed with language because it is the medium of intersubjectivity; he faults most professional students of linguistics because they refuse to acknowledge that an utterance conveys meaning fom one person's mouth to another person's ear.

4 Gabriel Marcel, another of Percy's early influences, speaks, in *Being and Having* (New York, 1965), pp. 18-21, of the curiosity that marks a total involvement in and acceptance of the mundane world. Heidegger, pp. 213-217, also speaks of that curiosity that is a fundamental characteristic of "everydayness," life as it is experienced by the alienated man. I have addressed Lance's enslavement to Heideggerian "everydayness" in "The Fall of the House of Lamar," in *The Art of Walker Percy*, ed. Panthea Reid Broughton (Baton Rouge, 1979), pp. 219-244.

5 In "Walker Percy and Modern Gnosticism," *Southern Review*, 13 (Autumn 1977), 677-687, Cleanth Brooks, in outlining the importance of the Gnostic temptation in Percy's fiction, identifies Lance as a modernday Gnostic quester. In "The Gnostic Vision in *Lancelot*," *Renascence*, 32 (Autumn 1979), 52-64, I demonstrate the use that Percy makes of Eric Voegelin's concept, in *The New Science of Politics*, of modern Gnosticism, which, he argues, derives from the "Eternal Evangel" of Joachim of Fiori.

6 In his interviews, Percy has credited Sartre's fiction and philosophical works as stimuli to his own fictional techniques. He has a fundamental disagreement with Sartre about conclusions, though; Percy accepts the existence of selfless love, intersubjectivity, and God, while Sartre rejects these concepts. I have described Lance's Sartrean understanding of love, lapse into sadism, and indulgence in the obscene in "The Fall of the House of Lamar."

7 Compare Jean-Paul Sartre, *Being and Nothingness*, trans. Hazel E. Barnes (New York, 1956), p. 402, and *Lancelot*, p. 235.

8 In another sense Lance is exactly the Lucifer-man at this point, according to the words of Gabriel Marcel, *The Mystery of Being* (Chicago, 1960), II, 198: "When, on the other hand, the presence of God is no longer—I shall not say felt, but recognized, then there is nothing which is not questionable, and when man models himself on Lucifer, that questioning degenerates into the negative will which I have already described. Can I hope to show this Lucifer-man his mistake? The truth seems to be that there is room for only one thing here, and that is a conversion which no creature can flatter himself he is capable of bringing about." I accept Marcel's conclusion and employ it to reach my assertion that at the end all Lance can do is stop talking, accept the mystery of grace, and start waiting.

[9]Percy makes this statement in an early essay, "The Message in the Bottle," p. 148, in *The Message in the Bottle*. A reading of this essay is most instructive to a reading of *Lancelot*, for in it Percy distinguishes between knowledge and news (including "good news"), faith as a form of knowledge, the role of the newsbearer as an authority. He concludes with a statement that is, I think, essential to the meaning of *Lancelot*: "And what if the news the newsbearer bears is the very news the castaway had been waiting for, news of where he came from and who he is and what he must do, and what if the newsbearer brought with him the means by which the castaway may do what he must do? When then, the castaway will, by the grace of God, believe him."

The Gnostic Vision in *Lancelot*

In "Walker Percy and Modern Gnosticism," Cleanth Brooks perceives a "basic resemblance" between Walker Percy and Eric Voegelin: "both writers see modern man as impoverished by his distorted and disordered view of reality."[1] Brooks then offers a most informative representation of their key shared idea, that the Gnostic vision has escaped its traditional religious context to invade the modern political world in secular philosophies. Because of the breadth of the subject, Brooks is understandably general in his treatment, although in conclusion he offers brief, extremely valuable identifications of Tom More (*Love in the Ruins*, 1967) and Lance Lamar (*Lancelot*, 1977) as Gnostic questers. He refrains from any direct application of Voegelin's theories to Percy's characters, for he says that, as far as he knows, Percy has never mentioned either Gnosticism or Voegelin.

There is some evidence to justify a somewhat closer association of Percy and Voegelin. In an early (1967) interview Percy does mention Voegelin; speaking of Will Barrett (protagonist of *The Last Gentleman*) to Ashley Brown, Percy says: "His disorientation in time has to do with a theory of Professor Eric Voegelin's about two senses of time. In his book Voegelin contrasts the unhistoric cyclical time of the Greeks and Orientals with the historic linear time of Israel—historical time began when Israel emerged."[2] This distinction occurs in *The New Science of Politics*; Voegelin asserts that Jewish-Christian philosophy envisioned "an end of history in the sense of an intelligible state of perfection. History no longer moved in cycles, as it did with Plato and Aristotle, but acquired direction and destination."[3]

As it happens, Voegelin distinguishes between history as a transcendental fulfilment and as an immanent process in the lengthy essay on Gnosticism that comprises the latter half of *The New Science*. The precise location of the distinction occurs in his discussion of Joachim of Flora, whom he identifies as the thinker who initiated the transformation of religious Gnosticism into secular millennialism. According to Voegelin, St. Augustine had established for Christianity a flexible conception of history that divided into a profane and a sacred track (*NSP*, 118). In the profane sphere, empires rise and fall without ordered cosmic process; in the sacred sphere there is a direction toward eschatological fulfilment. Joachim (1145-1202), an abbot fromm Calabria, attempted to reunite the two streams of history by a method that seems to derive from a mysticism of numbers. Taking the concept of "threeness" from Christian symbolism, he envisioned an actual historical epoch to correspond to Father, Son, Spirit, successively. Each epoch was invested with additional trinitarian symbolism. The net effect of Joachim's speculations was a fostering of a sense of certainty about the order which had structured the past and would structure the future.

Voegelin blames Joachim for creating "the aggregate of symbols which govern the self-interpretation of modern political society to this day" (*NSP*, 111). First, Joachim established the model of history as a sequence of three ages. Second, he envisioned the great man as the mysterious leader who would preside over the emergence of the final age. Third, he personified the prophet who could penetrate the appearance of secular history to detect the order struggling to emerge (frequently the prophet is also the leader). Fourth, he prophesied the emergence of brotherhoods of autonomous persons who, attaining spiritual perfection through their own efforts, not grace, would serve as the vanguard of the great change.

In support of his four generalizations Voegelin adduces the following specific data. 1) Humanistic, communist, and nazi philosophies have all conceived of history as a sequence of three ages. 2) Anticipation of the leader who will dominate the last age, the spiritual age, is common from Dante to the present. 3) The Gnostic prophet has, as secularization has increased, become the political philosopher or theoretician. 4) The dedicated band of those who transcend institutional authority is to be traced through medieval sects, to the Puritan sainthood, into every leadership cell in contemporary political life.

Voegelin explains the undiminished popularity of the Gnostic vision over the centuries as an implicit confession of weakness of faith. "Gnostic speculation overcame the uncertainty of faith by receding from transcendence and endowing man and his intramundane range of action with the meaning of eschatological fulfillment" (*NSP*, 129). Christianity replaced a "world full of

gods" (*NSP*, 121), a world in which man had felt secure because
he had seen those gods as manifestations of a natural, cyclical order. But Christianity offered only one god, who could be approached through faith alone. That dependence on faith has
been more than many could bear: "The life of the soul in openness toward God, the waiting, the periods of aridity and dullness,
guilt and despondency, contrition and repentance, forsakenness
and hope against hope, the silent stirrings of love and grace,
trembling on the verge of a certainty which if gained is loss—the
very lightness of this fabric may prove too heavy a burden for
men who lust for massively possessive experience" (*NSP*, 122).

Such men have turned to a consideration of the world as an
immanence. Early they adopted Christian heresies or secular
philosophies that announced cosmic progression; later they
adopted scientism, which increasingly purported to "know" the
world; now they worship a combination of the two, ideology and
technology. These two anti-transcendental attitudes fuel a modern world view that ignores what Voegelin calls the two great
principles governing existence: "What comes into being will
have an end, and the mystery of this stream of being is
impenetrable" (*NSP*, 167). The experience of life which ignores
these principles resembles nothing so much as a dream (*NSP*,
167-73); thus Gnostic-dominated society, as we experience it, is
characterized by "the weird, ghostly atmosphere of a lunatic asylum" (*NSP*, 170).

A reading of Voegelin's essay greatly enhances our response
to *Lancelot*. The setting of the novel is the "ghostly atmosphere
of a lunatic asylum." The entire novel is presented through the
consciousness of Lance Lamar, who immediately acknowledges
his concrete situation: "In short, I'm in the nuthouse."[4] He had
been confined there the year before, after a mysterious blast had
destroyed his home. Four bodies—his wife, movie actor Troy
Dana, movie actress Raine Robinette, and movie director Janos
Jacoby—had been found in the ruins; Janos Jacoby's throat had
been cut.

Lance's cell is given such a "ghostly atmosphere," such a phenomenological indistinctness, that the reader suspects that Lance
denies its actuality, accords reality only to his whirling thoughts.
Evidence of Lance's intensely subjective nature can be noted as
he conducts a monologue for Father John, a longtime friend, during a five-day sequence of visits. That stream of talk is com-
prised of 1) his recollection of the childhood shared by Father

John and himself, which Lance now interprets as Edenic, 2) his recital of his adult life so far, a period which Father John has spent in Africa, and 3) his revelation of an ideology that justifies his past actions and heralds his future actions.

There is no evidence that Lance was reflective as a youth. What thinking he did was based upon an easy, unexamined acceptance of the Southern Stoic tradition of his family.[5] He was aware that Harry (who becomes Father John) began to suffer from introspection, but he seems to have dismissed Harry's behavior as the result of mere Southern outlandishness or bad heredity. His own life remained active, as he excelled in athletics, academic studies, and campus social life; then he became a lawyer.

In keeping with his heritage, Lance was a romantic-idealist about women: there were ladies and there were whores. One consorted with whores, but one married a lady. In time Lance fell in love with Lucy Cobb, of Georgia, her first name suggesting the gleam that she revealed to her suitor, her eyes, those gateways to the soul, always attracting him. Lance had dreamed of an ideal type, and Lucy was so completely subsumed by it that she seems never to have become a real, autonomous presence to him. Though she bore him two children, he had wanted to continue thinking of her as a virgin (85). Her dying evoked no emotion from him, merely a sense that she gradually became pale and insubstantial (84). Thereafter he remembered her simply as a dancing figure within a bell jar (119), forever fixed in a closed world—his consciousness.

Lucy's death Lance now sees as the culmination of his innocent life, but at the time he found it merely "curious," exhibiting the same response as the alienated spectators of both Marcel and Heidegger. Lance had already fallen into "everydayness," so that he attached more significance to those ideas presented to him through the public media than to his own emotions, which were basically inauthentic. He was becoming an avid TV watcher, especially of newscasts. Like all of Percy's alienated protagonists, he attempts to view the world not directly, but through the medium of a viewing instrument (Binx Bolling sees "horizontally," sees the world as a movie, after abandoning the "vertical" vision offered by the microscope; Will Barrett employs his telescope; Tom More "reads" people with his lapsometer): each feels that only if the "It" is "certified" by a scientific/empirical apparatus does it become real. Small wonder that Lance confesses to Father

John: "Do you know what happened to me during the past twenty years? A gradual, ever so gradual, slipping away of my life into a kind of dream state in which finally I could not be sure that anything was happening at all. Perhaps nothing happened" (57).

A few years after Lucy's death, Lance met Margot Reilly, the daughter of a West Texas oil man. No longer capable of viewing the world idealistically, now reduced to viewing only so much as appeared through his empirical medium, he was immediately captivated by her pert, earthy behavior. Almost her first action must be symbolic to him; she steps out of her hoop skirt, as if shedding appearance. Her hand, conveying firmness, grittiness, grasps his; soon, when they lie down, her leg entwines his body, and one of her hands grasps an eight-inch iron key while the other grasps his penis. Her mouth opens to accept him (80), and he is drawn to kiss her pudendum, an act which he later establishes as his ritual of acknowledging the holy of holies, "the ark" (171). Phenomenologically, Lance feels himself swallowed up by the immanent, develops a sense of being incarnated in the specific to replace his former worship of transcendent forms, which had left him alienated when it disintegrated.

Marrying Margot, he then had a locality, a womb into which he could creep when he needed to feel protected. Although he could not decide upon her social definition, whether she was lady of whore, he did feel a phenomenological certainty: she was a body, never another person. In time he fell back into his televiewing. He was back in the depths of everydayness when he discovered that he did not sire the child that Margot had borne six years before.

In his description of his reaction to the discovery of Margot's infidelity, Lance employs a scientific analogy to liken himself to an astronomer (19). But his unintended imagery suggests that he is thinking of himself as one who uses a microscope. Speaking, apparently of sexual matters, he tells Father John: "It is a mystery which I ponder endlessly: that my life is divided into two parts, Before and After, before and after the moment I discovered that my wife had been rendered ecstatic, beside herself, by a man on top of her" (18-19). A minute later he repeats a reference to her "ecstasy" (21), then draws a conclusion: "Beyond any doubt she was both beside herself and possessed by something, someone? else. Such considerations have led me to the conclusion that, contrary to the usual opinion, sex is not a category at all. It is not merely an item on a list of human needs like food, shelter, air, but is rather a unique ecstasy, ek-stasis, which is a kind of possession" (21).

Lance's repetition of the word *ecstasy*, his reference to its root meaning, and his conclusion that copulation is not merely the manifestation of a physiological drive must be considered. If Margot is suddenly seen to be ecstatic, she is seen as more than just a woman writhing in passion; rather, she *stands out* out from the field of vision, in three dimensions, as if Lance suddenly adjusts the focus of his microscope on a specific object. She has, by her autonomous sexual activity, escaped Lance's "movie screen," escaped his possession; he can no longer hope to incarnate himself in her. Coincidentally he shakes himself from his bemusement to confess that for a year prior to his discovery of Margot's betrayal he had been suffering from impotence (66). Lance admits, then, that sexual activity is not an unconscious fulfillment of an instinct, but a phenomenological striving to control one's external world. As he begins to imagine her apprehended by his microscope or camera, he regains his capacity for erection, referring to his penis as "the worm of interest" (21).

Lance's subsequent actions toward his wife and her movie industry friends cannot therefore be viewed as behavior motivated by conventional sexual jealousy. First, his establishment of an elaborate TV system to spy on his wife must be dictated by his need to view the externals of his world through some "certifying" medium, rather than engage in a human encounter— talk—which would force the admission that he is dealing with another human being. The irony is that much of the data produced by the TV system is of ambiguous or incomplete meaning; Lance's description of the hazy, "ghostly" videotape images simply tells Father John what an incoherent vision of the world Lance had and still has. Second, his sparing of Robert Merlin, the man who first cuckolded him and sired Margot's child, springs from the fact that Merlin is now impotent, no longer capable of occupying the space that Lance must have to be incarnated. Third, the peculiarities of several actions associated with the crimes themselves will be mentioned when Lance's narration of his actions is presented.

Apparently Lance was committed to the "Center for Aberrant Behavior" after questioning by the authorities revealed that he was incompetent to stand trial. He alleges that he does not know how long he has been incarcerated before Father John visits his cell. Probably the actual amount of time is unimportant; it has been of sufficient length that Lance has been able to develop a very intricate ideology with which he interprets his past and predicts his future.   Although his ideology has its source in his dreams (36, 218, 220-21), he has absolutely no question of its validity.   When Father John apparently expresses some skepticism about the trustworthiness of dreams, Lance is quick to counter that dream revelation was used in the Bible.   He does not, however, wish to assert that his dreams are a message from God (221); that assertion would, after all, be an admission that God was simply informing him of what was to come to pass.   Rather Lance bases the integrity of his ideology upon his own "certain vision" (221); the degree to which his vision answers his deepest psychological needs is, of course, exactly the degree to which he is certain of its truthfulness.   Needless to say, his visionary construction, with its known, predictable processes, replaces God as the eidos of history.   He has become the Gnostic prophet.

Lance does not spring his new truth upon his visitor at once. Rather he feigns confusion and amnesia during their first day's meeting.   On the second day, though, he begins to slip his vision of history into his narrative.   He appears somewhat diffident at first, for he terms his vision only a "theory," his "sexual theory of history" (35).   But then he makes the visionary claim: "It applies to both the individual and to mankind."

The theory is a very significant revision of Christian orthodoxy.   In Lance's version of cosmic history, "first there was a Romantic Period when one 'fell in love' " (35).   Then there "follows a sexual period such as we live in now where men and women cohabit as indiscriminately as in a baboon colony—or in a soap opera" (35).   "Next follows catastrophe of some sort" (36); this shattering event sounds like the "Day of Yahweh" foreseen by Old Testament prophets, though Lance does not make the comparison.   This event may have happened while he has been isolated from society, Lance speculates, so imminent is its occurrence.   His speculation is reasonable enough, given his belief; if his truth applies to both individual and mankind, then since the catastrophe has happened to him, it should have happened to mankind.   If it has not happened yet, it surely will, to be just as surely followed by a desert world.   For he has had a dream in which he was "living in an abandoned house in a desert place, a ghost town which looked like one of those outlying Los Angeles neighborhoods Raymond Chandler describes" (36).   Yet immediately in the dream, a woman, "the New Woman," relieves the bleakness, and they start "from scratch" to make a new world.

In Lance's revelation of history several key features of the traditional Christian story are revised or ignored. First of all, he distinguishes between "romantic" and "sexual," thus creating a Gnostic dualism of spiritual and material, of light and dark. Lance gives no reason for the degeneration of the "romantic" into the "sexual" period; probably he thinks that the reason, an inherent contention between cosmic powers of good and evil, is self-evident. At any rate, he has in effect denied the doctrine of man's disobedience and fall from innocence. Rather than having sinned by a willful act, man suffers his falling-away by being created sexual. Beyond this lapse there is no cause for the catastrophe given; presumably it is to be visited upon mankind for its sexual wickedness as brimstone and fire were rained down on the Cities of the Plain. The result of both catastrophes will be the same; the modern world will be like Sodom and Gomorrah: "Most people will die or exist as the living dead. Everything will go back to the desert" (36). For the knowledgeable survivors, the post-catastrophic world will be a new Eden. Lance has dreamed that he will survive, so he has already picked out his new Eve, the girl in the next room, who has been so indoctrinated into the secret of the world that she would be a dependable helpmate. All Father John knows of her at this point is that she was repeatedly raped, forced to commit fellation, and left nearly dead by her attackers; Lance has not, though, revealed the great truth through which these crimes against Anna's person can be seen in a truly remarkable new light.

Having employed his interpretation of his personal experience to prophesy cosmic history, having leaped from the individual to mankind, Lance feels the need to strengthen the connection between the two absolutes by demonstrating how the former will save the latter. The sequence of the three periods may be observed in American history, he asserts: "The First Revolution in 1776 against the stupid British succeeded. The Second Revolution in 1861 against the money-grubbing North failed— as it should have because we got stuck with the Negro thing and it was our fault. The Third Revolution will succeed. What is the Third Revolution? You'll see" (157).

Like another twentieth-century Gnostic prophet, Lance dreams from a cell of the battle, the *Kampf*, that he will undertake to realize the Third Realm, the *Dritte Reich*. Lance is aware, when he speaks of a "new order" (156), that he will awaken Fath-

er John's memories of Nazism; he therefore specifically dis-
claims any similarity with that movement: "There is going to be
a new order of things and I shall be part of it. Don't confuse it
with anything you've heard of before. Certainly not with your
Holy Name Society or Concerned Christians Against Smut. This
has nothing to do with Christ or boycotts. Don't confuse it with
the Nazis. They were stupid." In fact, Lance concludes, his prophecy has "nothing to do with politics" (156). In his contempt
for "politics," Lance is like many a modern visionary, such as
Mao, who theoretically opposes (even his own) civil structures
of compromise and accommodation, those concessions to reality
that threaten the pure implementation of his vision. Like Marx,
Lance foresees a millennial epoch in which the withering away
of the state will have occurred and "politics" will have vanished.

But if Lance does not intend to capture control of existing political structures in order to introduce his "Reformation," how
will it be done? Here the fourth of Voegelin's characteristics of
Gnostic visionary movements, the "brotherhood of autonomous persons" (*NSP*, 112), appears in Lance's vision: "We?
Who are we? You will find out soon enough. It is enough for
you to know how it is going to be, for we are the new Reformation, which is to say we are going to tell you something and
show you something you should have known all along" (177).
"We know who we are and where we stand. There will be leaders and there will be followers. There are now, only neither
knows which is which. There will be men who are strong and
pure of heart, not for Christ's sake but for their own sake" (178).
United by their own shared gnosis, they will spurn the "sacramental mediation of grace" (*NSP*, 112) offered by the church.

Like other revolutionaries they will take to the mountains;
their Sierra Madre will be the Blue Ridge, the last redoubt
dreamed of by Confederate die-hards in '64 and '65: "A young
man is standing in a mountain pass above the Shenandoah Valley. A rifle is slung across his back. He is very tan. Clearly he
has been living in the forest. Though the day is very hot, he
stands perfectly still under a sourwood tree as the sun sets in the
west. He is waiting and watching for something. What? A
sign?" (221). There in the Shenandoah, after the catastrophe, the
Virginian will fight the last great battle: "The Virginian? He
may not realize it yet, but he is the last hope of the Third Revolution. The First Revolution was won at Yorktown. The Second
Revolution was lost at Appomattox. The Third Revolution will

begin there, in the Shenandoah Valley" (220).

But if the vanguard of the revolution is not organized by a traditional political structure or the institution of the church, what body of ideology will motivate it?

> What we are is the last of the West. What we are is the best of you, Percival, and the best of me, Lancelot, and of Lee and Richard and Saladin and Leonidas and Hector and Agamemnon and Richthofen and Charlemagne and Clovis and Martel. Like them we might even accept your Christ but this time you will not emasculate him or us. We'll take the Grail you didn't find but we'll keep the broadsword and the great warrior Archangel of Mont-Saint-Michel and our Christ will be the stern Christ of the Sistine. (178)

So fully is Lance committed to his vision that he already hears his marching men beyond his window (218). At that moment Lance still refrains from identifying himself as the leader of the revolutionary movement, but it seems clear when he uses the plural pronoun "we" that he is thinking of himself as the head of that body. When he starts singing along with his imagined followers (221), he seems finally oblivious of his actual surroundings.

Father John tries to recall Lance to their immediate, common world, but he succeeds only in stimulating Lance to reveal his "great secret" (222). It is this fundamental idea upon which all of his Gnostic vision rests; he tells Father John:

> It is the secret of life, the most astounding and best-kept secret of the ages, yet it is as plain as the nose on your face, there for all to see.
> You were onto it with your doctrine of Original Sin. But you got it exactly backwards. Original Sin is not something man did to God but something God did to man, so monstrous that to this day man cannot understand what happened to him. . . .
> The great secret of the ages is that man has evolved, is born, lives, and dies for one end and one end only: to commit a sexual assault on another human or to submit to such an assault. (222)

God, then, for Lance, is either the Demiurge, that mysterious subordinate divinity which originated evil in defiance of the Absolute Power, or the Absolute Power Himself Who instituted evil as the ruling principle of the universe. For, make no mistake about it:

God's secret design for man is that man's happiness lies for men in men practicing violence upon women and that woman's happiness lies in submitting to it.
      The secret of life is violence and rape, and its gospel is pornography. The question is, Can we bear to discover the secret?
      Do we have to accept the verdict of evolution, that the omega point is sexual aggression, the giving of it or the taking of it? (224)

Throughout the revelation of his fundamental idea, Lance recurs to the phrase *omega point* (223, 224). All during his monologue he has demonstrated a broad knowledge of scripture, theology, and patristic tradition; he is not therefore unconsciously alluding to the concept of omega. He knows that in the Book of Revelations the author quotes God as He proclaims Himself "Alpha and Omega, the beginning and the ending, . . . which is, and which was, and which is to come, the Almighty" (i.8) and then employs continual reference to the Alpha and Omega as an organizing principle of his entire book. Through the use of this refrain, the Revelations author establishes the eschatological theme, an eschatology that could have inspired Voegelin's two great principles governing existence: "What comes into being will have an end, and the mystery of this stream of being is impenetrable" (*NSP*, 167). Lance, then, is deliberately substituting his historical process of the three ages for the unknowable, yet inevitable, divine plan and his discovery of the "great secret" for the mystery that is God. What he wants is to force Father John to accept his vision as an apocalypse, as a redaction of the Revelation of Saint John.

Having related to Father John a history of mankind *and* having provided him with a radically new vision through which to interpret it, Lance is now prepared to speak of the future. What he tells his visitor is of the ultimate violent acts of the previous year. But the imagery that he uss to describe those events is strongly derivative of the Apocalypse of Saint John, so that while Lance is describing a specific past he is also implying the universal future. Thus the actions that he had performed the year before he would no doubt perform in the future on all who are so foolish as to oppose the immutable unfolding of his version of history.

Lance had begun his night of wrathful judgment ("Day of Yahweh"?) by arming himself with a Bowie knife. It is still his fantasy a year later that he had been handed the knife by a mysterious Lady of the Camellias, who, he must have thought, charged him to use his lance to quest for the Grail. Even a year later Lance is still enthralled by that imagined encounter with the Lady; he refers to the knife as a *"sword"* (226), clearly thinking of himself as the defender of the West. Catching himself calling the knife a sword, Lance laughs to imply to Father John that his work choice is simply a meaningless slip of the tongue. But it seems evident that Lance had thought of himself as the kind of divine figure who appears in Revelation (i. 16) with his "sharp twoedged sword."

Stressing the unusual atmospheric conditions and the stark black/white distinctions of that stormy night, Lance begins to narrate his activities. He had first mined his house by releasing natural gas into the air conditioning ducts. Then he had entered the room of Raine Robinette, whom he seems to have accepted only as a type, whore. Her name, Raine, *reins*, suggests her meaning to Lance, who loses little time in venting his hatred and sexual aggression upon her. He sodomizes her, "probing her for her secret" (236), until she acknowledges that she cannot tolerate any more pain and that she is therefore his inferior.

Then he goes to apprehend his wife, whom he has, in effect, treated as the "Son of God" treats the prophetess of Thyatira:

> And I gave her space to repent of her fornication; and she repented not.
>
> Behold, I will cast her into a bed, and them that commit adultery with her into great tribulation, except they repent of their deeds. (Revelation ii. 21-22)

Lance had, that afternoon, given his wife "space" to go to Virginia with him (208), but she had refused. Since he does not restrain her from her plans, he does, in a sense, "cast her into a bed" with Janos Jacoby.

When Lance begins to describe his stealthy entrance into Margot's bedroom, he begins to talk of "the beast" (239). Although the allusion immediately conveyed is of the "two-backed" beast (239) that Iago describes for another jealous husband, the cumulative effect of the several references to "the beast" continues the apocalyptic imagery that Lance imposes on his narration. He must have had a strong sense of divinity, for he describes himself as floating from one place to another, first to the bed, then in his fight with Janos. In due time he cuts his opponent's throat (and he may have emasculated him, for he quotes, in his narration, a newspaper headline: "DIRECTOR MURDERED AND MU-

TILATED! [105].   Such symbolic action would, of course, be consistent with Lance's insane sexual-phenomenological reasoning).   Then, as he talks to Margot, even of a trip that they could take, he strikes a match—and the catastrophe that concludes his second age has happened.

Thus Lance's entire vision is a "prophecy" that actually explains and justifies his own past experiences and excuses his future behavior even before it occurs.   He is cheery that last day when he and Father John meet, then, for he "knows" that he will go to Virginia to begin his new revolutionary movement in the third age.   He even seems somewhat conciliatory with Father John's orthodox Christianity, saying that he will wait to see if Father John's God will do anything about the present state of affairs.   Having completed his "simple scholastic syllogism" (255), Lance has some time for Father John: "So you plan to take a little church in Alabama, Father, preach the gospel, turn bread into flesh, forgive the sins of Buick dealers, administer com-munion to suburban housewives?" (256).   The effect of his lengthy description of the priesthood is to mock it, to challenge the priest's revitalized faith.   Father John, at last, looks directly into the eyes of his childhood friend.   Such a change of behavior encourages Lance to seek conformation for his doctrines, and Father John answers, for the first time, with simple assertions, a "yes" or a "no," rather than asking tentative questions.   Lance thinks that the responses conform to his statements, but in each case the priest could intend a much different meaning.   He knows, though, that any extended discourse would fail, for Lance is completely enveloped in his Gnostic vision.   Father John, as his last "yes" indicates, would like to tell Lance the good news of salvation.   But until Lance lets go of his certainty and really asks a question, there can be no hope for him.

Notes

[1] *Southern Review*, 13 (Autumn 1977), 677.

2 Ashley Brown, "An Interview with Walker Percy," *Shenandoah*, 18 (Spring 1967), 6.

3 Eric Voegelin, *The New Science of Politics* (Chicago: Univ. of Chicago Press, 1952), p. 118. Subsequent references to *NSP* are incorporated into the text of this essay. M. Bloomfield in "Joachim of Flora: A Critical Survey of his Canon," in *Joachim of Fiore in Christian Thought*, ed Delno C. West (New York: Burt Franklin, 1975), I, 77, notes a body of scholarship which asserts that the Grail Legend was originally inspired by Catharist and Joachitic ideas. Consciously or not, in using the Legend and Joachism, Percy has fought the heretics on their own ground.

4 Walker Percy, *Lancelot* (New York: Farrar, Straus & Giroux, 1977), p. 3. Subsequent page references are incorporated into the text of this essay.

5 Elsewhere I speak of Southern Stoicism in *Lancelot*. See "The Fall of the House of Lamar," in *Stratagems for Being*, ed. Panthea Reid Broughton (Baton Rouge: Louisiana State Univ. Press, 1979), pp. 219-44. In "Walker Percy's Silent Character," 33 (Spring 1980), 123-40, *The Mississippi Quarterly* I treat Father John, who by his eloquent silence opposes Lancelot's advocacy of a Joachitic Third Order, called in the Joachitic scholarship the "Eternal Evangel," the newly revealed "news" that supplants the orthodox "good news" of the Bible. Lancelot's many references to "good news" suggests that he deliberately baits John with his heretical belief.

Gnosis and Time in *Lancelot*

The presence of Eric Voegelin's ideas about modern Gnosticism in Walker Percy's fourth novel, *Lancelot*, has already been discovered. Lance Lamar, the protagonist, has been identified as a Gnostic quester whose dreams of millennial perfection plunge him into a nightmare of insanity.[1] Yet, despite the attention paid to the behavior of the man and the gnosis he hopes to realize through his behavior, not enough has been said about Lance's response to time, the trait that most clearly reveals his Gnostic psychology.

Walker Percy has directly referred to the distinction Voegelin draws between two conceptions of time: "the unhistorical cyclical time of the Greeks and Orientals with the historic linear time of Israel. . . . "[2] This statement is a close paraphrase of Voegelin's words: "History no longer moved in cycles, as it did with Plato and Aristotle, but acquired direction and destination."[3] Voegelin's distinction, however, characterizes only classical and Judeo-Christian time. What of Gnostic time, which differs from both? Voegelin offers little help with such a definition, for his chief concern is not to extract the characteristics of Gnosticism from its scriptures, but to trace the Gnostic impulse in the texts of modern Western political theory. Percy, therefore, may have depended solely upon his own intuitions to imagine the kind of time-sense that controls Lance Lamar's mind. But if he did turn to recent Gnostic scholarship, he might have found Henri-Charles Puech's "Gnosis and Time," an analysis that greatly illuminates Percy's protagonist.[4] Puech's introductory statement serves as an excellent intermediate step between Voegelin and Percy:

> the Greek world conceived of time as above all cyclical or circular, returning perpetually upon itself, self-enclosed, under the influence of astronomical movements which command and regulate its course with necessity. For Christianity, on the contrary, time is bound up with the Creation and continuous action of God; it unfolds unilaterally in one direction, beginning at a single source and aiming toward a single goal: it is oriented and represents a progression from the past toward the future; it is one, organic and progressive; consequent-

ly it has a full reality. Then comes Gnosticism. With its need for immediate salvation, it rejects the servitude and repetition of Greek cyclical time as well as the organic continuity of Christian unilinear time; it shatters them both into bits (the figure is no exaggeration). More succinctly, the first representing time by a circle, the second by a straight line, the third by a broken line.[5]

Puech's image of time blown to bits is exactly appropriate to *Lancelot.* After the explosion of Belle Isle, home of an old Louisiana landed family, and the discovery of four bodies in the rubble, Lance Lamar is held for questioning about the murder and mutilation of Janos Jacoby, one of the people whose corpse could be identified. The authorities place Lance in his present confinement, a Center for Aberrant Behavior. There he reveals during the five days of the novel that his mind, like his house, had reached a point of explosion. As he delivers a monologue for a visiting childhood friend, Harry Percy—now Father John, a Catholic priest and psychiatrist—Lance attempts to explain, in a narrative that can only be called a broken line, how he came to be where he is.

During the first day's visit Lance does not refer to the events that led to his confinement. Rather, in good spirits, seemingly content to reestablish ties with his old friend, whose visit he had requested, he appears at home with his "little view" out the window. Indeed, he welcomes limitation: "Have you noticed that the narrower the view the more you can see?"[6] A day or so later, Lance helps to explain his easy adjustment to his cell by revealing that he really does not experience himself in that particular place at that particular time. Both he and the cell, he says, are like the head of a tape recorder: the pure possibility of the future (outside the window) is converted into the banality that is the past (in the hospital corridor) by its mere passage through his consciousness/the cell (the present)—" a small empty space with time running through it and a single tiny opening on the world" (107). Since the Gnostic mind regards life as a prison of unconnected instants, Lance does not find his actual confinement all that extraordinary: he could conceive of no other present. Only after much whirling talk does Lance confess that not quite all has been well: "You see, I've been rather depressed and 'in the dark' and only lately have managed to be happy just living in this room and enjoying the view." (5). In subsequent days Lance reveals that he has divided his history into periods of Darkness and Light.[7]

On the second day Lance tells his old friend: "Seeing you was a kind of catalyst, the occasion of my remembering" (13). He offers two segments of the past that the visit stimulates him to recall: first, "the circumstances under which I discovered that my wife had deceived me, that is, had had carnal relations with another man" (15) and, second, the times he and Father John spent in the pigeonnier on Belle Isle. The two segments are related both as actual events and as symbol-systems. That Lance's discovery of his wife's unfaithfulness occurs in the pigeonnier becomes essential to an understanding of his entire reconstruction.

In *Theaetetus* (196C-199C) Plato likens the mind to a pigeonnier: a person catches a pigeon, places it with his other pigeons, then later attempts to catch it in the cage—only to pick up another by mistake. Thus Plato argues that a person can truly learn something, yet make a false judgment of what he has learned. Since it is Lance's disposition to think of his mind as a building, he might well be thinking of Plato's image as he begins to attach symbolic value to the pigeonnier. The pigeonnier represents not only an actual building in which much action occurs, but also his mind as a container and (at least in part) a product of the past. Thus he reminds his old friend of their shared adolescent retreat: "When you and I went there, it was still being used by the pigeons, six inches deep in pigeon shit upstairs, and the cooing-chuckling going very well with Joyce and Miller read aloud. Downstairs was a junk room, an accumulation of the detritus of summer, crumbling hammocks and badminton sets and busted croquet balls" (17-18). Lance is evidently implying that in his youth, his unawakened state, the past had no vital or appreciated impact on his experience of the present.

Indeed, in a moment, he again implies that the past was insignificant to him at the time:

> Do you remember poking around the junk in the pigeonnier and finding what looked like the original Bowie knife? Maybe it was. My ancestor did know Bowie, even had a part in the notorious Vidalia sand-bar duel in which Bowie actually carved a fellow limb from limb. At any rate, my grandfather made a good story of it when I showed him the knife, claimed it was one of the originals made by Bowie's slave blacksmith (though it wasn't : the original was made from a rasp and still showed the grooves), and displayed it as part of his spiel to the tourists whom he used to lead around Belle Isle at a dollar a head. [18]

The grandfather has falsified the banal to create the mythical, Lance says, implying that his own version of the past is free from subjective distortion. Yet Lance's entire outlook on life, including the interpretation buried in his comments above, is radically colored by the other event he can now remember: his discovery of his wife's unfaithfulness.

Sitting in the study that Margot, the erring wife, has had fashioned out of the junk room of the pigeonnier, Lance discovers quite by accident that he cannot possibly be the father of the daughter Margot bore several years into their marriage. The inescapable conclusion that his wife has been unfaithful prompts Lance to see Margot's act as resulting "from a kind of possession," a "possession by Satan," he implies (21). At once he had begun to disregard the actuality of the erring wife to view her error as evidence of cosmological evil.

A year later, while describing his discovery, Lance cannot stay on the subject and occasionally has to be prompted by Father John to return to it. As a Gnostic, though, Lance is constructing an exactly appropriate stream of narrative.[8] The narrative becomes progressively more insane and violent as Lance relives the crisis he is describing and reaches its climax with the blow-up of Lance's mind. The onslaught of the hurricane and the explosion of the house represent the same event in cosmic, mythological images. Of course, to isolate specific themes and treat them sequentially is to distort the narrative. Yet there seems to be no other way to describe the complexity (frequently caused by the inherent contradiction) of Lance's thought.

On Father John's second visit Lance discusses his discovery of his wife's infidelity. He recalls that he was killing time in the pigeonnier, reading *The Big Sleep* for the fifth or sixth time; he implies that time was killing him by instants: he is so aware of its discontinuous nature that he thrice specifies the exact minute of discovery (18, 19, 27).[9] Lance even used various checks to verify his discovery, although he had known at once that his deduction was irrefutable. Perhaps, though, he emphasizes those checks in relating the tale to explain the emotional response he describes. He specifically denies feeling "the appropriate emotion—shock, shame, humiliation, sorrow, anger, hate, vengefulness" (21) to stress that he felt only the interest an astronomer might feel upon discovering a dot of light in an unexpected position on one of his photographs.[10] Then Lance wanders away from the discovery to weave into his narration, among other things, a scheme of periods of time and the recounting of a dream that, he is convinced, is a prophecy (35-36). His narration becomes so abstract, so mythic, that it seems finally to dissipate.

Lance returns after the break to a discussion of the discovery. Again he stresses that he did not feel the appropriate emotion.[11] This time, however, he does admit to a "curious sense of expectancy, a secret sweetness at the core of dread" (41). The feeling now reminds him, he says, of his childhood discovery of his father's bribe-taking.

When Lance's accounts of the time of discovery are tested for Gnostic traits, several conclusions may be drawn. For one thing, his alleged lack of "appropriate emotion" simply does not follow. On the contrary, his unsolicited denial suggests that he was so affected with those emotions that, even a year later, he cannot admit that they occurred. Later, Lance makes a distinction between Father John and himself that is useful here: "From the beginning you and I were different. You were obsessed with God. I was obsessed with—what? dusky new graygreen money under interwoven argyle socks? Uncle Harry and Lily in the linoleum-cold gas-heat-hot tourist cabin?"(216). These two latter obsessions, the alleged bribe-taking of his father and the alleged adultery of his mother, Lance gradually equates with Margot's infidelity, thus blending all three events into a mythological drama of the ineradicable evil of the universe. "The Gnostic is haunted by an obsessive sense of evil; he never stops asking himself: 'Whence comes evil? Why evil?' "—Puech's generalization aptly applies to Lance at this point.[12] Moreover, if Lance is destined from childhood to quest for evil, then his reaction to the discovery can be explained, though he implies that he still does not know why he had felt pleasure (167). But the discovery must have pleasurably fulfilled an expectation that illustrates his essential way of looking at the world. Lance implies that he felt the same emotion when he discovered the bribe money in his father's sock drawer (42).

On the third day Lance again stresses that his "only 'emotion'" at the discovery "was a sense of suddenly coming alive, that peculiar wakefulness when a telephone rings in the middle of the night" (90). Such a vivid image of sudden wakefulness builds upon his occasional reference to *The Big Sleep* and to a twenty-year dream state in which he had been confined (57). Such an event is obviously sufficient to interrupt time, so that he would think that it divided his life into two parts, "Before and After" (19).

Lance does admit on the third day that he did experience "an all consuming curiosity" (90). Up to this time he has been speaking almost flippantly of "interest" and "curiosity" as characteristics of the age, but here he uses "curiosity" in an altogether different way: it appears to be an intellectual activity, but it obviously has the intensity of involvement appropriate to such emotions as shock, anger, shame. *Curiosity* has become another way of describing his obsessive quest to discover Evil: "I had to know. If Merlin 'knew' my wife, I had to know his knowing her" (90).[13]

By this point in the narrative, Lance has also begun to hint at another revelation associated with his awakening: "I discovered my wife's infidelity and five hours later I discovered my own life. I saw it and myself clearly for the first time" (51). After his 5:01 discovery Lance goes to dinner as usual and is pretty much ignored. In the past he always left the table first to go upstairs to visit his (no, Margot's) daughter and his father-in-law, and he returned to the pigeonnier in time for the ten o'clock news (49)—the routine of a time-dominated man.

But on this night Lance goes into the dark parlor, where he can see through a mirror the diners still at table. What he sees of them is suggestive but not conclusive. What else he sees is starkly clear:

> It was a man at the far end of the room. He was watching me. He did not look familiar. There was something wary and poised about the way he stood, shoulders angled, knees slightly bent as if he were prepared for anything. He was mostly silhouette but white on black like a reversed negative. His arms were long, one hanging lower and lemur-like from dropped shoulder. His head was cocked, turned enough so I could see the curve at the back. There was a sense about him of a vulnerability guarded against, an overcome gawkiness, a conquered frailty. Seeing such a man one thought first: Bigheaded smart-boy type; then thought again: But he's big too. If he hadn't developed his body, worked out, he'd have a frail neck, two tendons, and a hollow between, balancing that big head. He looked like a long-distance runner who has conquered polio. He looked like a smart sissy rich boy who has devoted his life to getting over it.
>   Then I realized it was myself reflected in the dim pier mirror. [63-64]

What he has seen is his *pneuma*, his "ghastly image" (64), a Whiteness lost and isolated in the Darkness of the Second Moment.

He had gone to see the child and the old man, and afterwards had taken a different path back to the pigeonnier, along the levee, there to sense the true measure of time, the incredible lengthiness of cosmic time as proved by the distance of Arcturus and the speed of light (57). At that moment he experiences *epignosis:* "Then for the first time I saw myself and my life just as surely as if I were standing in the dark parlor and watching myself sitting at the table with Margot. Do you know what happened to me during the past twenty years? A gradual, ever so gradual slipping away of my life into a kind of dream state in which finally I could not be sure that anything was happening at all. Perhaps nothing happened" (57).

Lance now knows that he has fallen into a world of time, of carnality, of evil. But he also knows that the angelic, preexistent part of his being can still be reclaimed by action. After returning to the pigeonnier, he studies his wretched appearance and tests his muscles (65). The test he uses could hardly be more mythic/ historic: with his right hand, he drives the Bowie knife into the wood; with his left, he tries to draw it out. He cannot. He knows that it will be a struggle to recapture the prowess possessed by the ancestor who, he comes to fantasize, had used the Bowie in paradisal times.

That night Lance subjects himself to his own baptism and to ritual punishment to reawaken his senses (66). He has made his second great discovery: "A year ago (was it a year?) I made my two great discoveries: one, Margot's infidelity; two, my freedom. I can't tell you why, but the second followed directly upon the first. The moment I knew for a fact that Margot had been fucked by another man, it was as if I had been waked from a twenty-year dream. I was Rip van Winkle rubbing his eyes. In an instant I became sober, alert, watchful. I could act" (107). Lance has experienced the Gnostic *eleutheria*, the freedom from domination by this world and the freedom to do anything in order to achieve and maintain total independence.[14]

By the time he has breakfast with his wife the next morning, Lance has become the completely free man. As he watches Margot eat, showing not the slightest nervousness at the evil he knows she hides, he exhibits the "indifference" and "impeccability" possessed by the Gnostic quester. Lance is no longer bothered by the time his watch announces, though he is so habituated to it that he still marks the moment (87). He seems to think no more of Margot than of the fly that crawls on his arm (88-89);

in his knowledge, because of his knowledge, he is free of sin and free to judge all who are in its possession.

By that afternoon he has decided upon his plan: he will use a family employee, the young black man Elgin, as a spy. The following day, while waiting for Elgin's first report, Lance begins to face the problem most mocking to any Gnostic. He admits to Father John that he was, after all, suffering from an "appropriate emotion": "Do you know what jealously is? Jealousy is an alternative in the very shape of time itself. Time loses its structure. Time stretches out." But the solution is not the retrieval of the object which caused the jealousy: "It was not Margot I was thinking about but time, what to do with time" (122-23).

When Elgin's report places Margot in Jacoby's room, Lance proceeds to the next step. By a stratagem he sees to it that all his wife's movie friends are forced to take rooms in his house and that certain rooms are rigged for secret videotaping. Whereas they have been treating him as an object while they dissembled, both in their movie and in their lives, now he will treat them as objects, cast them in a movie in which they will unwittingly play no role but themselves. Lance is elaborate in his discussion of technical details and therefore all the more shocking the next time his hidden fury bursts out. Reverting to his discovery of freedom, he proclaims: "I cannot tolerate this age. What is more, I won't. That was my discovery: that I didn't have to" (154). Then he describes how his great-great-grandfather used a Bowie knife (154-155)—just as Jim Bowie had in Lance's earlier story. Lance thus apparently sublimates historic individuals and facts into the myth that will supplant the actual past.

Elgin is soon able to bring Lance the desired videotapes. Fond of contrasting the movies of his youth (as innocent as every other part of paradise) with the movies of this age (so sexually explicit as to convince him of the utter depravity of the Darkness), Lance is pleased to nurse his *schadenfreude* by saying that he went to the movies when he viewed the videotapes. The movie screen aptly represents Lance's newly awakened mind. Just as he has discovered himself as a Light image nearly swallowed by the Darkness in the parlor, now he sees creatures of Darkness as dark images, "reddish" (185) as from the fires of Hell. These images and the words they speak are so indistinct as to defy certainty about what really is going on, but Lance is predisposed to see sexual depravity, and so he does.

Since the evil occurs in matter and in time, the only recourse

for the Gnostic is, as Puech says, to shatter them to bits. Lance
has acknowledged already that his ultimate concern was not Margot, but the endurance of time. Now his actions reveal that he
has begun to think of himself as the savior who will appear at
the end of one piece of the broken line that is time.

In an apocalyptic frame of mind, Lance begins to see signs in
the heavens. The hurricane that approaches must be a portent,
as is the exodus of bird life. With the moment of judgment imminent, Lance goes about to save the deserving in a scene reminiscent of the winnowing that occurs in Mathew 24. Citing the
approaching hurricane as the reason for the need to leave, Lance
achieves the removal of his father-in-law, Margot's daughter, Elgin and his parents, his daughter Lucy, and even Merlin, now
impotent and therefore undeserving of Lance's single-minded
vengeance. Then he attempts to persuade Margot to leave with
him, to flee to Virginia, which has come to represent the new
Eden in his myth.

Lance clearly intends to destroy only those he associates with
utter sexual depravity: Raine Robinette, Troy Dana, and Janos
Jacoby (Margot is excused because Lance has considered her to be
possessed). He will destroy them by fire, enacting a plan for blow-
ing his house to bits by using the capped-off natural gas well in
the basement. He could see such an event symbolically, as the
renewal of the explosive energy that once characterized the
house of Lamar.

Margot refuses to leave, and Lance returns to the pigeonnier.
There he experiences the visit of "Our Lady of the Camellias,"
who seems to be Lance's version of the woman who proclaims,
"Mystery, Babylon the Great, Mother of Harlots . . . " (Rev. 17).
Lance says that the appearance was "no mystery" (210), but it
does seem to be, in the apocalyptic sense of *mystery*, an eschatological revelation. For it is the Lady of the Camellias who reveals that Lance's mother Lily, the pure, had been so possessed
of the sexual impulse that she betrayed Lance's father. Lance alleges that the visitor said that his mother was not a dove (that
token of the spirit): "Maybe more like a lovebird. She lived for
love. Literally" (212). So Lance has reached the ultimate, a climax as intense as an orgasm: "now, in the pigeonnier and in the
eye of the storm, the sense at last of coming close to it, the sweet
secret of evil, the dread exhilaration, the sure slight heart-quick-
ening sense of coming onto something, the dear darling heart of
darkness—ah, this was where it was all right" (216). Lance's

Gnostic explanation of the fall of paradise by woman's sexuality is nowhere better expressed. It is the Lady of the Camellias, the whorish voice of the past, Lance says, who directed him to use the sword: *"The sword?* Ha ha. It was the Bowie knife" (226).

Lance then proceeds to execute his plan. Through the house he moves, as undetected as the gas that he has released; all is darkness except for a safety lamp and the lightning. He first slips into Raine's room, to discover Troy "OD'd" and Raine drunk (231). Since it is not yet the fullness of time, Lance really does not know what to do: "Time seemed to pass both slowly and jerkily" (234). Although Raine wants to fornicate, Lance is apparently unaroused; according to his theory of sexuality, "lust" is founded on hatred. Since she looks so childlike, so unconnected to past or future, he has lost the hatred she aroused as a symbol of depravity. But when he catches sight of his daughter's ring on her finger, his hatred is rekindled. Now aroused, he subjects her to anal penetration until she collapses in pain, "like a burned leaf" (236). The image suggests both her crumpled body and the death by fire so often imposed upon sexual transgressors.

Still, Lance must continue to his wife's bedroom. There in the darkness, in a repetition of his awakening in the parlor, he looks at the bed through a mirror, likening the lightning to camera flashes, thus seeing the "movie" with his own eyes. Earlier he had jested about what would happen if the Holy Grail were to be discovered; now he discovers the "Unholy Grail" for which he has quested, Janos' jockey shorts on the rug—"an ancient artifact it was" (238). Othello was mistaken about the meaning of the handkerchief, but Lance is not mistaken about his discovery; he has the ocular proof of "the strangest of all beasts, two-backed and pied, light-skinned dark-skinned, striving against itself, holding discourse with itself in prayers and curses" (239). The discovery certainly represents Puech's "median moment, in which Light is attacked and conquered by Darkness and the two unengendered and atemporal substances are mixed. . . . "[15]

If Lance has seen signs in heaven, he now sees a sign of the beast, the "Babinski sign" (239) provided by Margot as she experiences orgasm, thereby revealing just how possessed she really is. Then he lies down on top of the "beast," which is, like Adam and Eve, "all at once watchful and listening." Margot knows that she has fallen, for her first words are, "Oh my God . . . " (240). In a dream-like sequence, Lance and Janos fight. Still possessed of his "indifference," Lance cuts Janos' throat, experienc-

ing no more emotion at the dying breath moving the hairs on
his hand (243) than he had when the fly had crawled on it (89).
After the explosion, he most likely mutilates the corpse, perhaps
even dismembers it, in the fulfillment of the Bowie-Lamar legend.

Having recaptured his wife (who merges into the image of
his mother, the entire Southern tradition of womanhood, the
Gnostic image of Divine Sophia), Lance is ready to take Margot
from the house. According to Lance, she is still so terrified that
in effect she addresses him as God (244). Then, regaining her self-
possession, Margot tells him that he has never accepted her simply as a woman (245); in his Gnostic fashion, Lance has always
transformed her into a symbol. Lance, however, is so caught up
in his dream of going to Virginia, the new Eden, that he really is
not listening to the words a real person might say. His distance
from his immediate environment (or, conversely, his total involvement in a mythic life) is revealed when he blithely lights
the match that causes the explosion. As he remembers the moment: "Without a sound the room flowered. All was light and
air and color and movement but not a sound. I was moved.
That is to say, for the first time in thirty years I was moved off
the dead center of my life. Ah then, I was thinking as I moved,
there are still great moments. I was wheeling slowly up into the
night like Lucifer blown out of hell, great wings spread against
the starlight" (246). Lance has gotten rid of the Darkness. The
Christian story is that Satan fell from Heaven (Luke 10: 18)—but
for a Gnostic, to be exploded off the earth would finally be a
"great moment," a break in time. The deliverance could only be
into myth—as he sees himself emulating the Original Gnostic
—and into madness.

Miraculously Lance escapes serious injury and seems to have
been burned at all only because he had waded into the burning
rubble to retrieve his Bowie knife (246). As the symbol of the
true way of dealing with evildoers, the "broadsword" (178), or
knife, would be needed in the next age. The "miracle" of being
unharmed convinces him that he has survived the apocalypse.
And—tumbling one delusion on top of another—his success at
escaping into a new age confirms both the "cosmological" and
the "soteriological" myths that have begun to dominate his
thinking.[16]

Consequently, when he talks to Father John, Lance uses not
only circumstantial details but also ideas derived from dreams

and speculation to tell his story. After a while Father John must realize that Lance, as a Gnostic, regards the "knowledge" gained through intuition as having greater significance and validity than knowledge gained only from circumstantial evidence.

Such *gnosis*, as Lance gradually parcels it out, provides a cosmological myth. At the very foundation of the myth, of all truth, lies sexual aggressiveness (222). It must be emphasized that Lance does not regard the sexual act as a communion, as a chosen means of expression between two people who have graduated to the ultimate immanent intimacy. Instead he regards sexual activity as the result of an evolutionary drive (223) that must be seen as either a force independent of God's plan or absolute proof of God's evil nature (176).

As a universal, eternal force, sexual activity thus becomes infinity, both infinite good and infinite evil (129). Its nature depends upon how it is managed. *Gnosis* has revealed to Lance that both the individual and the entire human race evolve in a three-phase sequence. First there is a Romantic Period, in which whores and ladies are carefully distinguished: one is to be acknowledged as carnal, the other as spiritual. In Lance's private myth, his first wife Lucy and his mother Lily personify Light. In the second period "men and women cohabit as indiscriminately as in a baboon colony—or in a soap opera" (35). The operative idea here is "indiscriminately": the absolute distinction between lady and whore is breached. Lucy had been a virgin at marriage, but Lance makes no such claim for Margot. Thus she must be a whore. Nevertheless, Lance thinks that she can be a lady as well: it is possible that Light can be incorporated into Darkness or, better still, that Light can transform Darkness. Twice, therefore, he refers to Margot's genitalia as the place of Communion (81, 171), fooling himself into thinking that she can be both a Colonial Dame and a two-minute screw in a bathroom. After the screwing-in-the-bathroom episode, Lance eats his apple pie while Margot the Dame gives her speech (67): Lance must have thought himself still in Eden, a mindless spasm before the apple. His discovery that she has acted the whore with someone else disabuses him of the notion that Light can be incorporated into Darkness; rather, the concepts are now confused and ambiguous, as in his "movie"—Margot the Light becomes Margot possessed by Darkness. Even Our Lady becomes Our Lady of the Camellias. Similarly, if Margot has dissembled, why should he have any confidence that his mother behaved any differently? He therefore generates the myth about her betrayal of his father with "Uncle Harry." "Next follows catastrophe of some sort" (36)—the apocalypse Lance has achieved. The world will now enter the millennial period, in which awakened men (222, 224), will use it in the only way it can be understood, as a mode of force. The girl Anna, in the next room, traumatized by repeated rape, has—according to Lance—been purified by the violence done to her and therefore understands the nature of the future. His dreams tell him that she will be the woman whom he is to take to the Shenandoah, the Paradise he will regain through his knowledge and total freedom of action.

In Lance's vision of things, an intermediate sequence of phases exists between the individual and the universal. It is a *gnosis* of American (more particularly, Southern) history (157, 220):

(1) The First Revolution, 1776-1781, won
(2) The Second Revolution, 1861-1865, lost
(3) The Third Revolution, 1976-

In other words, Lance sees his own life as identical in structure not only with universal history but with his own nation's history. He is thus impelled to believe that his destiny and that of the nation are inseparable and mutually revealing. Since *gnosis* enabled him to save himself, it will enable him to save the country. Like other visionary leaders before him, Lance thus begins to speak of a "new order" (156), by which he will redeem the country's honor and return it to a prelapsarian, mythic state. That he is beset by a nagging memory of the lost mother and the stranger male who captured her is to be inferred; such a conclusion provides a possible explanation for his psychosexually motivated actions.

Lance's plans to save the country rest upon his soteriological myth. Against the iron law of material depravity caused by sexuality must be placed a tradition of spiritually awakened men who have always chastised an age in an effort to give humanity a chance to start over: the true believer understands the necessity of devastation as purification. Lance acknowledges his "precursors": Lee, Richard the Lion-Hearted, Saladin, Leonidas, Hector, Agamemnon, Richtofen, Charlemagne, Clovis, Martel (178).[17] The confusion of chronology, of the historical and the legendary, suggests just how mythical the scheme is. What Lance really desires is an Arthurian or a Hitlerian Last Great Battle in the West, out of which will emerge a world fit for the elite. Although he has only himself so far, he has of course gained his greatest convert; with utter confidence in himself as prophet and leader, he will gain the necessary cadre through his charisma. Those few will be devoted to him, the only one who can save them. The image of Christ with the sword must be his self-conception at that moment, but in his opposition to Father John, he is of course revealed as the Anti-Christ. With great wrath, thinking no doubt of his pigeonnier, of his dishonored role as son and husband, Lance lashes out at Father John: "Don't talk to me of love until we shovel out the shit" (179).

Thus Lance reveals just how totally detached from time he is and just how caught up in myth he has become. Since he knows the future, he has no serious question to ask Father John, when finally he stops talking. He will admit one puzzling result of his quest: neither during the night at Belle Isle nor since has he felt anything except a numbness, a coldness. There was "nothing at the heart of evil" (253). What he says at this point would be as significant to Father John in his role as psychiatrist as in his role as priest. For though Father John can recognize the barrenness of Lance's soul, he can also understand just how insane Lance is. A multitude of symptoms—confusion of the sequence of time, experience of internal states as external objects, hallucination, projection, personality disintegration and bodily numbness, and an elaborate *Weltuntergang* fantasy—suggests that Lance is trapped in schizophrenia.[18] Finding himself confined in time, Lance has blown it to bits. But that action merely strips him of any comforting sense of placement. Hence he is revealed at the conclusion in an even harsher, inescapable confinement, as a man sick in mind and soul, spurning any intercession.

Notes

[1] See Cleanth Brooks, "Walker Percy and Modern Gnosticism," *Southern Review* 13 (1977): 677-87; Lewis A. Lawson, "The Gnostic Vision in *Lancelot*," *Renascence* 32 (1979): 52-64.

[2] Ashley Brown, "An Interview with Walker Percy," *Shenandoah* 18 (Spring 1967): 6.

[3] *The New Science of Politics* (Chicago, 1952), p. 118.

[4] In *Man and Time*, ed. Joseph Campbell (New York, 1957), pp. 38-84. This volume is the third in a Bollingen Series of translations from the *Eranos Yearbook*. Puech indicates that the first version of his essay was given at the Seventh International Congress for the History of Religions, on 5 September 1950. In his acknowledgements, Voegelin indicates that he studied in Europe in the summer of 1950, but I do not know that he attended the conference.

[5] Puech, pp. 39-40. Hereafter references to "Gnosis and Time" are cited by page.

[6] *Lancelot* (New York, 1977). Subsequent references are cited in the text by page.

[7] For a Gnostic, all responses to the visible world are conditioned by one's certain knowledge of the *Urzeit*, in which the *Ursprung* occurs. In the beginning, Light was free of Darkness; now, Light is corrupted; with the Apocalypse, Light will once again be free. Since all history accords with a plan, every human action contributes either absolute Light or absolute Darkness. The Gnostic must judge absolutely.

[8] Lance's narrative—"half abstract, half concrete, half personal, half impersonal"—presents "fragments of time or spatialized or hypostatized periods of time," a "mythological drama" in which "historical individuals and facts are sublimated into something half way between the real and the symbolic" (p. 82).

[9] In Gnosticism, man's discovery of time is as abrupt as an awakening. Opening his eyes, the Gnostic senses that he is in an "abode of servitude, of exile, of oblivion, ignorance, and sleep" (p. 64). Since he is in such a loathsome, evil situation because he is confined to a body, he despises it (and every other form of matter) and cares not when it or all will be destroyed.

The Gnostic also knows at once that his spirit has fallen from an eternal state; unless he had experienced some previous condition, how could he know that his present condition is so infinitely inferior (p. 73)? That fall occurs when spirit is put into body through the sexual act. Sex, then, is the force through which the Evil Principle achieves its hatred of mankind (p. 65). The Gnostic thus can possess opposing views toward sexual activity: the awakened man knows that the act is essentially evil and that there must be a universal ban against it if the Spirit is to overcome the World; the awakened man is free, though, to engage in its every form, for his knowledge protects him from its seduction (p. 79).

At the moment of awakening, resurrection has taken place. Since the body is corrupt, it certainly will not be resurrected. Only the spirit lives eternally: once it has awakened, it has saved itself. There is no need, then, for a Savior who will at some future time raise the dead (p. 81). In effect, the Gnostic is already past the Apocalypse—the end of the age has come for him and in him (p. 82).

[10] When he becomes aware of his entrapment in time, the Gnostic is assaulted by extreme emotion, "disgust or hatred, terror, anguish and despair, and piercing nostalgia" (p. 68).

Lance's comparison of his reaction to an astronomer's detached interest is not the free association it might seem. His father was a stargazer who, according to Lance, tolerated a wife's infidelity. Since Lance has another reason for having an ambiguous attitude toward his father, he might be implying that he expunged his father's stargazing feebleness.

[11] Fundamentally, the Gnostic makes an absolutely unreasoning reaction. But his repulsion is so strong that he cannot allow himself to admit that he could even have such an experience. Thus he refuses to accept the authenticity of emotions and instead insists that he is completely intellectual and that only knowledge is needed to save him (p. 73). He may thus appear to be intellectual and be convinced that he is only intellectual, while he is in fact wildly emotional. The more he spins out elaborate schemes of "ultimate truths," the more he confesses his emotionalism.

[12] Puech, pp. 63-64.

[13] Since ignorance led to his fall, the Gnostic is obsessed with knowledge, which he understands in two senses: *gnosis* indicates the possession of "an absolute Truth, a total Knowledge, to which all riddles raised by the existence of evil are solved" (p. 73); *epignosis* indicates the possession of oneself: "It is an interior and individual illumination, a revelation of oneself to oneself, a sudden, gratuitous act which is accomplished by a predestined individual and which presupposes no previous condition or preparation in time" (p. 76). One then understands the *Urzeit* and one's role in the *Ursprung*.

[14] Discovering the true nature of time enables a Gnostic to be a "spiritual" or "perfect" man (p. 70) who possesses "*adiaphoria*, 'indifference,' and *apatheia*, 'impeccability'. . . . The Gnostic is free in all things and judges all things" (pp. 77-78).

[15] Puech, pp. 82-83.

[16] With the Gnostic's discovery of himself in time and his certainty that he must and can escape it come two myths. The "cosmological" myth explains the imperfection of the world: either Darkness pre-exists Light (the dualist explanation) or some aspect of Light deteriorated (the emanatist explanation). The "soteriological" myth reassures the Gnostic that though he is now captive in a body in a material world he has the knowledge and the freedom to use any means to save himself (pp. 74-75).

[17] Puech, pp. 79-80.

[18] See Thomas S. Szasz, *Pain and Pleasure: A Study of Bodily Feelings* (New York, 1975), p. 127: "loss of bodily feelings may also signify the ego's experience of its essential dissolution, as does the *Weltuntergang* fantasy. The unrelatedness to the body in these instances does not signify a recent, actual object loss, but simply express *the inner experience of personal dissolution at the*

periphery with a tendency toward retrenchment and survival in progressively narrower areas of ego and object." This observation may explain Lance's fondness of his "little view" at the very beginning of his monologue.

Walker Percy's Physicians and Patients

For thirty years Walker Percy has been writing about a gap in medical education, the same gap that concerns many physicians, nurses, and health services specialists. In five novels and several dozen essays he has explored the relationship between physician and patient, recording the inadequacy that often exists in the present relationship and thereby implying a vision of what it could be. Stated all too simply, he believes that the relationship suffers from compartmentalization: the physician is trained to be a specialist and the patient is expected to be a consumer. The solution, also stated too simply, must be wholeness: physicians who are themselves whole—an integration of body, mind, and soul—must recognize that each patient is likewise a whole, whose suffering in one area must be related to the other areas of his being. Having been both physician and patient, Walker Percy knows whereof he speaks. Yet he is still fairly unknown among the very audience who would most benefit from his ideas. What follows, then, is an introduction to Walker Percy, the physician whose illness restricted him to reading and freed him to write.

Walker Percy graduated from Columbia's College of Physicians and Surgeons in 1941, but within a year his internship was interrupted by tuberculosis. After a convalescence of two years, a relapse, and another convalescence, he was forced to abandon any plans for an active practice. Instead, he turned to writing. In time he began to get essays accepted, in the journals of several very diverse disciplines and systems of value; some of the best known are collected in *The Message in the Bottle* (1975), which treats man as a language-user. He also began to write fiction; he has published a string of five very well-received novels—*The Moviegoer* (1961), *The Last Gentleman* (1966), *Love in the Ruins* (1971), *Lancelot* (1977), and *The Second Coming* (1980).

It might be concluded that Walker Percy's scientific interests and medical inclinations would have lapsed, as he necessarily occupied himself with the concerns of his new profession. Noth-

ing could be further from the truth, though, for his writing
makes it clear that while he has been attentive to both practice
and theory in literature he has also remained alert to developments in medicine, especially psychiatry. Indeed he admits a continuing bent for science and still conceives of himself as a physician,[1] who happens to spend all of his time writing. That self-
image would explain his continued listing in *The American
Medical Directory*.

What has changed in the four decades is Walker Percy's understanding of illness and of medicine. His own experience
taught him that there are several different aspects to illness, not
merely a physical, not merely a physical *and* a mental, but a physical *and* a mental *and* a spiritual (for want of a better word), and
that every illness is a unique combination of those three elements. He began to realize, too, that while each aspect is studied
by numerous specialists, all too often each specialist fails to consider the other aspects, precisely because of the blinding truths of
his own discipline. Walker Percy's writing documents the evolution of his thinking about illness and medicine, about physicians and patients, an apparently simple theme, but one that is
still too often ignored: that any serious illness possesses a mixed
nature, affects different aspects of the human entity, and is best
treated by a response that acknowledges the several possible mal-
functions. What he has been studying is a reality that defies the
research techniques of modern science. The study of so many
cases of angina pectoris reveals a set of general symptoms that is
sufficient for an adequate diagnosis of a single example of the
condition, but the study of so many cases of heartsickness does
not reveal information that enables the individual sufferer to
treat his own illness. On the contrary, it transforms an individual's sickness of heart into a sociological datum. Since Walker
Percy has had to depend upon his own experience to analyze
both the actuality of suffering a mixed illness and the varied responses that a physician, limited by the truths of modern science,
may make to it, he has, in more than one sense, been writing
about himself. Any consideration of his major theme must begin, therefore, with a brief biography.

After the suicide of his father, in 1929, in his Birmingham,
Alabama home, the thirteen-year-old Walker was taken into the
Greenville, Mississippi home of his father's cousin, William
Alexander Percy. When Percy's mother died, two years later, he
was adopted by his "Uncle Will," who, though a bachelor, devot-

ed himself to his paternal role. Although heir to a large estate, "Uncle Will" rejected the uninvolved life he could have afforded and might have preferred, because of his physical frailty and introspective nature; instead, motivated by a code that Percy has called Southern Stoicism,[2] he used his legal training to aid those less favored by fate. Thus he taught his son that human behavior must be inspired by unchanging moral absolutes, especially duty; as Percy grew older, he understood that in order to make his own small contribution he should become either a lawyer or a physician.

Although "Uncle Will" accepted the scientific picture of an evolving phenomenal world, he was basically indifferent to cosmology. He could be the model for that recurrent father figure in Percy's fiction who gazes at the immensity of the starry sky, only to be reminded of man's tininess and loneliness in the universe.[3] In reality "Uncle Will" did not like change; only nature's timeless grandeur—Mount Etna at sunset, for example—claimed his poet's regard. Ironically, though, his romantic reverence for natural beauty taught his son to love science.[4] When, therefore, Walker chose a career, it was medical science, although the law was a stronger family tradition.

As a teenager, Percy was an avid reader of such well-known advocates of the new science as H. G. Wells, Arthur Eddington, and James Jeans, and he also read such fictionalizations of medical science as Sinclair Lewis's Arrowsmith (1925), a tribute to Dr. Paul de Kruif. At the University of North Carolina, from which he graduated in 1937, he majored in chemistry, minored in mathematics, took as much work as he could in physics and biology. The scene in the biology lab in his first novel catches that engrossment he had known as a dedicated student. The scientific outlook, he now says, had become "a religion": "I believed that any problem, anything wrong, could be solved by one or another of the sciences."[5] For Percy thus to describe his attachment to science is no exaggeration; he responded intellectually to the truth of process, but beyond that he responded emotionally to its beauty, "its constant movement . . . in the direction of ordering the endless variety and the seeming haphazardness of ordinary life by discovering underlying principles which as science progresses become ever fewer and more rigorously and exactly formulated. . . . "[6] This movement, called the "vertical search" in The Moviegoer, was, Percy says quite simply, "the first great intellectual discovery of my life."[7]

In the fall of 1937 Percy entered Columbia's medical school, noted at the time, he says, "for its emphasis on the mechanics of disease, . . . a very beautiful and elegant idea, that disease can be explained as the response of the body to an invading organism." Both his intellectual and his aesthetic needs were still being served by the same activity: "It's a beautiful concept—you can categorize a great deal of pathology as response to an invading body, a foreign element. I was going to go into pathology, and I loved the idea of looking at a microscope slide and seeing all those beautifully stained cells, the tubercle bacilli, the lung tissue responding to it, which you could draw a picture of and explain by chemistry, by transactions among the bacteria, the membranes and the lung cells."[8] He was learning to abstract man out of his very body: "Under the microscope, in the test tube, in the colori-meter, one could actually see the beautiful theater of disease and even measure the effect of treatment on the disease process."[9] Percy's behavior was taking a form familiar to those who have read his fiction: there is a recurrent character who thinks that by putting a 'scope—microscope, telescope, lapsometer—between himself and the extended world he can draw it nearer. But the character discovers that, on the contrary, such technology pushes the world away, so that it resembles a movie screen; the "movie-goer" is Percy's brilliant image of the modern man who is alien-ated by the very scientific-empirical, "spectator" method that he has embraced.[10]

Despite his fascination for the objectivity offered by the scien-tific technique, Percy probably was not, even at Columbia, totally fulfilled by his participation in research. For he felt the need to submit himself to Dr. Janet Rioch, a psychoanalyst. Of this deci-sion he has said: "I had seen Harry Stack Sullivan, a friend of Uncle Will's. He suggested Dr. Rioch. He wasn't sure what ailed me, and I wasn't either. I must say that after three years, five days a week, Dr. Rioch and I still weren't sure."[11] Consider-ing that there are several characters in Percy's novels who con-sult psychiatrists, not because they have a specific distress, but be-cause they simply have trouble making their world view cover the world viewed, it seems a fair speculation that Percy's disquiet might have been a symptom of his failure to be completely satis-fied by the "beautiful concept" that he loved so much.

In the fall of 1941 the new Dr. Percy joined eleven others as in-terns in the pathology laboratory of Bellevue Hospital, where autopsies on the derelicts of the city were performed. In January of 1942 "Uncle Will" died, and soon after Dr. Percy was diagnosed as tubercular.   During the few months of his internship, he had conducted more than a hundred autopsies, many of which must have been on bodies in an advanced, if not ultimate, stage of tuberculosis. Laboratory precautions against infection must not have always been thorough, for four of the twelve interns contracted the disease.   Given the frequency of contact and the prevalence of infection among the group, it is not surprising that Dr. Percy was infected. It is of course idle speculation to wonder if there was a psychosomatic connection between the death of the man who, in assuming a father's role, had taught respect for science as the ultimate in rationality and the physical breakdown of a son who knew that he should be faithful to that view, even if science had not been able to keep a relatively young "Uncle Will" alive.   It could be wondered, too, if once again the totality of Walker Percy's being was rebelling against the limitation placed upon it by a strictly scientific point of view—as if the body were taking up the rebellion that the mind had earlier begun. Thirty years after the fact, Dr. Percy thus refers to the results of his illness: "Let's just say I was the happiest doctor who ever got tuberculosis and was able to quit [medicine]";[12] "I contracted a minimal amount of TB and that stopped the internship. . . . It was a great excuse to quit medicine . . . ";[13] "TB liberated me."[14]

But those are statements of a man making an interpretation of an event thirty years after the fact, an event, moreover, which has had a very successful outcome. At the time Dr. Percy may not have been so quick to emphasize the beneficial aspect of the crisis that he was undergoing. He was, after all, in the clutches of an illness that might leave him an invalid or even cost him his life. He was, as a visiting friend, Shelby Foote, observed, "gaunt and pale," "living the life of a hermit."[15] And it must have been every bit as much an existential as a biological crisis.   For he must have felt a sense of reversal, even of betrayal: as a confident, *untouched* scientist he had always looked—with pure intellectuality, without affect—at *a* body being invaded by disease; now he was *the* body being invaded, not abstractly, but immediately.   Rather than penetrating the world to know it spatially, he was being penetrated by the world and being taught by pain to know himself temporally. It was as if his consciousness was being reincarnated, as if he was reconciling the split in his being that the scientific method had developed.

A reference to Descartes at this point is not extravagant.   In his most telling description of how he felt about his condition *then*, Dr. Percy says: "I was in bed so much, alone so much, that I had nothing to do but read and think.   I began to question everything I had once believed.   I began to ask why Europe, why the world had come to such a sorry state."[16] Dr. Percy knows and must have known at the time that René Descartes provided the groundwork for modern scientific methodology.   Indeed, in *Love in the Ruins*, Dr. Percy alludes to a specific Cartesian context, the first and second of the *Meditations Concerning First Philosophy* (1641).[17] There Descartes uses systematic doubt to strip his consciousness of everything except the *cogito*, the starting point of his reconstruction of the world.   Dr. Percy, without intention, but by virtue of his illness, underwent a process of doubt equally as radical; in one place he admits that at the time the illness was seen as a "misfortune . . . in terms of its consequences for one's inner life, the area of the deepest convictions and the unspoken assumptions by which every man lives his life (and if a man thinks he has no such assumptions, they are all the stronger for not being recognized)."[18] In other words, Dr. Percy doubted the world that Descartes's doubt had created.

Whatever the richness of Descartes's intended meaning for "I think, therefore I am," the declaration has too often been accepted as *proving* the primacy of the intellect, not simply among the different modes of human knowing, but even over against the extended world.   Gradually the idea has developed that science has a sacerdotal function; it is not just the only knower of ultimate reality, but also the mediator between that reality and the layman.   As a consequence the layman is now taught that he is essentially a consumer, who should respond to the stimuli provided him; private consciousness, as manifested in individuality, is shameful, and seems to be tolerated only when it engages in shameful fantasies.   There may indeed be a connection between the decline of the humanities and the outburst of pornography: now that the layman does not learn the traditional values by which his spirit may know its freedom, he must try to satisfy his hunger for freedom with fantasies of body freedom.[19] All the while, science continues to tear down the world in order to rebuild it according to its own specifications. Each new discovery is announced with such fanfare that it is tempting to think that a new reality has been discovered. Dr. Percy has frequently noted that such thinking has led to what Whitehead described as "the fallacy of misplaced concreteness," the delusion that a scientific abstraction has more reality than do the data upon which it is based.

Dr. Percy lay there, suffering from pain of body and pain of mind, the sources thought by Cartesians to be irreconcilable, yet the pain—as anyone knows in his heart—easily blended, to awaken his spiritual pain. It was then that he made what he has called his second great intellectual discovery[20]: "I saw one day— maybe it was something of a breakthrough, something of a turning of a corner—that science can say so much about things, objects, or people, but by its very method can only utter a statement about a single object, a glass or a frog or a dogfish—or a man—only insofar as it resembles other things of its kind."[21] Perhaps his personal attitude toward what had happened is best revealed by that homey phrase, "a turning of a corner," which is often used to indicate that a person has passed the crisis of an illness, which in its Latin equivalent, "conversion," also suggests a radical change for the better. The reminiscence is still abstract, though; it needs a personal reference—something Dr. Percy said to Bradley Dewey in an interview locates his intellectual discovery in his body: "Suffering is an evil, yet at the same time through the ordeal of suffering one gets these strange benefits of lucidity, of seeing things afresh."[22]

Time and again in his essays Dr. Percy has written of the person who "comes to himself" as a physical danger threatens his life. Most often that person has suffered a heart attack, as in this sketch from his well-known "Man on the Train": "the commuter on the New York Central had a heart attack and had to be taken off at Fordham station: Upon awakening, he gazed with astonishment at his own hand, turning it this way and that as though he had never seen it before."[23] The specific details of the sketch may be based on an observation during his medical school days; but the action of lifting one's hand to gaze at it in wonderment is so typical of someone who has been laid flat by sickness that Dr. Percy must be thinking of his own experience when he uses it. What the scene *means* to him is expressed in another of his essays; he writes of the commuter:

> One day he is on his way home on the five-fifteen. He has a severe heart attack and is taken off the train at a commuter's station he has seen a thousand times but never visited. When he regains consciousness, he finds himself in a strange hospital surrounded by

> strangers. As he tries to recall what has happened, he catches
> sight of his own hand on the counterpane. It is as if he had never
> seen it before: He is astounded by its complexity, its functional beau-
> ty. He turns it this way and that. What has happened? Certainly
> a kind of natural revelation, . . . which can only be called a revela-
> tion of being . . . [24]

Notice that the hand is now credited with those two qualities,
beauty and complexity, that had earlier been reserved for the
scientific method.   Just as scientific observation had been for
Percy a "religious" action, so the appearance of his hand is a "revelation," a "natural revelation," rather than a divine revelation,
but nevertheless a "revelation of being." Even the action, lifting
the hand, is palpable proof, a "manifestation," a word of great significance in the New Testament.   As the hand "exists," *ex +
sistere*, stands out from the background of *en soi*, so the entire being of which the hand is a part has been reclaimed from the ster-
ile space of scientific abstraction. Dr. Percy could by this time certainly appreciate the significance that Heidegger attaches to
"handedness" in *Being and Time:* it is when *Dasein* wills to pick
up the things about him to make them his tools that he creates
his own world.

By virtue of his systematic doubt, then, Dr. Percy awakened to
this *cogito:* "I hurt, therefore I am." From that assertion these
(simplified) inferences may be drawn: (1) that the external force
which causes the pain preexists the consciousness, (2) that pain
isolates, but not in the way that science alienates—pain will
bring even the most alienated observer back to his body, will reincarnate him, and (3) that pain awakens the consciousness to *its*
time—quite apart from world time—and ultimately to its time's
end, death. So often, when looking at his hand, Dr. Percy must
have meditated upon the wisdom of language in the New Testament: there the concept of time (and immediate choice) is per-
sonalized by using the phrase *at hand*. Indeed there is a wisdom
in the folk usage of the "hands" of the watch that will be lost
when they are replaced by "digitals" (also a human reference, but
long since lost). Several times, in discussing his crisis, Dr. Percy
has referred to an observation by Kierkegaard: "Hegel . . . explained everything under the sun, except one small detail: what
it means to be a man living in the world who must die."[25] Dr.
Percy must have concluded as much about the scientific view.

Because of an illness, then, Dr. Percy had experienced an ordeal that truly introduced him to life—and to his lifetime

theme. In a candid, yet typically impersonal way, he discusses the concept of ordeal with an interviewer:" . . . that touches on a subject I have been interested in for a long time—a theme I use in all my novels: the recovery of the real through ordeal. It is some traumatic experience . . . in each case. You have the paradox that near death you can become aware of what is real."[26] What happens in time of crisis? Dr. Percy, in another place, gives his answer: "When the novelist writes of a man 'coming to himself' through some such catalyst as catastrophe or ordeal, he may be offering obscure testimony to a gross disorder of consciousness and to the need of recovering oneself as neither angel nor organism but as a wayfaring creature somewhere between."[27] Is that still too imprecise? Then the common usage of language offers some clarification. To "come to" means primarily to awaken from unconsciousness, but it implies a recovery of self-awareness. Closely aligned is the expression "to come to one's senses," which stresses a recovered sense of values and implies a need for action. Both folk expressions are caught up in Heidegger's *Befindlichkeit*, the discovery, in a crisis, that one is inescapably in actuality, but discovering at the same moment that one has possibility. "Coming to himself" in Percy's thought, then, is recovering the spirit: one is not all body ("organism"), responding to universal physical stimuli, nor is one all mind ("angel"), responding to universal psychological stimuli; rather one is ultimately a unique wayfarer. It is exactly appropriate that Jesus says of the Prodigal Son (Luke 15:17), that "he came to himself," realized his alienated condition and decided to return to his father.

When he was released from his second convalescence, Dr. Percy returned to Greenville, to find that he no longer had a home there. Somewhat at loose ends, he went to New Mexico, a healthy climate for his lungs. But the shadowy meanings of his novels hint that he felt no better in his heart. The desert suggested too much the "empty space" pictured by the scientific method, and the very hour—right at the time of the explosion at Alamogordo—argued that the scientific method, if unchecked, would render the whole world a wasteland. There is in his work that apocalyptic scene that fuses Oppenheimer and Yeats's "rough beast." In ordeal himself, Percy must have envisioned a total ordeal. For he seems to have undergone a "conversion" out there, a total religious experience. Like many another, Walker Percy went to the desert to endure the demons and returned a dedicated man—he ridicules Toynbee's easy generalization, "Withdraw-al-and-Return," doubtless because he knows just how painful the process really is and how doomed to failure any generalization about it will be, but in his case it really happened.

After a year he returned to Mississippi, married, and moved to New Orleans. Soon after he became a Catholic. His subsequent move to Covington, Louisiana, seems to be a clear statement that he finally knew his place in the world—like the priest Father John (once Harry Percy), in *Lancelot*, who decides that his place is to be a parish in Alabama, ministering to ordinary folks. To know where one belongs depends upon knowing what one is supposed to be doing. Walker Percy was settling down to write, at first essays, but soon novels. For he realized that essays, though personal, are too easily taken as generalizations, while the truth that he wanted to convey was a truth that had to remain personal. So he had to write a series of novels, in which he would confess his ordeal, not in a direct way—which was sure to offend—but in an indirect way, which might nevertheless affect the interested reader.

His novels have—for all their humor, their savage social comment, their existential insights (each devotee has his own favorite reason for reading Percy)—been dissertations upon sickness, both the physical sickness that flesh is heir to and the sickness unto death that Percy found so profoundly described in Kierkegaard.[28] In a vast oversimplification, here are the novels and the sickness-theme which inhabits each.

(1) *The Moviegoer:* how can a person be sick, if medical science has not established any symptoms by which his sickness can be defined and how can such a person be treated?

(2) *The Last Gentleman:* what good can psychiatry do, if a patient is suffering not from "accepted," recognized symptoms but from "family," which is not usually thought to be a disease?

(3) *Love in the Ruins:* how can medical science be taught that distress of consciousness is not always a psychological malady, to be treated with drugs, but a sign of spiritual life, to be fostered by both physician and patient?

(4) *Lancelot:* how can a psychiatrist who recognizes that a condition is primarily spiritual, not psychological, best treat his patient?

(5) *The Second Coming:* how can a "sick" person determine if his inherited depressed condition is so forceful that he will inevitably be controlled by its dictates?

Such an arbitrary isolation of a theme from a group of novels does great violence to the richness and diversity of the world pictured, of course. But the risk is taken here, in order to identify a specific subject for a specific audience. For this audience—physicians, nurses, health services professionals—would have its own experience enhanced by the exploration of the world of sickness provided by Walker Percy. They would better understand that the title "Walker Percy's Physicians and Patients" refers not to two different classes of people, but to Percy's contention that a person, if he will be whole, must realize that he must be both physician and patient. In Percy's eyes, wholeness begins when a person realizes that he must do some things for himself, but that he cannot do everything for himself.

Notes

[1] See my early piece, "Walker Percy: The Physician as Novelist," *South Atlantic Bulletin*, 37 (May 1972), 58-63, for Percy's argument that scientific research, medical diagnosis, and fiction writing are essentially identical activities.

[2] See my "Walker Percy's Southern Stoic," *Southern Literary Journal*, 3 (Fall 1970), 5-31, and "William Alexander Percy, Walker Percy, and the Apocalypse," *Modern Age*, 24 (Fall 1980), 396-406, for an introduction to the importance of the Stoic attitude in Percy's background.

[3] In his introduction to *The Stoic Philosophy of Seneca* (New York: W. W. Norton, 1958), p. 13, Moses Hadas observes: "The orderly grandeur of astronomical phenomena seemed to the Stoics a most immediate proof of the direction of the universe by a rational and powerful providence, and hence study of celestial and other natural phenomena was an essential part of their program. Seneca repeatedly recommends it, not only as a means for assimilating man's reason to the great directing reason from which it derives, but also as an ethical exercise. Stargazing gives a sense of proportion; as Seneca's admirer Emerson said, its moral is, 'Why so hot, little man?' " Whether consciously or unconsciously, Walker Percy has provided his Stoic figure with a telling characteristic.

[4] Walker Percy's most extended appreciation of William Alexander Percy is his "Introduction" to the reissue of William Alexander Percy's *Lanterns on the Levee* (Baton Rouge: Louisiana State University Press, 1973), pp. vii-xviii.

[5] Quoted in Robert Coles, *Walker Percy: An American Search* (Boston:

Little, Brown and Company, 1978), p. 62.

[6] One of the best sources of information about Percy's regard for science is the early "From Facts to Fiction," *Book Week*, 4 (December 25, 1966), 5, 9. Reprinted in *The Writer*, 80 (October 1967), 27-28.

[7] Ibid.

[8] Quoted in Marcus Smith, "Talking about Talking: An Interview with Walker Percy," *New Orleans Review*, V, No. 1 (1976), 13-18.

[9] "From Facts to Fiction."

[10] See my "Moviegoing in *The Moviegoer*," *Southern Quarterly*, 18 (Spring 1980), 26-42, and "Walker Percy's *The Moviegoer*: The Cinema as Cave," *Southern Studies*, 19 (Winter 1980), 331-54, for a discussion of Percy's "picture" of modern man as the spectator.   An excellent treatment of the "spectator attitude" is provided by John Dewey in *The Quest for Certainty: A Study of the Relation of Knowledge and Action*, the Gifford Lectures for 1929 (New York: Putnam, 1960).

[11] Coles, p. 63.

[12] Quoted in Carleton Cremeens, "Walker Percy: The Man and the Novelist: An Interview," *Southern Review*, n.s., 4 (Spring 1968), 271-90.

[13] Quoted in David Chandler, "Walker Percy's Southern Novel Has a Lunatic Hero and Other Gothic Touches," *People* , 7 (May 2, 1977), 95-96.

[14] Quoted in Alfred Kazin, "The Pilgrimage of Walker Percy," *Harper's Magazine*, 243 (June 1971), 81-86.

[15] Coles, pp. 65-66.

[16] Ibid.

[17] See my "Tom More: Cartesian Physician," *Delta*, 13 (November 1981), 67-81, for a discussion of Percy's response to Descartes.

[18] "From Facts to Fiction."

[19] After I wrote the first draft of this paper, Walker Percy's "The Promiscuous Self," *Vanity Fair*, 46 (May 1983), 49-52, appeared.

[20] "From Facts to Fiction."

[21] Quoted in John Carr, "An Interview with Walker Percy," *Georgia Review*, 25 (Fall 1971), 317-32.

[22] Quoted in Bradley R. Dewey, "Walker Percy Talks about Kierkegaard: An Annotated Interview," *Journal of Religion*, 54 (July 1974), 273-98.

[23] Walker Percy, "The Man on the Train," in *The Message in the Bottle* (New York: Farrar, Straus and Giroux, 1975), p. 88.

[24] "Notes for a Novel about the End of the World," in *The Message in the Bottle*, p. 109.

[25] "From Facts to Fiction," but see, also, Dewey.

[26] Quoted in Zoltán Abádi-Nagy, "A Talk with Walker Percy," *Southern Literary Journal*, 6 (Fall 1973), 3-19; but see, also, Dewey.

[27] "Notes for a Novel about the End of the World."

[28] See my "Walker Percy's Indirect Communications," *Texas Studies in Literature and Language*, 11 (Spring 1969), 867-900; but see, also, William Buckley, "The Southern Imagination: An Interview with Eudora Welty and Walker Percy," *Mississippi Quarterly*, 26 (Fall 1973), 493-516.

Index